The "Million Dollar Inmate"

The "Million Dollar Inmate"

The Financial and Social Burden of Nonviolent Offenders

Heather Ahn-Redding

LEXINGTON BOOKS

A division of
ROWMAN & LITTLEFIELD PUBLISHERS, INC.
Lanham • Boulder • New York • Toronto • Plymouth, UK

LEXINGTON BOOKS

A division of Rowman & Littlefield Publishers, Inc.
A wholly owned subsidiary of The Rowman & Littlefield Publishing Group, Inc.
4501 Forbes Boulevard, Suite 200
Lanham, MD 20706

Estover Road
Plymouth PL6 7PY
United Kingdom

British Library Cataloguing in Publication Information Available

Library of Congress Cataloging-in-Publication Data

The hardback edition of this book was previously cataloged by the Library of
Congress as follows:

Ahn-Redding, Heather.
   The "million dollar" inmate : the financial and social burden of non-violent
   offenders / Heather Ahn-Redding.
      p. cm.
   Includes bibliographical references.
   1. Prisoners. 2. Prisons. 3. Prison sentences. I. Title.
HV8665.A45 2007
365'.973—dc22   2007032099

ISBN 978-0-7391-1496-4 (cloth : alk. paper)
ISBN 978-0-7391-1497-1 (pbk. : alk. paper)
ISBN 978-0-7391-5775-6 (electronic)

Printed in the United States of America

♾™ The paper used in this publication meets the minimum requirements of
American National Standard for Information Sciences—Permanence of Paper
for Printed Library Materials, ANSI/NISO Z39.48-1992.

Contents

List of Tables

Preface

All one has to do is to turn on the television or thumb through a newspaper to conclude that the United States is a frightening, dangerous, and increasingly violent nation.[1] It is no wonder then that the solution to our "crime problem" seems so evident: punish, punish, punish! But how accurate are Americans *really* when gauging the true rates of crime and violence? Let's take a look at school shootings. According to a *Wall Street Journal*-NBC News poll in 1998, over two-thirds of Americans believed a school-shooting like that at Columbine High School could occur at a school in their own community.[2] In taking a closer look, however, we find that out of 52 million school children in 2002 there were 16 school-related violent deaths, indicating that the probability of being a victim of a school-related incident was one in three million.[3] In fact, between 1976 and 2005, 19.6 percent of homicide victims under the age of eighteen were actually killed by family members[4] and not by the evil stranger lurking in a dark alleyway, an icon of fear that we are all too familiar with, or by the lone gunman rampaging through school hallways. An even more unfortunate statistic is during the same period, 61 percent of murder victims who were under the age of five were killed by a parent.[5] While school shootings are indeed horrific and traumatic events, as evidenced by a recent series of devastating school shootings in 2006, over 99 percent of youth homicides occur when children are not in school,[6] thus suggesting that children are actually safer at school than at home! But as the poll suggests, Americans' perception of public safety has been tainted by media images that sensationalize, dramatize, and distort the prevalence of otherwise rare events, such as school shootings and violent murders.[7] It is no wonder that the reaction to crime in the United States is fueled by so much unrelenting anger and fear, and that we have sent millions of nonviolent offenders to prison with relative ease, scant hesitation, and little afterthought.

Violent crime rates have been decreasing since 1994,[8] yet media pundits proclaim, "*Beware! You too could be the next victim!*" So, the next time you are in a busy public area (say, a movie theater or a restaurant), take a close look at the teens and adults around you. Are there any ominous, sinister-looking deviants skulking about, ready to strike at the next vulnerable victim—perhaps even you or your loved ones? Probably not. Even yet, people may be watching *you*—trying to discern whether *you* are a threat because of your gender, the color of your skin, your age, or the manner in which you dress or speak. Though you may not realize it, you most likely encounter ex-inmates on a regular basis because a disturbing 2.7 percent of the entire adult American population who pass your way—or 1 out of every 37 U.S. adults—has spent time in a state or federal prison.[9] Among adults in their late 30s, there is a high likelihood that 3 or 4 percent have spent some portion of their lives in state or federal prison.[10] More astonishing, Austin and Fabelo predict that one in three black males (32.2 percent), 1 in 6 Hispanic males (17 percent), and 1 out of every 9 white males (11.3 percent) will be incarcerated at some point during their lifetime (see table 0.1).[11] If this isn't unnerving enough, 6 out of every 100 children born in the United States during this millennium are predicted to go to prison.[12] What is most striking and perhaps even more unsettling is that these ex- or future inmates are not dangerous psychopaths who would mug, rob, rape, maim, or murder given the opportunity, but are instead nonviolent individuals who are (or will be) involved in low-level drug-related, property, or public-order offenses. So, despite what we may hear, feel, or even personally experience, the average American is actually in no more serious danger of

Table 0.1.   Lifetime Chance of Going to Prison (State or Federal) for the First Time in the United States, 1974–2001

	1974	*1991*	*2001*
Total	1.9%	5.2%	6.6%
Males			
White	3.6	9.1	11.3
Black	13.4	29.4	32.2
Hispanic	4.0	16.3	17.0
Females	0.3	1.1	1.8
White	0.2	0.5	0.9
Black	1.1	3.6	5.6
Hispanic	0.4	1.5	2.2

Source: Austin and Fabelo. 2004. "The Diminishing Returns of Increased Incarceration: A Blueprint to Improve Public Safety and Reduce Costs." Washington, DC: JFA Institute: table 2, page 7 (table reprinted with permission).

becoming a victim of a violent crime than a decade ago. In 2004, the FBI reported that crime rates for serious offenses[13] were 32 percent lower than those recorded in 1995.[14] The majority of ex- or future-inmates then are not representative of the dangerous criminal elements repeatedly portrayed on the nightly news, but are ordinary men, women, and children swept up in the emotionally charged atmosphere of an increasingly disproportionate justice system that has altered the lives of the 5.6 million U.S. adults who have seen the inside of a prison at some point during their lifetime.[15] This perpetual tide of incarceration has created a precarious yet monstrous system in which close to seven million people are currently on probation or parole, or are locked up prison or jail.[16]

Now, consider the funding that has poured into the coffers of the criminal justice system—especially corrections—that has been used not just to punish but to castigate in the harshest manner permitted by the public and the Constitution. In a frantic haste to toughen laws, extend prison terms for less violent offenses, and construct enough prisons to hold our growing prison population, the costs of such efforts have been passed on to otherwise supportive (or uninformed) taxpayers. After all, in our fear-mongering culture where Americans are warned to be suspicious of everyone and everything, why not use our hard earned tax dollars to buffer the divide between the criminals and their victims? Why not pour billions of dollars into the construction and maintenance of correctional facilities if they can shelter society from those who threaten our safety, endanger our children, and weaken the moral foundation of society? Because, as I have pointed out, crime is and has been waning (and not because of increased incarceration, as we shall later see), and an overwhelming proportion of offenders who do see the inside of modern, state of the art, multimillion dollar correctional facilities are there for nonviolent offenses. As we shall see, the overincarceration of the American public has unlocked a Pandora's box, out of which a multitude of financial and social costs have emerged, placing a tremendous burden on the whole of society.

This book explores the visible and less-visible costs of incarceration. Rather than focus on the correctional system in its entirety and the costs of sending every type of offender to prison, I have intentionally narrowed my examination to the financial and social costs of incarcerating *nonviolent* offenders (although I do review the expenses associated with our prison system as a whole). These are drug-related, property, and public order offenders whose incarceration is accruing massive costs every day, month, and year that they linger behind bars. As a society, we do not like to acknowledge costs; we prefer to postpone or ignore them, and push them out of sight. We are as averse to owning up to the costs of our social policies—cost-effective or not—as we are disposed to seeking instant gratification and rewards. Therefore, we have turned to prison as an instantaneous response to crime, a solution that facilitates the invisibility of its costs by remaining, as the cliché goes, out-of-sight, out-of-mind.

This book attempts to shed light on the flaws in this traditional approach and suggest alternative recommendations. It addresses the *real* costs of locking up nonviolent offenders, especially those who could otherwise serve community-based sanctions while receiving treatment, contributing to their communities, supporting their families, and raising their children. There are no definitive figures, as it is impossible to measure every cost and benefit with exact precision, but our prisons have been in a state of fiscal crisis for years. This is exacting an enormous toll on prisoners, families, and communities, and while these social costs are especially difficult to measure, they are certainly significant and real. As the costs of incarceration continue to rise, we must ask: *Should we spend as much on nonviolent prisoners as we do on violent offenders? Have prisons been effective in reaching their stated goals? Are we spending too much on a system that has shown few tangible social benefits? What would happen if we stopped building prisons? What measures are in place within the prison system that might indicate whether our spending has exceeded the benefits of prison? What might these measures reflect about our current correctional system?*

To address these questions, the goals of this book are fourfold and attempt to:

1. Examine historical sentencing and penal practices to understand the origins of our current sentencing and correctional systems (Parts I and II),
2. identify the implicit and explicit financial and social costs of incarcerating nonviolent offenders (Part III),
3. review the goals of our prison system and relevant empirical literature to determine whether they have been met (Part IV), and
4. review and suggest alternative methods of corrections for nonviolent offenders (Part V).

This book attempts to identify the social and financial costs of incarcerating nonviolent offenders and to unravel the effect that mass incarceration has had on prison environments, families, communities, and on individual prisoners. When referring to the expenses of imprisonment, we must identify the costs to the fullest extent. Among explicit costs include the construction, transportation, maintenance, and upkeep of correctional facilities, such as salaries of correctional workers, food, mental health costs, medical costs, and treatment programs. Less visible costs include losses of legitimate employment when individuals are incarcerated, the toll incarceration takes on family members, especially children, and potential anomie in communities where a disproportionate number of residents have been uprooted and imprisoned. While these latter items are not traditionally factored into calculations of prison expenditures, they are nonetheless tangible costs with potentially devastating financial implications.

Part I of this book introduces the "Million Dollar Inmate" and discusses the development of current sentencing policies that have played an integral part in the creation of the world's largest prison population. Part II examines today's sentencing structures and prison conditions, with a focus on overcrowding, supermax prisons, prison violence, and mental illness. This section attempts to reveal the inner workings of our correctional system, exposing numerous costs along the way. While the prisoners described in this section are both violent and nonviolent, it is crucial to remember that in many prisons, these offenders exist and live side-by-side. Thus, the conditions that affect violent offenders will also affect those with no such histories. Part III will review the financial and the less visible costs of incarceration. This section will also describe certain prison populations who have been disproportionately affected by harsh sentencing laws, such as women and drug-offenders, and who incur enormous expenses throughout their incarceration. Part IV of this book discusses the various goals of our prison system, the financial and/or social costs associated with attempts to adhere to these multiple philosophies of punishment, and whether these goals have been met and the expenses justified. Finally, Part V will attempt to comprehensively explore the costs and benefits of prison and examine alternative methods of punishing nonviolent offenders.

First and foremost, this book challenges lawmakers, politicians, academicians, and voters to hold themselves accountable for the criminal justice system that we have together created, sustained, and promoted through our reactive attitudes and our tax dollars. As exclaimed by Merlo, "Americans love prisons."[17] And so, we must demand higher standards of performance[18] within our correctional system while also demonstrating our support of promising alternative programs, many of which may be community-based. We must all accept the consequential realities of our penal system and their long-term effects on communities and families. Further, we must challenge our own "tough on crime" beliefs by disallowing the media to distort our already fragile sense of safety. When people are afraid, they naturally desire to see stern punishment, even when offenders are nonviolent. We must confront our stereotypes, myths, and unrealistic perceptions of safety and crime in order to shape our penal system into one that is efficient and based on the realistic needs of society. Do we *need* to send nonviolent offenders to prison? Do we *need* to spend billions of dollars to incarcerate individuals who pose very little physical threats to society? And as we fulfill our seeming *need* to build more prisons, what benefits are we reaping? These questions cannot be answered in full, and other unrecognized long-term costs of incarceration will inevitably transpire within the next few decades, but these are issues that we must force ourselves to consider and confront with open minds.

NOTES

1. Mauer 1999; Glassner 1999.

2. CNN 2001.

3. Schiraldi 2001.

4. "Homicide trends in the U.S, Age trends." Washington, D.C.: Bureau of Justice Statistics, U.S. Department of Justice. Retrieved October 24, 2007 (http://www.ojp.usdoj.gov/bjs/homicide/teens.htm).

5. BJS 2004m; BJS website 2004 (http://www.ojp.usdoj.gov/bjs/homicide/children.htm).

6. Schiraldi 2001.

7. Mauer 1999; Glassner 1999.

8. BJS 2004n.

9. Bonczar 2003; Austin and Fabelo 2004: 6.

10. Bonczar 2003.

11. Austin and Fabelo 2004: 6.

12. Ibid.

13. These include murder, rape, robbery, and assault.

14. Frieden 2005.

15. Bonczar 2003; Austin and Fabelo 2004.

16. See BJS website 2006c. "The number of adults in the correctional population has been increasing" (http://www.ojp.usdoj.gov/bjs/glance/corr2.htm).

17. Cited in Pollack 1997: 36.

18. See Logan 1993.

I

INTRODUCTION AND EARLY SENTENCING

1

An Introduction to the "Million Dollar Inmate"

Prisoners, whatever their crimes may be, constitute one of the most expensive, financially draining populations in our nation. When offenders enter the correctional system, they instantly become the responsibility of the state (or federal system) in which they are incarcerated. Once offenders become custodians of the state or federal government, their lives are reduced to an almost infant like existence; they require everything from the most basic amenities, like food and clothes, to the more expensive services, such as medical care. They are stripped of their personhood, their identities are replaced with identification numbers, and in many respects they become property of the state or federal government for the duration of their imprisonment. Because incarceration extinguishes an individual's ability to function and act independently, a tremendous amount of resources are needed on a daily basis to shelter, secure, feed, and care for millions of prisoners, many of whom will never exit the system. As such, the daily costs of incarceration per inmate, which was on average $62.05 among state prisoners in 2001,[1] can easily accumulate when offenders are serving decades-long sentences or life terms. Based on average rates of spending in the state and federal correctional systems, a nonviolent offender who is sentenced to 45 years in prison will cost the state or federal government over one million dollars (in today's dollars) and, most notably, yield few economic or social benefits in return. Yet too few voices have dared to ask the question: *Is there a limit to how much we as a society should spend on each inmate when we are already sacrificing billions of dollars that could otherwise be spent on education, health care, and other social programs? Can we continue to justify supporting the "million dollar inmate" despite the costs?*

So, who is this "Million Dollar Inmate"? Initially, one might conjure up the image of a serial murderer, a child killer, or a murderous sociopath who unleashes terror upon innocent, unsuspecting targets. Terrorists like Timothy McVeigh, cannibals such as Jeffrey Dahmer and Albert Fish, serial killers like Witchita's Dennis Rader, and sniper John Allen Muhammad are only a few of the most obvious who come to mind. Indeed, most would agree that they are deserving of an austere lifetime behind bars, at minimum. Fortunately, these individuals are the exception, rather than the norm, and most prisoners today are nothing of the sort. However, the manner in which we are treating nonviolent offenders is beginning to approximate the way in which the system bestows punishment upon its violent offenders (aside from executions, of course).

The amount of lethal violence experienced in the United States is higher than in many other countries;[2] therefore it is no wonder that we possess a mammoth prison population. This book however is not about the people who deservedly belong in prison, such as our aforementioned notorious offenders. Rather, it is about people who, I will argue, are deserving of punishment yet do *not* necessarily belong in prison cells. These are nonviolent drug abusers/users caught in a powerful war on drugs. They are nonviolent property offenders whose damage may be miniscule in comparison to the resources the government is willing to expend to put them behind bars.

Let me introduce you to the "Million Dollar Inmate." A prime example of the "Million Dollar Inmate" is a young mother of two who receives a 20-year federal prison sentence due to peripheral involvement in a drug deal orchestrated by her boyfriend. Other "Million Dollar Inmates" are:

- a young man who has permanently exited the workforce due to a life sentence under "three-strikes" legislation for three nonviolent burglaries;
- a substance abuser who tangentially participates in a drug sale, receives 15 years to life, and requires treatment for HIV;
- an aging inmate who will require ongoing geriatric medical care until he serves his life sentence by dying in prison;
- a mentally ill inmate who has not been able to adapt to life in prison and is sent to a multimillion dollar supermax prison for misbehavior; and
- a pregnant woman whose unborn child will require years of foster care while she is incarcerated for 20 years.

The "Million Dollar Inmate" is not merely a nonviolent, nonthreatening prisoner, but one whose incarceration incurs massive financial and social expenses without giving anything in return to society.

THE BURDEN OF THE "MILLION DOLLAR INMATE"

The "Million Dollar Inmate" is a prime representation of the inefficiencies of America's criminal justice system, a product of our nation's impetuous reactions to solving social problems, tribulations that are both real and socially constructed. Rather than restructure sentencing practices to limit the use of incarceration—especially for non-violent offenders—our country has done quite the opposite by remaining grounded in an obstinate "tough on crime" position.

Within the last five decades, we have become overly reliant on corrections as a solution to crime, drug abuse, and other social ills. Prison has become a simple, fast, and hidden solution to crime problems that, for the most part, have been largely exaggerated by the media, politicians, and others who benefit from social fear[3] or what Cohen aptly termed "moral panic."[4] Incarceration, in essence, has become its own addiction, yet our dependence on it has elevated to the point where its financial costs are dangerously high. Like addicts, we are depleting our financial resources to feed our incarceration habits, and we are draining the life out of many individuals, families, and communities. Eventually, our justice system's proclivity toward locking up offenders will bite the proverbial hand that feeds it—namely the taxpayers who continually support the funding of new prisons and tough on crime initiatives. As the financial toll of our correctional system is becoming increasingly evident, the social ramifications of mass incarceration are emerging as well. Overlooked as real and tangible consequences, the effects of this current correctional era on families and communities are becoming clearer as more people are encountering the correctional system—either as offenders or family members of those incarcerated.

Despite our society's unremitting disdain for criminal offenders (as expressed through harsh sentencing laws), our addiction to the media has drawn us into a world where crimes are sensationalized, dramatized, and entertaining, and where social problems, rather than practical solutions, have become the main attraction of the evening news. One has only to turn on a local news channel to feel unsafe. When murder rates decreased from 1990 to 1998 by nearly 50 percent, the media's coverage of homicide increased by 600 percent.[5] In a survey conducted in 1997, 80 percent of the respondents reported that their fear of victimization increased after watching news segments on violent crime.[6] Ironically, as much as we loathe crime and criminals, we also love exploring the darker side of humanity[7] and immersing ourselves in the thrills of a good courtroom drama. For example, NBC's 14-year running "Law and Order" attracted more than 15 million viewers in 2004,[8] while newer and increasingly graphic crime series bombard viewers every night with grizzly and realistic images of death and gratuitous violence, often mixed with sex. We all love a good mystery (who doesn't love a good Agatha Christie novel?)—and crime definitely sells—yet the more we have permitted crime to entertain us, the more fearful we have become of each other and of the world. As a result of this media-driven fear, Glassner notes, the "price tag for our panic about overall crime has grown so monumental that even law-and-order zealots find it hard to defend."[9]

After watching television, reading a newspaper, or skimming through a magazine—in essence, immersing one's self into American culture—one has every reason to be afraid of potential dangers ranging from medical malpractice and toxic drinking water to school shootings and sexual predators. We are all wary of leaving our property unattended; we secure our doors and windows during the day, we never leave our cars unlocked, and we tightly grip our pocketbooks and conceal our wallets as we make our way down busy streets. Contrary to common perception, however, victimization rates for theft and burglary have been declining since the early 1970s and violent crime rates have been falling since 1994.[10] As Beiser succinctly observes, "It's not crime that has increased; it's punishment. More people are now arrested for minor offenses, more arrestees are prosecuted, and more of those convicted are given lengthy sentences."[11]

In 2005, according to the Bureau of Justice Statistics (BJS), there were 23 million crimes reported by U.S. residents who were age 12 or older.[12] Among these victimizations, 77 percent (18 million) were property crimes, 22 percent (5.2 million) were violent crimes, and 1 percent (227,000) were personal thefts. Additionally in 2005, there was one rape or sexual assault, two assaults with injuries, and two robberies per every 1,000 individuals who were age 12 or older, and 6 murders per 100,000 individuals.[13] While these numbers may appear staggering at first glimpse and may be disturbing to anyone unfortunate enough to be part of these statistics, most of these offense rates are at record low levels.

Table 1.1 shows trends in property and violent crime since 1973 based on the National Crime Victimization Survey (NCVS). Among all categories, crime rates have decreased. From table 1.1 we can see that violent and property crime victimization rates[14] decreased overall from 1973 to 2003.[15] Victimization rates of violent crimes (including murder, rape, robbery, aggravated assault, and simple assault) per 1,000 households have been decreasing since the mid-1990s, and property crime victimization rates (including burglary, theft, and motor vehicle theft) have been falling continuously since the mid-1970s. It is important to note that homicide rates have taken a similar downward trajectory in the past few decades. First, if we examine homicide trends (see table 1.2), we can see that the homicide rate per 100,000 population increased by 21.7 percent from 1950 to 2002 and that the actual number of homicides increased by 131 percent. However, homicide rates have been steadily declining over recent years, from a rate of 10.2 per 100,000 population in 1980 to 5.6 in 2002.

Table 1.1. National Crime Victimization Survey: Violent and Property Crime Rates per 1,000 Households, 1973–2003[a],[b]

Year	Total Violent Crime	Rape[c]	Robbery	Aggravated Assault	Simple Assault	Total Property Crime	Burglary	Theft	Motor Vehicle Theft
1973	47.7	2.5	6.7	12.5	25.9	519.9	110.0	390.8	19.1
1974	48.0	2.6	7.2	12.9	25.3	551.5	111.8	421.0	18.8
1975	48.4	2.4	6.8	11.9	27.2	553.6	110.0	424.1	19.5
1976	48.0	2.2	6.5	12.2	27.0	544.2	106.7	421.0	16.5
1977	50.4	2.3	6.2	12.4	29.4	544.1	106.2	420.9	17.0
1978	50.6	2.6	5.9	12.0	30.0	532.6	103.1	412.0	17.5
1979	51.7	2.8	6.3	12.5	30.3	531.8	100.9	413.4	17.5
1980	49.4	2.5	6.6	11.4	28.8	496.1	101.4	378.0	16.7
1981	52.3	2.5	7.4	12.0	30.3	497.2	105.9	374.1	17.2
1982	50.7	2.1	7.1	11.5	29.8	468.3	94.1	358.0	16.2
1983	46.5	2.1	6.0	9.9	28.3	428.4	84.0	329.8	14.6
1984	46.4	2.5	5.8	10.8	27.2	399.2	76.9	307.1	15.2
1985	45.2	1.9	5.1	10.3	27.9	385.4	75.2	296.0	14.2
1986	42.0	1.7	5.1	9.8	25.3	372.7	73.8	284.0	15.0
1987	44.0	2.0	5.3	10.0	26.7	379.6	74.6	289.0	16.0
1988	44.1	1.7	5.3	10.8	26.3	378.4	74.3	286.7	17.5
1989	43.3	1.8	5.4	10.3	25.8	373.4	67.7	286.5	19.2
1990	44.1	1.7	5.7	9.8	26.9	348.9	64.5	263.8	20.6

(continued)

Table 1.1. *(continued)*

Year	Total Violent Crime	Rape[b][c]	Robbery	Aggravated Assault	Simple Assault	Total Property Crime	Burglary	Theft	Motor Vehicle Theft
1991	48.8	2.2	5.9	9.9	30.6	353.7	64.6	266.8	22.2
1992	47.9	1.8	6.1	11.1	28.9	325.3	58.6	248.2	18.5
1993	49.1	1.6	6.0	12.0	29.4	318.9	58.2	241.7	19.0
1994	51.2	1.4	6.3	11.9	31.5	310.2	56.3	235.1	18.8
1995	46.1	1.2	5.4	9.5	29.9	290.5	49.3	224.3	16.9
1996	41.6	0.9	5.2	8.8	26.6	266.4	47.2	205.7	13.5
1997	38.8	0.9	4.3	8.6	24.9	248.3	44.6	189.9	13.8
1998	36.0	0.9	4.0	7.5	23.5	217.4	38.5	168.1	10.8
1999	32.1	0.9	3.6	6.7	20.8	198.0	34.1	153.9	10.0
2000	27.4	0.6	3.2	5.7	17.8	178.1	31.8	137.7	8.6
2001	24.7	0.6	2.8	5.3	15.9	166.9	28.7	129.0	9.5
2002	22.8	0.7	2.2	4.3	15.5	159.0	27.7	122.3	9.0
2003	22.3	0.5	2.5	4.6	14.6	163.2	29.8	124.4	9.0
% Change, 1973–2003	−53.2	−80.0	−62.3	−63.2	−43.6	−68.6	−72.9	−68.1	−52.8

[a]Based on population age 12 and older.
[b]Rape, robbery, and assault data are from the National Crime Victimization Survey (NCVS).
[c]Rape excludes sexual assault.
Sources: Bureau of Justice Statistics [BJS]. 2006. "Key Crime and Justice Facts at a Glance." Washington, DC: Bureau of Justice Statistics, U.S. Department of Justice (http://www.ojp.usdoj.gov/bjs/glance.htm#Crime); BJS. 2004d. "Key Facts at a Glance: National Crime Victimization Survey, Property Crime Trends, 1973–2003" (http://www.ojp.usdoj.gov/bjs/glance.tables/proptrdtab.htm); BJS. 2004e. "Key Facts at a Glance: National Crime Victimization Survey, Violent Crime trends, 1973–2003" (http://www.ojp.usdoj.gov/bjs/glance.tables/viortrdtab.htm).

Table 1.2.   Homicide Rates, 1950–2002

Year	Homicide Rate per 100,000 Population	Estimated Number of Homicides
1950	4.6	7,020
1955	4.1	6,850
1960	5.1	9,110
1965	5.1	9,960
1970	7.9	16,000
1975	9.6	20,510
1980	10.2	23,040
1985	8.0	18,976
1990	9.4	23,438
1995	8.2	21,606
2000	5.5	15,586
2001	5.6	16,037
2002	5.6	16,204
% Change, 1950–2002	21.7	131

Source: Bureau of Justice Statistics [BJS] (website). 2004o. "Homicide Trends in the U.S.: Long term trends" (http://www.ojp.usdoj.gov/bjs/homicide/tables/totalstab.htm).

Because our incarceration rates have been climbing more rapidly than violent and property crime rates are falling, it might appear that these decreasing crime trends are a result of incarceration—therefore validating our million-dollar prisons—but this has not been the case (this will be discussed in greater depth in chapter 9).

The mass incarceration of nonviolent offenders has yet to convincingly produce a significant effect on increasing public safety and is arguably one of the most ineffective forms of crime control for many nonviolent offenses. Nonetheless, two million men, women, and children are currently in prison or jail. Considering the entire world's penal population totals nine million,[16] this is an astonishing figure, one that is indicative of a potentially bleak future of correctional budget shortfalls, jammed courthouses, and overflowing prisons. Our methods of sentencing and corrections are in jeopardy of self-destruction—from overcrowding, budget constraints, prison violence, high rates of staff overturn—yet we persist by locking up more offenders each year as we adamantly adhere to a harsh and unforgiving stance on punishment. Our nation, one that rests on the foundation of equality and justice for *all*, has succeeded in incarcerating more people than any other industrialized or developing nation in the world. We have become a country where from 1985 to 2000, increases in state spending on corrections outpaced growth in spending on higher education by six-fold despite a paucity of empirical evidence that incarcerating nonviolent offenders efficiently and significantly reduces crime.[17]

Not every country depends on the use of incarceration as we do. In a comparison of incarceration rates and prison populations of nations around the world, the United States outranks every other country (table 1.3). It should be noted that the figure for the United States does not include juveniles in custody, prisoners in jails in Native American territories, and those held in

Table 1.3.   International Prison Populations and Incarceration Rates

Country	Prison Population[a]	Incarceration Rate[b]	Year
United States[c]	2,135,901	724	2004
Argentina	56,313	148	2002
Australia	23,362	117	mid-2004
Belarus	52,500	532	2003
Brazil	330,642	183	2004
Canada	36,389	116	2003
China	1,548,498	118	2003
Colombia	68,545	152	2004
Costa Rica	7,619	177	2004
Czech Republic	19,226	188	2005
England & Wales	75,187	142	2005
Finland	3,719	71	2004
France	55,028	91	2004
Germany	79,329	96	2004
India	313,635	29	2003
Iran	133,658	191	2004
Israel	13,603	209	2004
Japan	73,734	58	2004
Korea	57,902	121	2004
Kuwait	3,700	148	2003
Mexico	191,890	182	2004
Netherlands	19,999	123	2004
Pakistan	86,000	55	2004
Panama	10,630	354	2003
Peru	32,129	114	2004
Poland	79,807	209	2004
Romania	39,015	180	2005
Russia	847,000	594	2006
Saudi Arabia	23,720	110	2000
South Africa	186,739	413	2004
Sweden	7,332	81	2004
Taiwan	57,037	251	2004
Thailand	168,264	264	2004

[a]Includes pretrial detainees/remand prisoners.
[b]Per 100,000 national resident. The years used to determine rates may vary slightly.
[c]Includes state and federal prison and jail inmates.
Sources: Walmsley. 2003. "World Prison Population List," 5th edition. Research, Development, and Statistics Directorate, Home Office (http://www.homeoffice.gov.uk/rds/pdfs2/r234.pdf). Statistics used with permission.

immigration or military facilities.[18] It should be noted that the figure for the United States includes individuals in jail and prison, as well as pretrial detainees. Russia's respective incarceration rate of 594 per 100,000 national population is the closest in the world to our rate of 724, yet, their jail and prison populations are miniscule when compared to our 2 million.[19]

As the latter half of the twentieth century has come to an end and we are progressing into the new millennium, it is becoming increasingly evident that the gravity of our correctional spending has compromised our nation's ability to focus on other social needs. In 1952, 3.5 percent of state and local spending was directed toward higher education while only 1.5 percent went toward prisons.[20] By 2000, however, state and local governments increased their spending on prisons by 187 percent, whereas the percent of local and state expenditures directed toward education only increased by 80 percent.[21] Altogether, 45 states increased their spending on corrections by 100 percent from 1983 to 2000 and 18 states experienced at least a 200 percent increase.[22]

In the 1990s, institutions of higher education across the country felt the backlash of the Violent Crime Control Act and Law Enforcement Act, signed by President Clinton in 1994, which channeled even more money into state prison construction. In California, for example, 21 prisons were built from 1984 to 1994—a result of a 209 percent increase in funding—yet only one state university was constructed.[23] Unsurprisingly, state universities only received a 15 percent increase in funding during that time period. Similarly, New York during the 1990s increased its budget for prisons by $761 million while decreasing higher education expenditures by $615 million.[24] It was in 1995 that for the first time in our nation's history, total state spending on the construction of new prisons ($2.6 billion) surpassed the amount spent on constructing universities ($2.5 billion).[25]

From 1997 to 2001, "total state and local expenditures for corrections increased by 1,101 percent compared to 448 percent for education, 482 for

Table 1.4. Annual per Capita Costs for State Expenditures, 1986–2001

	Cost per Resident				
	Corrections	Prisons	Health	Public Education	Welfare
1986	$65	$49	$78	$843	$425
1991	98	76	109	998	632
1996	113	91	141	1143	849
2001	134	104	154	1315	914
% Change, 1986–2001	106	112	97	56	115

Source: Stephan. 2004. "State Prison Expenditures 2001." Washington, DC: Bureau of Justice Statistics Special Report, U.S. Department of Justice: table 1, page 2.

hospitals and healthcare, and 617 percent for public welfare."[26] Our country spent $374 billion on education, $260.3 billion on public welfare, $43.7 billion on health costs,[27] and nearly $56 billion on corrections in 2001—a $48 billion increase since 1982. With these rising costs come increases in state per capita spending. Table 1.4 compares annual state[28] expenditures per state resident on corrections, prisons, health, education, and public welfare. From 1986 to 2001, per capita spending on education increased by 56 percent, while per capita spending on prisons and corrections increased by 112 and 106 percent, respectively (table 1.4). Throughout the nation, state spending on corrections has exceeded that directed toward higher education. Only in Maryland and New Mexico did the spending on higher education increase more than corrections from 1980 to 2000.[29]

Not only have taxpayers paid a phenomenal price to sustain a growing correctional system over the last 50 years, but so too have children and students across the country.

The magnitude of the expenses incurred by our correctional population is endemic. In 2001, each of the 1.25 million state prisoners cost their respective state an average of $22,650. Since the early 1990s, our country has spent over $30 billion annually on correctional facilities despite little evidence that our prisons are effectively reducing recidivism, deterring offenders, and providing safe environments for prisoners.

WHERE ARE THE RETURNS?

Most governmental expenditures involve the expectation of some human, social, or financial capital return. We funnel billions of dollars into social and welfare programs each year with the expectation that recipients will become law-abiding, taxpaying, and contributing members of society. In other words, we expect something in return for our social investments. Yet, the dollar amount allocated to each welfare recipient is negligible in comparison to what we spend each year to incarcerate prisoners whose potential for future success, by many social standards, are generally perceived as low.

The United States has been putting prison spending ahead of other social agendas in order to house millions of offenders. In 1998, according to the Justice Policy Institute,[30] our nation's 1.2 million nonviolent prisoners cost 50 percent more than the amount the federal government spent on 8.5 million welfare recipients ($16.6 billion), and six times the amount allocated to child care for 1.25 million kids.[31] On the one hand, 99 percent of families receiving government assistance under the Temporary Assistance for Needy Families (TANF) program received a monthly average of $351 in 2001.[32] Families with four or more children received an average of $519 per month. If an individual in 2001 sought food stamps like 17 million other

Americans that year, he or she might have received $74.82 in benefits per month, or $897.84 for the entire year.[33] On the other hand, if that same individual were to commit a nonviolent felony, the government might spend more to incarcerate him than the average person would receive from any form of government welfare in a given lifespan.

Correctional spending stands alone among other governmental expenditures due to its infrastructure in which there is a consistent incongruence between the stated goals and actual observed outcome. Most large-scale operations utilize some standards of performance in order to measure success or failure.[34] Prisons, on the other hand, continue to receive state and federal support despite poor performance levels. Over 50 percent of state prisoners who were released on parole in 2000 were returned to prison or jail (42 percent) or absconded (9 percent).[35] If 42 percent of our high school students failed to graduate or find employment, or if 42 percent of welfare recipients failed to find legitimate work, each respective system would undoubtedly undergo restructuring at the public's behest. What is the chance that our government and voters would continue to finance a program with the foreknowledge that the expected yield of their investment would be negligible? Yet, our penal system, in which over 40 percent of state prisoners recidivate, continues to operate on immense budgets that, on average, are only getting larger.

Fluctuations in governmental expenditures generally reflect changes in societal needs, such as more classrooms, more highways, or more police officers. With violent and property crime rates at their lowest in over 30 years, do we *need* additional prison beds? Do we truly *need* to incapacitate 1.2 million nonviolent prisoners in facilities that are systematically overloaded, expensive to maintain, violent, and potentially psychologically damaging? Gainsborough and Mauer claim there is little empirical evidence suggesting that "massive prison construction is the most effective way to reduce crime,"[36] so as the need for more prison beds increases, we must consider how much we are willing to sacrifice to be tough on violent *and* nonviolent prisoners.

Prior to the 1970s, correctional departments justified their spending through attempts to rehabilitate offenders. Indeterminate sentencing, practiced by every state until the 1970s, was driven by the belief that offenders could be reformed and the system could indeed reduce crime rates. States invested heavily in treatment, education, and rehabilitation programs with an expected return—namely, the molding of law-breaking individuals into honest, productive, and respectable citizens. Since the 1970s, when the efficacy of treatment programs came under heavy scrutiny (see chapter 2), our country's penal philosophy has rapidly embraced a more punitive approach to sentencing, replacing the once dominant philosophy of rehabilitation.

To justify current harsh sentencing legislation and correctional spending, most lawmakers and politicians—who are almost always in favor of tough on crime' initiatives (see chapter 12)—are standing by these sentencing laws and publicizing their supposed deterrent effects when research suggests otherwise. And because of these sentencing laws, 9.4 percent of prisoners in state or federal prisons are serving life sentences, which is 83 percent more than in 1992.[37] Of these 127,677 lifers, 33,196 (26.3 percent) will never be eligible for parole. Unsurprisingly, "imposing a life sentence carries with it a potential cost to taxpayers of $1 million."[38] The costs of confining an individual for his or her natural life will be discussed in more detail in chapter 6.

Today's sentencing and penal goals can be classified into five categories, each adhering to a different philosophy of punishment.[39] In short, these goals are:

1. Retribution ("just deserts," equity, proportionality)
2. Incapacitation (crime control, public safety)
3. Deterrence (specific and general)
4. Rehabilitation and treatment
5. Restitution

Part IV discusses retribution, incapacitation, deterrence, and rehabilitation, while Part V touches upon issues regarding restitution. While we have been increasingly skilled in punishment, our current system has not shown the deterrent capability espoused by public figures. Actually, very few of the above goals set forth by our correctional system have come close to full actualization. Many sentencing policies designed to deter potential offenders have shown few deterrent effects, if any; attempts to rehabilitate offenders have been compromised by the incapacitating and harsh environments in which treatment takes place;[40] and incapacitation as a primary sentencing goal is a costly decision.

Many nonviolent "Million Dollar Inmates" will never see the outside world again, never contribute significantly toward the workforce, and will have difficulty supporting their families. What financial sense does it make to increase spending on an already overburdened system that shows little or no returns on its investment? Perhaps the absence of any future crimes nonviolent offenders may commit is a viable financial or social benefit (an argument that will be explored later), but a record-breaking number of prisoners are serving life sentences with no possibility of parole, thus arguably costing the state much more than the losses associated with any potential criminal activity. While we should not discount the gravity of these potential crimes, we do need to ask ourselves if there are less expensive ways of preventing them. From an economic perspective and that of a taxpayer, the opportunity costs— or better uses—of our increased prison expenditures are considerably vast.

Clinging to our passionate belief that prisons are the only solution to crime, we continue to allocate billions of dollars annually to the construction and maintenance of new state-of-the-art correctional facilities. But, vulnerable prisoners in these facilities often experience a process of psychological and physiological decay and many of these nonviolent offenders will someday be released back into the community. Despite some initiatives to provide treatment and educational programs in a more rehabilitative environment, the prison experience damages one's sense of dignity, humanity, and individuality, exposes prisoners to conditions that are both physically dangerous and mentally taxing, and often leads to physical deterioration. Do we want these prisoners returning to their communities mentally and physically broken from their prison experience? Can we expect them to contribute to society upon release when they have endured years of deprivation,[41] when they have become estranged from their children or families, and when their substance abuse problems are worse than when they entered prison? People do find ways to reenter society after incarceration, of course, but the difference between serving a community-based punishment and serving time in prison can drastically shape an individual's ability to succeed in society.

NOTES

1. Stephan 2004.
2. Lynch 1995.
3. Deyoung 2003.
4. Cohen 2002.
5. Glassner 1999: xxi; Beiser 2001.
6. Beiser 2001.
7. Goode 1995.
8. NBC website: http://www.nbc.com/Law_&_Order/about/index.html.
9. Glassner 1999: xvii.
10. Rennison 2002.
11. Beiser 2001.
12. BJS 2006b.
13. Ibid.
14. Per 1,000 persons.
15. BJS 2004.
16. Walmsley 2003.
17. JPI 2002: 4.
18. See International Centre for Prison Studies [ICPS]. *World Prison Brief.*
19. Walmsley 2003.
20. JPI 2002: 3.
21. Ibid: 3–4 (table 1).
22. Ibid: 6.
23. Ibid: 2.
24. Ibid: 2.

25. Ibid: 2.
26. Austin and Fabelo 2004: 2.
27. Stephan 2004: 2.
28. BJS 2004.
29. JPI 2002: 7–8 (table 4).
30. JPI 2000.
31. Camp and Camp 1999.
32. Administration for Children and Families 2001.
33. Food & Nutrition Service 2004.
34. Forst 2004; Logan 1993.
35. BJS 2003c.
36. Gainsborough and Mauer 2000: 3.
37. Mauer et al. 2004b.
38. Mauer et al. 2004b: 3.
39. BJA 1998; Forst 1995.
40. See DiIulio 1993 on the multiple roles assumed by prison staff.
41. See Sykes 1958.

2

Punishment in the Twentieth Century: Run-On Sentences

The development of sentencing practices in the United States and the shaping of penal philosophies are deeply embedded within a landscape rich with passionate reformers, faith in an innate human goodness, investments in the capacity of individuals to find redemption, and at times, a raw and unforgiving fervor of harsh intolerance and condemnation. Over the past two centuries, the rehabilitative ideal—the belief that social deviants could redeem themselves through religion, hard labor, or treatment—has ebbed and flowed amidst a series of political transformations, social movements, and economic hardships. While the history of punishment in the United States is far beyond the scope of this chapter, we shall take a look at sentencing practices over the past century.

INDETERMINATE SENTENCING

During the early 1900s, when the nation lifted itself from the ashes of the Depression, rehabilitation as a goal of imprisonment emerged through the practice of indeterminate sentencing. Prisoners were engulfed in institutions that promoted reformation (or at least made a concerted effort) and that would later be branded *correctional facilities*.[1] It was believed that, with a helping hand of the state, people could change their deviant lifestyles if given a second chance (see chapter 6).

From the 1930s to 1970s, indeterminate sentencing was the primary method of sentencing used throughout the United States.[2] The concept of indeterminate sentencing was based on an individualized approach to rehabilitation[3] through incarceration whereby judges had the authority to dictate the maximum sentence to be served but would otherwise not provide a fixed release date. Through indeterminate sentencing, judges were able to consider an offender's individual circumstances when devising appropriate punishments.[4] They could thus hand down very different sentences to offenders who had committed very similar offenses. In calculating appropriate sentences, judges would weigh the severity of the offense, the offender's criminal history, and aggravating circumstances against relevant mitigating factors. Probation officers and parole boards were also endowed with a significant degree of discretion.[5] Prison staff, for example, could recommend that an inmate receive time off his or her sentence for good behavior. Judges would therefore hand down sentencing decisions under the assumption that the prison's staff would make the ultimate determination as to prisoners' release dates. For this reason, judges would often only give minimum and maximum sentence ranges.

Eventually, swelling prison populations and a declining faith in rehabilitation would usher in a new era of sentencing, making rehabilitation efforts difficult to implement and sustain. Prisons would later slam their doors in the face of reform and instead adopt measures founded on the ideals of incapacitation, retribution, and deterrence that still characterize sentencing today.

FROM INDETERMINATE TO STRUCTURED SENTENCING

The social unrest that occurred during the 1950s and 1960s[6] culminated in the sentencing reform movement that would begin to unfold in the 1970s. Lilly et al. describe "a host of . . . dramatic social and cultural shifts,"[7] such as the Civil Rights movement, which gained momentum in the mid-1950s, President Kennedy's assassination in 1963, and the United States' involvement in the Vietnam War,[8] that left many in a state of skepticism over the stability of social institutions.[9] Furthermore, the amount of control the state exercised over incarcerated individuals came into question.[10] This waning trust in the government, in conjunction with rising crime rates during the 1960s,[11] stirred up growing concern over the appropriateness and effectiveness of penal practices and methods of social control employed by the state.[12]

Two main issues arose in the 1970s that would launch widespread reform in sentencing laws and parole practices. First, sentencing was criticized for being too arbitrary, unfair, and for producing disparities in sentence lengths.[13] Criminologists insinuated that the lower class and minorities were being unfairly punished under the guise of rehabilitation and proposed significant policy changes in order to bring about more judicial consistency. A 1958 senatorial publication documented cases in which federal judges handed down sentences that were disparate in length.[14] The judges, each with different perspectives on rehabilitation, sentenced offenders with different degrees of leniency or severity. Research by the National Academy of Sciences Panel on Sentencing Research concluded that judges indeed had a greater impact on sentencing than any other factor[15] and were empowered by "unchecked discretion."[16] Ultimately it was concluded that the sentence an offender received depended largely on the judge residing over the case, a finding that caused great consternation regarding the equitable application of punishment.

Second, doubt over the efficacy of prison treatment programs arose among penologists, other academics, and politicians. Martinson's infamous publication in 1974 reported that "with few and isolated exceptions, the rehabilitative efforts that have been reported so far have no appreciable effect on recidivism."[17] The following year, Lipton et al. observed, "the field of corrections has not as yet found satisfactory ways to reduce recidivism by significant amounts."[18] If rehabilitation and treatment programs were yielding no noticeable effects, then handing down indeterminate sentences—a practice that was wholly based on the notion of personal reform—seemed to make little sense. While Martinson's findings were often quoted out of context and the methodological problems plaguing the studies included in his meta-analysis overlooked (see chapter 6), the belief that rehabilitation efforts were dead in the water was used to fuel many agendas in multiple forums.

After examining the "fundamental questions about the wisdom of maintaining a sentencing policy"[19] that was deemed ineffective, and with conservatives broadcasting the system's seeming failure to control crime, the country set out to reexamine "punishment, deterrence, and incapacitation as justifications for sentencing."[20] From the political front, critics charged that sentencing was too lenient, that judges and parole boards were too soft on crime, and that prison terms should be harsh and predictable.[21] Proponents of indeterminate sentencing, on the other hand, advocated for the continued utilization of judicial discretion, arguing that offenders should be treated as individuals—not just statistics—who could be reformed. Further, they stated that by limiting judicial discretion, the government was undermining the ability of judges and parole board members to professionally and effectively perform their jobs. However, there was also an increasing concern over discretionary parole boards, which were portrayed by critics as unsystematic, arbitrary, and ineffective in identifying which offenders were truly rehabilitated. Parole board members would generally make decisions through a voting system without being held accountable for their decisions.[22] Studies, such as an American Friends Service Committee report in 1971, found no evidence suggesting that current sentencing practices and parole decisions could effectively identify those who were rehabilitated and those who were still in need of treatment and incapacitation.

In response to the widespread debate over the correctional system's rehabilitative capacity,[23] "unchecked discretion" among judges,[24] accusations of arbitrary and racially discriminatory sentencing practices, and ethical concerns regarding indeterminate sentencing, state courts began to introduce structured sentencing in the 1970s. By adopting more structured and determinate sentencing, states sought to eliminate what they believed were unfair methods and replace them with practices that would yield more fixed and consistent punishments for similar offenses. Within a short span of time, the discretionary power that was once embraced by judges and prison officials quickly slipped away.

Despite a general consensus that modifications in sentencing procedures were desperately needed, developing a system that would address the grievances of liberals, conservatives, politicians, and academics proved a near impossibility. From the academic camp, scholars argued that sentences should be fixed, predictable, and consistent. Von Hirsch[25] and the Committee for the Study of Incarceration argued against both indeterminate sentencing and the rehabilitation ideal. They suggested that judges should have limitations placed on their discretionary power and argued that punishments should be less severe. From the political and conservative sidelines, judges were criticized for being too lenient on criminals and were pressured to deliver more punitive sentences. After all, "wicked people exist," according to James Q. Wilson,[26] and therefore had to be dealt with in a swift, judicious, and severe manner. As a response, the nation questioned the use of "punishment, deterrence, and incapacitation as justifications for sentencing"[27] and courts began to adopt a *just deserts*—or retributive—approach to punishment. From this perspective, the severity of a sentence would be directly proportionate to the nature and gravity of the offense. States adopted the goal of handing out like sentences for like crimes in order to produce fair and predictable punishments and to reduce racial disparities in sentence lengths. In addition to the concept of proportionality, the penal goals of incapacitation, retribution, deterrence, and truth-in-sentencing (TIS) became the predominant philosophies of punishment.[28]

At the federal level, major reforms were also reshaping the structural core of sentencing. Judge Marvin Frankel, in *Criminal Sentences: Law without Order*,[29] urgently called for the development of a commission to create sentencing guidelines; these guidelines would ultimately usurp the discretion of federal judges and parole boards,[30] thereby increasing uniformity and proportionality across sentences. The Federal Sentencing Guidelines, a product of the Sentencing Reform Act of 1984[31] and its newly established Sentencing Commission,[32] defined its goals as

1. "to reflect the seriousness of the offense, to promote respect for the law, and to provide just punishment for the offense;
2. to afford adequate deterrence to criminal conduct;
3. to provide the public from further crimes of the defendant; and

4. to provide the defendant with needed educational or vocational training, medical care, or other correctional treatment in the most effective manner."[33]

Over the next several years, states entered a period of experimentation[34] with structured sentences, such as flat-time sentencing,[35] voluntary sentencing, fixed-term mandatory sentencing, and presumptive sentencing, in order to fetter "fundamentally unjust" sentencing practices.[36] More importantly, sentencing commissions were formed throughout the nation to create sentencing guidelines that would, in essence, provide judges with formulaic sentencing procedures. To claim that sentencing commissions and their guidelines had a large impact on corrections is a gross understatement,[37] for they paved the way for a plethora of new and innovative sentencing practices. Major reforms were enacted in Maine, where determinate sentencing was adopted and parole abolished in 1975;[38] in Minnesota, where presumptive sentencing was enacted in 1978;[39] in California, which passed the Uniform Determinate Sentencing Law in 1976;[40] and in states where sentencing guidelines were adopted, such as Oregon, Minnesota, and Washington.[41]

Notoriously harsh sentencing laws, such as the 1951 Boggs Act that introduced mandatory minimum sentences for offenses relating to marijuana, the 1956 Narcotics Control Act, the 1973 Rockefeller Drug Laws in New York, Massachusetts' 1975 Bartley-Fox Amendment, Michigan's 1977 Felony Firearms Statute, and the 1998 Anti-Drug Abuse Act, were just a few examples of mandatory sentencing laws listed by Mauer and The Real Cost of Prisons Project that were devised to get "tough on crime."[42] In 1971, the same year as the Attica prison riot, President Nixon declared drugs "Enemy number one" and in 1973 created the Drug Enforcement Agency (DEA).[43] Neither the Reagan administration's war on drugs, waged in 1981, nor the crack cocaine frenzy that hit the streets in the mid-1980s, weakened the tough on crime movement.[44]

After 1975, 14 states abolished the use of discretionary parole boards,[45] and additionally harsh sentencing laws were passed by states and the federal government such as the notorious "three strikes" policies which was first adopted by Washington State in 1993 and California soon after.[46] By 1994, every state had some variation of mandatory sentencing, which was designed to send more drug offenders to prison and to prolong their sentences. This has been a successful undertaking to a certain extent; from 1980 to 1992, the possibility of being incarcerated following a drug arrest increased by 447 percent.[47] TIS, which was first adopted in Washington State in 1984, was also implemented throughout the country to extend the proportion of an offender's sentence that would actually be served (see chapter 3). As a result of TIS, inmates are now serving longer percentages of their prison terms.

Discretion has always played an integral part of the criminal justice system—from the preliminary decision to monitor a crime suspect to future decisions as to which offenders should be prosecuted, which inmates should be granted parole,[48] and whose probation should be revoked. At the sentencing phase, the removal or reduction of judicial discretion through new sentencing laws has directly affected many defendants who, under older laws, would have received probation rather than prison. The next chapter reviews the implications of sentencing structures that are in place today throughout the United States.

Now that we have reviewed the history of sentencing in the United States, we shall turn to sentencing structures that are in place today and current prison conditions.

NOTES

1. See Johnson 2002: chapter 2.
2. Tonry and Hatlestad 1997.
3. Walker 1993.
4. Tonry and Hatlestad 1997.
5. Forst 1995.
6. See Lilly, Cullen and Ball 1995: chapter 4; Cullen 2002.
7. Lilly et al. 1995: 94.
8. U.S. involvement lasted from 1964–1973.
9. Lilly et al. 1995: 93–95.
10. Cullen 2002.
11. Donziger 1996.
12. See Cullen 2002.
13. Bedau 1993.
14. BJA 1998.
15. Forst 1995.
16. Walker 1993: 115.
17. Martinson 1974: 25.
18. Lipton et al. 1975: 627.
19. Forst 1995: 376.
20. Walker 1993: 115.
21. Morris 1993.
22. Davis 1969.
23. Tonry 1999a.
24. Walker 1993: 115.
25. Von Hirsch 1986.
26. Wilson 1975.
27. Walker 1993: 115.
28. Bedau 1993; Mauer 1999; Tonry 1999b.
29. Frankel 1974.

30. USSC 2004a: 2.
31. The federal sentencing guidelines were implemented in 1987.
32. Bedau 1993; Mauer 1999; Forst 1999b.
33. USSC 2004b: 12. See 28 U.S.C. § 991(b)(1).
34. Lubitz and Ross 2001.
35. Walker 1993.
36. Morris 1993: 306.
37. It should be noted that in 2005, the Supreme Court ruled that parts of the federal sentencing guidelines were unconstitutional (Barbash 2005). See *U.S. v. Booker* (2005).
38. Walker 1993.
39. Walker 1993; Morris 1993.
40. Tonry and Hatlestad 1997; BJA 1998
41. Walker 1993.
42. Mauer 1999: 57, 62. Also see The Real Cost of Prisons Project.
43. See The Real Cost of Prisons Project.
44. See Mauer 1999.
45. Ditton and Wilson 1999.
46. BJA 1998.
47. Mauer 1999; BJA 1998.
48. Walker 1993.

II

SENTENCING AND PRISONS TODAY

3

Sentencing Today: A Sentence Is a Sentence—Period!

Today, there is a widespread consternation over what Americans have willingly accepted as an escalating crime problem. By now, however, we have established that crime rates are historically low, although by just examining our sentencing practices and correctional trends one might easily believe otherwise, and understandably so! When crimes are sensationalized, statistics distorted, and fear reinforced—almost ritualistically—it is no wonder that the public continues to support our increasingly punitive system of punishment with little thought as to the potential aftermath of decades of mass incarceration.

As was touched upon earlier, our incarceration rate[1] surpasses every other nation in the world. Penologists, policymakers, and politicians of any other era would be utterly astounded at our correctional monstrosities and our willingness to process, categorize, feed, and secure millions of human bodies—young and old, male and female, black and white, etc. Since rising crime rates are not the driving forces behind our country's bulging prison body, this chapter shall turn to trends in conviction and incarceration rates,[2] as well as recent innovations in sentencing practices.

Over the past 25 years, incarceration rates in the United States have increased by 249 percent, from 139 per 100,000 resident population in 1980 to a current rate of 486 (see table 3.1).[3] The Sentencing Project observes that the rise in incarceration from 1992 to 2001 was due in whole to changes in sentencing policies instead of crime rates.[4] One of the most pressing questions therefore is: *Why, since crime rates are low, are we still incarcerating so many people?* For one, sentencing policies—like many other laws—are generally driven by the public's fear of crime. The public's support of these initiatives is often fueled by raw emotions, as well as a tendency to seek out im-

Table 3.1. State and Federal Incarceration Rate per 100,000 U.S. Population, 1980–2004

1980	139
1981	154
1982	171
1983	179
1984	188
1985	202
1986	217
1987	231
1988	247
1989	276
1990	297
1991	313
1992	332
1993	359
1994	389
1995	411
1996	427
1997	444
1998	461
1999	476
2000	478
2001	470
2002	476
2003	482
2004	486
% Change, 1980–2004	249.6

Source: BJS website. 2005a. "Key Facts at a Glance: incarceration rate, 1980–2004". Washington, DC: Bureau of Justice Statistics, U.S. Department of Justice (http://www.ojp .usdoj.gov/bjs/glance/tables/incrttab.htm).

mediate solutions rather than fund social programs or even entertain the idea of forgiveness and leniency. To answer this question further is to explore the historical context in which these changes are unfolding, thus unraveling the many complexities of the criminal justice system and revealing the inner mechanisms that maintain the churning of the judicial wheels. First, we must touch upon a history fraught with indecisive attitudes toward offenders and their deserved fates.

The criminal justice system is made up of a succession of major decision points,[5] from search and arrest to incarceration and finally probation.[6, 7] In many states these decisions are no longer in the hands of judges and parole boards but reside under the auspices of state legislatures. The era of rehabili-

Table 3.2. Felons Sentenced to State or Federal Prison and Mean Maximum Sentence Lengths by Most Serious Conviction Offense, 2000

Most Serious Conviction Offense	Percent of Felons Sentenced to Prison/Jail		Mean Maximum Sentence Length for Incarcerated Felons In Months	
	State	Federal	State	Federal
All offenses	68	83	36	58
Violent offenses	78	92	66	86
Property offenses	64	59	27	23
Drug offenses	67	92	30	76
Weapon offenses	70	91	25	91
Other offenses	66	83	22	33

Source: Durose and Langan. 2003a. "Felony Sentences in State Courts, 2000." Washington, DC: Bureau of Justice Statistics, U.S. Department of Justice: page 3.

tation has faded into a new preoccupation with stiff punishments and incapacitation. As explained in chapter 2, the 1970s debate over the rehabilitative capability of our prisons and floating concerns over disparate sentencing practices led to the introduction of structured sentencing that would ideally produce more predictable and uniform sentences. Rather than hand out individualized sentences reflecting a specific defendant's personal characteristics, life situation, and other such factors unique to each offense, courts began to mete out consistent sentences for similar offenses.[8] In efforts to increase the punitive nature of our correctional system and to reduce disparities between sentences received and actual time served, offenders are now expected to serve lengthier proportions of their original sentences. The culmination of sentencing reforms has left prisons throughout the country in overcrowded conditions and has galvanized efforts by state legislatures to orient sentencing practices towards proportionality and truth-in-sentencing (TIS).[9]

These efforts have not been in vain. In 2000, there were over 900,000 individuals who were convicted of felonies in state and federal courts.[10] Table 3.2 compares the percentage of state and federal felons sentenced to prison (as opposed to other sanctions), as well as the mean maximum sentences received (in 2000). A higher percentage of federal felons (83 percent) were sentenced to prison or jail than state felons (68 percent),[11] and their average maximum sentences (58 months) were longer than those received by the average state felon (36 months). Among violent felons, 92 percent of those convicted in federal courts and 78 percent convicted in state courts received prison or jail time. State property offenders, on the other hand, had a higher likelihood of going to prison or jail (64 percent) than did federal property offenders (59 percent). The largest gap in the percent of state and federal convictions resulting in incarceration by crime type was among drug offenses. Of

Table 3.3.   U.S. District Courts and Outcomes, 1980–2001ª

Year	Total	Convicted	Imprisonedᵇ	Imprisoned as Percent of Convicted
1980	39,172	29,943	13,766	46.0
1985	51,243	40,924	20,605	50.3
1990	58,704	47,494	28,659	60.3
1995	56,480	47,556	31,805	66.9
2000	76,952	68,156	50,451	74.0
2001	77,145	68,533	51,057	74.5
% Change, 1980–2001	97	129	271	62

ªIncludes class A misdemeanors handled by U.S. magistrates.
ᵇThis figure includes offenders who were incarcerated and who received a community corrections sentence
Source: Bureau of Justice Statistics website. 2003a. Federal Criminal Case Processing, 2001 with trends
  1982–2001, Reconciled Data. (http://www.ojp.usdoj.gov/bjs/glance/fedipc.htm).

those convicted in federal courts, 92 percent were incarcerated, compared to 67 percent of drug offenders convicted in state courts. Federal drug offenders received an average maximum sentence of 76 months, while state offenders were sentenced to 30 months on average. Overall, a higher percentage of federal felony convictions resulted in prison/jail for all offense categories except property offenses than did state convictions. Further, federal felony offenders received lengthier mean maximum sentences than state felons, but once again with the exception of property offenses.

By 2003, there were 161,673 individuals in federal prisons.[12] The federal government has been using prison at a continually high rate as the number of convictions continues to rise, even though it has been estimated that "nearly three-fourths (72.1%) of federal prisoners are serving time for a nonviolent offense and have no history of violence."[13] The number of offenders convicted in federal courts increased by 129 percent from 1980 to 2001, yet the percentage of convicted offenders actually sent to prison increased by 62 percent—from 46 percent in 1980 to 74.5 percent in 2001 (table 3.3). According to the Sentencing Project, "While many states are experiencing a slowing of the rate of growth of their prison population and some a small decline, the federal prison population continues its rapid expansion."[14] Much of this growth has been attributed to the public-supported government's campaign against drugs and a growing number of federal prosecutions, which increased from 1984 to 1999 by 147 percent.[15]

Since the early 1990s, however, the percentage of offenders receiving prison sentences in state courts for many crime categories has decreased despite an increasing number of convictions (see table 3.4). In state courts during the 1990s, there was a 3.5 percent increase in felony convictions, from 893,630 in 1992[16] to 924,700 by 2000.[17] The offenses for which these

Table 3.4. Number of State Felony Convictions and Percent Sentenced to Prison by Offense Type, 1992 and 2000

Offense[a]	Number of State Felony Convictions		Percent Sentenced to Prison	
	1992	2000	1992	2000
All Offenses	**893,630**	**924,700**	**44**	**40**
Violent Offenses	**165,099**	**173,200**	**60**	**54**
Murder	9,079	6,400	93	93
Manslaughter	3,469	2,100		
Rape	21,655	10,600	68	70
Other sexual assault	20,900			
Robbery	51,878	36,800	74	74
Armed	13,810	10,400		
Unarmed	20,154	11,000		
Unspecified	17,914	15,300		
Aggravated assault	58,969	79,400	44	40
Other violent	20,049	17,000	39	42
Weapon Offenses	**26,422**	**28,200**	**40**	**41**
Property Offenses	**297,494**	**262,000**	**42**	**37**
Burglary	114,630	79,300	52	52
Residential	16,649	10,900		
Nonresidential	45,159	16,300		
Unspecified	52,822	52,100		
Larceny	119,000	100,000	38	33
Motor vehicle theft	19,332	11,900		
Other theft	99,668	88,100		
Fraud	30,245	82,700	31	29
Forgery	33,619	40,500		
Drug Offenses	**280,232**	**319,700**	**42**	**38**
Possession	109,426	116,300	33	33
Trafficking	170,806	203,400	48	41
Marijuana	16,376	25,300		
Other	125,333	54,400		
Unspecified	29,097	123,700		
Other Offenses	**124,383**	**141,600**	**35**	**32**

[a]Represents most serious conviction offense.
Sources: Langan and Graziadei. 1995. "Felony Sentences in State Courts, 1992." Bureau of Justice Statistics, U.S. Department of Justice: tables 1, 2, 4; Durose and Langan. 2003a. "Felony Sentences in State Courts, 2000." Bureau of Justice Statistics, U.S. Department of Justice: tables 1, 2, 4.

individuals were convicted in 1992 were as follows: 18.4 percent violent, 33.5 percent property, and 31.3 percent drug-related.[18] Among those convicted of felonies in 2000, 18.7 percent were for violent offenses, 28.3 percent were property crimes, and 34.6 percent for drug offenses.[19] From 1992 to 2000, the percent of convicted felony offenders who received prison terms decreased from 44 to 40 percent, and those receiving probation increased from 30 to 32 percent.[20] During this same period, the percent of violent offenders receiving prison sentences decreased from 60 to 54 percent, as did the percent of property offenders decrease from 42 to 37 percent and the percent of drug offenders decrease from 42 to 38 percent.[21] Thus, the overall percentage of individuals given prison sentences for state felonies over the past 15 years has decreased among violent, property, and drug offenders.

Though the federal system appears more punitive in sentence lengths, given the data presented in table 3.2, the percentage of prison sentences actually expected to be served has increased in state courts since 1992, notably among non-violent offenders (see table 3.5). Table 3.5 shows the mean prison sentences given to state offenders in 1992 and 2002, as well as the estimated percentage of sentences and number of months expected to be served. In 1992, the mean prison sentence for all felonies in state prisons was 79 months, with an average 38 percent expected to be served in prison (or 30 months).[22] In 2002, the mean prison sentence for all state felonies had decreased to 53 months, but the estimated percent of the sentence to be served was 51 (or 27 months), a 34 percent increase since 1992.[23] For violent offenders, the estimated percent of sentences served in prison increased from 46 (58 months) in 1992 to 62 (52 months) in 2002, a 34.7 percent increase. For drug offenders in 1992, it was estimated that they would serve 32 percent (21 months) of their sentences in prison, but this figure increased to 43 percent (20 months) in 2002, a 34 percent increase. Among those convicted of drug possession, the estimated percent of sentences to be served in prison increased from 27 (15 months) in 1992 to 40 (14 months) in 2002, a 48 percent increase. Finally, property offenders were expected to serve an average 34 percent (23 months) of their sentences in prison in 1992, but 49 percent (20 months) in 2002, a percentage increase of 44. While the absolute number of estimated months served by convicted state felons decreased from 1992 to 2002, the percentage of the original sentence to be served in prison has increased, especially among those convicted of drug possession and property offenses. Furthermore, the increase in the estimated percentage of sentences to be served was greater among property offenders (44.1 percent) than violent offenders (34.7 percent).

This overall trend may reflect states' attempts to eliminate the traditional early release process in prisons by requiring offenders to serve a greater portion of their sentences and by seeking more TIS. On a different note, how-

Table 3.5.   State Court Mean Prison Sentence, Estimated Percent to Be Served, Estimated Time Actually Served, 1992 and 2002

Offense[a]	Mean Prison Sentence (months)		Estimated % of Sentence to Be Served		% Increase of Sentence to Be Served	Estimated Time Served (months)[b]	
	1992	2002	1992	2002	1992–2002	1992	2002
All Offenses	79	53	38	51	34.2	30	27
Violent Offenses	125	84	46	62	34.7	58	52
Murder	251	225	44	63	43.2	110	142
Rape	164	132	50	68	36.0	82	90
Robbery	117	91	46	58	26.1	54	53
Aggravated assault	87	54	48	66	37.5	42	36
Other violent	88	51	46	61	32.6	40	31
Weapon Offenses	55	38	46	63	37.0	25	24
Property Offenses	67	41	34	49	44.1	23	20
Burglary	76	50	35	49	40.0	27	24
Larceny	53	34	33	52	57.6	17	18
Fraud	69	38	30	44	46.7	21	17
Drug Offenses	67	48	32	43	34.3	21	20
Possession	55	35	27	40	48.1	15	14
Trafficking	72	55	34	45	32.4	24	24
Other Offenses	53	38	42	50	19.0	22	19

[a]Represents most serious conviction offense.
[b]Calculated by multiplying mean prison sentence by estimated percent of prison time served
Sources: Langan and Graziadei. 1995. "Felony Sentences in State Courts, 1992." Bureau of Justice Statistics, U.S. Department of Justice: tables 1, 2, 4; Durose and Langan. 2004. "Felony Sentences in State Courts, 2002": table 4; Durose and Langan. 2003a. "Felony Sentences in State Courts, 2000": tables 1,2, 4.

ever, the mean prison sentences decreased (or increased only slightly) from 2000 and 2002, as did the estimated percent of sentences to be served. This turnaround may indicate that state courts and prisons are recognizing their functional and operational limitations in housing offenders. Nonetheless, the percentage of sentences expected to be served in prison in 2002 were substantially higher than in 1992, as were the actual number of persons incarcerated.

THE CURRENT STATE OF SENTENCING

In many states, sentencing today is an unforgiving and unrelenting practice in which professional judicial discretion has been replaced by formulaic legislative decisions that dictate sentence lengths for specific crimes. However, the path to our current statutes has not been straightforward, nor has it been consistent across states. This section reviews the developments in sentencing practices that have led to these current correctional trends.

Sentencing Commissions and Guidelines

Sentencing commissions have emerged in the federal government and several states in order to formulate legislatively determined sentencing guidelines,[24] many of which adhere to presumptive or voluntary sentencing. By adopting sentencing guidelines, state systems and the federal government have sought to control discretion, increase the fairness of sentencing, and to adhere to the principles of punishment, incapacitation, and rehabilitation.[25] After all, what was the "wisdom of maintaining a sentencing policy"[26] if it was ineffective? The Bureau of Justice Assistance[27] and Lubitz and Ross[28] cite the various goals that have been espoused by states that have adopted sentencing guidelines which include 1) increasing judicial accountability by reducing racial, gender, and socioeconomic sentencing disparities and by increasing uniformity across sentences; 2) lengthening or shortening sentences for various types of crimes and classes of offenders; 3) implementing TIS; 4) increasing the use of intermediate sanctions and community corrections; 5) reducing crowding in prison; 6) adopting the penal philosophies of just deserts, incapacitation, and rehabilitation; 7) and clarifying sentencing procedures and rationales.[29] Whether these goals have actually been actualized continues to be widely debated and varies by state.

Federal Sentencing Guidelines

Within the federal government, the goal of rehabilitation was once pervasive, yet issues of sentencing disparities were also prevalent. Prior to the federal sentencing reform era of the 1980s, sentences were prescribed with great discretion under the assumption that parole authorities would determine when offenders should be released, a practice that "exacerbated the lack of uniformity."[30] These concerns were addressed through the Sentencing Reform Act of 1984, which created the United States Sentencing Commission (USSC),[31] an "independent agency within the judicial branch of the federal government" charged with "promulgating guidelines to be used for sentencing within the statutorily prescribed maximum sentence."[32] As a result, a system of presumptive sentencing was implemented that bound judicial sentencing to punishments set forth through guidelines. The new guidelines, implemented in 1987,[33] were intended to create more uniform and predictable sentences and to deter, as well as provide offenders with necessary treatment, training, or education.[34] More specifically, however, the Commission was instructed to create a system of sentencing that would reflect the following: 1) the severity of the offense, 2) aggravating/mitigating circumstances, 3) harm caused by the offense, 4) the community's perspective on the crime and public concern stemming from the crime, and 5) the general deterrent potential of the sentence.[35] Furthermore, there were

> eleven additional factors for the Commission to consider in establishing categories of defendants, including, but not limited to, age, education, mental and emotional condition, physical condition, role in the offense, and criminal history. The SRA [Sentencing Reform Act] prohibited the Commission from considering the race, sex, national origin, creed, and socioeconomic status of offenders, and instructed that the sentencing guidelines should reflect the general appropriateness of considering certain factors that might serve as proxies for forbidden factors, such as current unemployment.[36]

The resulting guidelines, which Tonry describes as "[o]ne of the commission's worst blunders,"[37] took the form of a "sentencing table with 43 offense levels and six criminal history categories."[38] The level of the offense was based upon details of the criminal incident and the severity of the crime; the level could be enhanced based on additional factors, such as whether a weapon was used during the commission of a crime.[39] Despite attempts to standardize sentencing procedures, reduce disparities in punishments, and increase the predictability of punishments, the federal government managed to commission one of the most notoriously harsh sentencing structures that significantly diminished the role of discretion in sentencing decisions. Judges were bound by these sentencing guidelines, even if they believed the sentence was too severe, unless there were special aggravating or mitigating circumstances.[40] This would be the general trend until a recent Supreme Court decision (which will be discussed momentarily), which restored some of this usurped discretion. Under the traditional federal guidelines, judges were permitted to impose sentences for behaviors that were never presented to the jury; for example, if the judge believed the defendant lied in court, sentence enhancements could be added to the penalty.[41] However, this practice was found to be unconstitutional by the Supreme Court because "the mandatory application of the federal sentencing guidelines violated the right to trial by jury under the Sixth Amendment."[42] In January of 2005, the Supreme Court ruled in *United States v. Booker*[43] that "district courts, while not bound to apply the Guidelines, must consult those guidelines and take them into account when sentencing."[44] Thus, the guidelines serve an advisory rather than mandatory role.[45]

While the impact of this decision is still under evaluation, the USSC has found that a "majority of federal cases continue to be sentenced in conformance with the sentencing guidelines";[46] sentences, on average, have increased;[47] the rate at which prison sentences are being handed down has not declined; and "the rate of imposition of above-range sentences doubled to a rate of 1.6 percent after *Booker*."

SENTENCING STRUCTURES

The reforms within the federal system are not unique, as different states have taken different sentencing routes. Yet, most of these paths have led to the implementation of structured sentencing policies that have only expanded the use of incarceration. There are four types of sentencing structures that can be identified throughout the Unites States, which are categorized as presumptive, voluntary, indeterminate, and determinate.[48]

Presumptive Sentencing

According to the 1996 National Survey of State Sentencing Structures, 17 states have adopted presumptive or voluntary sentencing.[49] Under the presumptive sentencing structure, state legislatures establish sentencing guidelines that set forth a range of determinate and indeterminate sentences for specific crimes. The objectives of presumptive sentencing include uniformity, proportionality, and unbiased sentencing practices. Judges must choose a sentence within the range specified by the guidelines, and if they deviate they are required to formally justify their reasons for doing so. The sentencing guidelines used by the federal system determine the length of presumptive sentences by examining the severity of the crime and the defendant's criminal history.[50] The USSC[51] has identified the guideline goals that have already been accomplished, including increased rational and transparent sentencing and more certain and severe punishments.[52] Goals that have been "partially achieved" are sentencing disparity reductions and increased uniformity in sentencing.[53]

Voluntary Sentencing

Within the framework of voluntary sentencing, judges are provided with recommended sentences. However, they are not legally compelled to follow the recommendations and may hand down determinate or indeterminate sentences. Many judicial decisions are based on outcomes of prior cases with similar circumstances.

Indeterminate Sentencing

Through indeterminate sentencing, judges may hand down a maximum sentence, or a minimum and maximum sentence. Judges can give defendants long sentences rather than statutorily predetermined sentences, thus ultimately rely upon discretionary parole boards to determine when the offenders are fit for release. Over 35 states and the District of Columbia use indeterminate sentencing, and most states still retain the use of discretionary parole. All but two states (Hawaii and Utah) still grant inmates good time credits.[54]

Determinate Sentencing

Determinate sentences are fixed and inmates are often ineligible for parole, but inmates in some states can earn good time credits.[55] In addition to the sentencing structures described above, various determinate sentencing practices have unfolded in efforts to enforce "tough on crime" agendas and to deter offenders. These include mandatory minimums, TIS, and three-strikes laws.

Mandatory Minimums

Mandatory minimum statutes, which FAMM (Families against Mandatory Minimums) describes as a "one-size-fits-all" approach to punishment,[56] require specific offenders to be given preset sentences for predetermined crimes, with no option of parole and with no allowance for judicial discretion. The crimes that are punished through mandatory minimum laws are generally drug- and gun-related,[57] yet there is little evidence that mandatory minimums effectively reduce gun- and drug-related crimes, nor do they always increase the probability of imprisonment. The use of mandatory minimums under the Narcotic Control Act of 1956 showed no appreciable effect in reducing drug offending[58] but Congress nonetheless embraced mandatory minimum policies in 1984[59] which were subsequently found in every state by 1994.[60]

The federal system also launched a massive strike against drug-related offenses in the 1980s—especially those involving crack cocaine—which was described as "a violence inducing, highly addictive plague of inner cities."[61] Congress passed crack-related mandatory sentencing laws in 1986 and 1988 and rejected a USSC recommendation in 1995 to "equaliz[e] the quantity ratio that would trigger the mandatory sentences."[62] Under the federal guidelines, a first-time offender could receive a ten-year mandatory minimum prison sentence for 50 grams of crack cocaine, yet it would only require 5 kilograms of powder cocaine to receive the same sentence.[63]

In 2002, the USSC stated that these crack-related mandatory minimums "exaggerate the relative harmfulness of crack cocaine" and affect many low-level drug offenders and minorities.[64] However, in 2003, there were over 5,400 individuals who were sentenced in federal courts for offenses involving crack cocaine, of whom 75 percent were given mandatory five-or ten-year prison sentences.[65] King and Mauer explain that the outcome of *Booker* permits judicial discretion only when "a mandatory sentence does not apply" or "in the consideration of enhancements beyond the baseline sentence in a vast majority of cases where a mandatory does apply."[66]

As of November 2004, there were nearly 78,000 sentenced drug offenders in federal prison. These offenders made up 54.1 percent of the total federal prison population. In fiscal year 2004, the USSC reported on 18,137 drug offenders sentenced prior to *Blakely*.[67] Among these cases, 28 percent of the offenders were African American (5,061), 27.4 percent white (4,979), and 41.5 percent (7,528) Hispanic.[68] Among the 4,019 federal offenders sentenced for powder cocaine offenses in 2004, only 16.9 percent were white whereas 26.3 percent were African American and 55.3 percent Hispanic. Among the 3,698 sentenced for crack cocaine offenses, 6.8 percent were white, 83.1 percent were African American, and 9.2 percent Hispanic. Broken down by gender, 13.4 percent of those sentenced for federal drug offenses were female (2,422) and 86.6 percent were male (15,707).[69] Of the 3,698 crack cocaine offenders, 8.8 percent were female, and of the 4,020 powder cocaine offenders, women comprised 12.6 percent.[70]

In 2004, the average federal crack cocaine sentence was 129.2 months, whereas the average powder cocaine sentence was 85.1 months.[71] Approximately 49.5 percent (1,833) of crack cocaine offenders received a mandatory minimum sentence of ten years or more, the highest percent among all drug categories, and 44.1 percent of powder cocaine offenders (1,773) received ten-year mandatory minimum sentences.[72] Approximately 29 percent (1,164) of powder cocaine and 28 percent (1,035) of crack cocaine offenders received five-year mandatory minimum sentences. Those sentenced on marijuana charges received an average of 343.5 months, those sentenced on heroin charges received 66.3 months, and those sentenced for methamphetamine offenses were given an average of 101.2 months.[73] Approximately 64 percent (3,066) of marijuana offenders, 38.4 percent (494) of heroin offenders, and 26.9 percent (952) of methamphetamine offenders received no mandatory minimum sentences.[74] However, 25.7 percent (1,232) of marijuana offenders were given five-year mandatory minimum sentences and 10.5 percent (502) received ten-year mandatory minimum sentences. Among heroin offenders, 27.5 percent (353) were given five-year and 34.1 percent (438) received ten-year mandatory minimum sentences, as were 25.6 percent (908) and 47.5 percent (1,681) of methamphetamine offenders, respectively.

It is especially interesting to note that agents within the state and federal systems, especially judges, have employed the use of discretion in order to circumvent sentences they believe are too harsh.[75] Tonry's research on mandatory sentencing found that arrest rates decreased following the enactment of mandatory sentencing laws.[76] He also reported that while mandatory sentencing laws resulted in longer and harsher sentences, more defendants chose to go to trial rather than plea-bargain and that the probability of incarceration did not significantly increase. A 1993 study[77] reviewed by Vincent and Hofer found that while mandatory minimums in New York increased the likelihood of conviction and the severity of the sentences, "there were declines in the volume of arrests, the rate of indictment upon arrest, and the rate of conviction upon indictment. The result was that the overall probability of imprisonment after the law's enactment was lower than before the law."[78]

On the other hand, mandatory minimums have contributed significantly to the rising number of women going to prison. In 1986, 2.9 out of every 100 women arrested for drug-related crimes were imprisoned. By 2000, the rate of incarceration among arrested female drug-offenders had increased to 9.1 per 100, a 214 percent growth.[79] In a startling yet similar streak, the number of women who were arrested and subsequently imprisoned for public order offenses increased by 250 percent from 1986 to 2000.[80] The consequences of the rise of the number of women in prison have been staggering and will be addressed in more detail in chapter 6.

There has been much doubt cast upon the efficacy of mandatory sentencing, as it has arguably added to the complexities and dysfunctions of the criminal justice system.[81] Thousands of low-level federal offenders have been affected by mandatory minimum statutes, many of whom are nonviolent and without criminal histories.[82] Vincent and Hofer report on 10,670 federal offenders who were convicted under mandatory sentencing statutes in 1992.[83] Of the 9,359 offenders sentenced for drug trafficking, 4 percent (340) had minimal roles, 9 percent (881) had minor roles, 9 percent (776) had "manager" or "leader" roles, and only 23 percent of the offenses involved weapons.[84] Further, 49 percent of those sentenced for drug trafficking had no "criminal history points,"[85] and 12 percent had one criminal history point.[86] Altogether, Vincent and Hofer conclude that federal mandatory minimum statutes have little or no effect in reducing crime rates and deterring offenders, nor do they appropriately target offenders who are truly "in need of incapacitation."[87] Tonry also concluded that "mandatory penalties do not work" and that they do little in the way of reducing serious crime.[88]

Truth-in-Sentencing

TIS was originally implemented in Washington State in 1984. In addition to incapacitation,[89] the rationale behind TIS is to narrow the gap between the length of a sentence given to an offender and the proportion of the sentence that is actually served. TIS generally comes hand-in-hand with the elimination of discretionary parole boards and earned-time credits.[90] By abolishing discretionary parole boards, TIS ensures that certain offenders serve a larger percentage of their sentences. Indiana abolished parole in 1977, followed by Maine (1975) and Illinois (1978). During the 1980s, Florida, Minnesota, Oregon, and Washington abolished parole; Arizona, Delaware, Kansas, Mississippi, North Carolina, Ohio, and Wisconsin all followed suit in the 1990s.[91] By 2000, discretionary parole boards had been abolished in 16 states.[92]

The Violent Offender Incarceration and Truth-in-Sentencing Incentive Grants Program provided grants to states that met the federal TIS standards.[93] By 1998, 27 states and the District of Columbia met these federal TIS standards.[94] Delaware, Minnesota, Tennessee, Utah, and Washington were already using TIS prior to 1994. Table 3.6 shows state TIS requirements (as of 1999). In some states and in the federal system, 85 percent of a sentence must be served under TIS, while other states may only require 50 percent or some other predetermined percentage. Arkansas, for example, requires 70 percent of a sentence to be served for certain violent offenses.[95] In Colorado, offenders with two prior violent convictions are required to serve 75 percent of their sentence, whereas those with only one prior conviction serve 56.25 percent.

Table 3.6. State TIS Requirements

Required Time Served				
85%		50%	100% of min.	Other
Arizona	Missouri	Indiana	Idaho	Alaska
California	New Jersey	Maryland	Nevada	Arkansas
Connecticut	New York	Nebraska	New Hampshire	Colorado
Delaware	North Carolina	Texas		Kentucky
D.C.	North Dakota			Massachusetts
Florida	Ohio			Wisconsin
Georgia	Oklahoma			
Illinois[a]	Oregon			
Iowa	Pennsylvania			
Kansas	South Carolina			
Louisiana	Tennessee			
Maine	Utah			
Michigan	Virginia			
Minnesota	Washington			
Mississippi				

[a]Qualified for federal funding only in 1996.
Source: Ditton and Wilson. 1999. "Bureau of Justice Statistics Special Report: Truth in Sentencing": table 1 (http://www.ojp.usdoj.gov/bjs/pub/pdf/tssp.pdf).

TIS has been effective in increasing the percentage of sentence time served, especially among certain categories of offenders. Approximately 70 percent of inmates entering state prisons for violent offenses are now required to serve at least 85 percent of their sentence. However, while violent offenders are serving a higher percentage of their sentences in states with TIS than in non-TIS states, they are serving less absolute time in TIS states, on average, than in non-TIS states. Table 3.7 shows that violent inmates in 1999 served an average of 53 months in TIS states and 55 months in non-TIS states. What table 3.7 indicates is that TIS states are accomplishing their goal of increasing the percentage of sentences that violent offenders are supposed to serve, but that violent offenders in non-TIS states are in actuality serving more time (in months) than those in non-TIS states.

Three-Strikes Laws

Three-strikes laws, which have been implemented in the federal system and in over 20 states, are based on the belief that "[o]ffenders convicted repeatedly of serious offenses should be removed from society for long periods of time, in many cases for life."[96] According to FAMM, three-strikes laws were enacted by the federal system to incarcerate "high level" drug traffickers who in actuality only make up 11 percent of the drug offenders in federal prisons. Three-strikes laws found throughout the United States are diverse and complex and each state has its own variation of the three-strikes concept with different offenses eligible as *strikes*.[97] In addition, the number of strikes needed before an offender is *out* varies by state. In some states, *out* may result in a mandatory life sentence with no possibility of parole; in other states it could lead to a long sentence with the eventual possibility of parole. For example, one only has to commit two strikeable offenses in South Carolina to be *out*—meaning mandatory life in prison with no possibility of parole. In Nevada, on the other hand, three strikeable offenses must be committed for the court to sentence an offender to either life without parole, life with eligibility for parole after ten years, or 25 years with the possibility of parole after 10 years.

Table 3.7. Mean Time Served and Percent of Sentence Served for Violent Offenders: 1993, 1996, and 1999

	Mean Time Served (in Months)			Percent of Sentence Served		
	1993	*1996*	*1999*	*1993*	*1996*	*1999*
TIS states	46	50	53	46	52	56
Non-TIS states	53	54	55	42	48	54

Sources: BJS. 2001a. *Trends in State Parole*, 1990–2000. Washington, DC: U.S. Department of Justice: page 6.

California's controversial three-strikes law is another prime example of the shift from the rehabilitation paradigm to current punitive sentencing practices. In 1994, California's Governor Pete Wilson passed the "Three Strikes and You're Out" legislation[98] with the intent of "getting tough" on repeat offenders: "*It sends a clear message to repeat criminals. Find a new line of work, because we're going to start turning career criminals into career inmates.*"[99] On the other hand, Walker describes three-strikes policies as "represent[ing] all the worst aspects of the 'get tough' approach to crime" because the laws are not applied consistently, they result in the incarceration of many nonviolent offenders, and they impose great costs on criminal justice systems.[100] Nonetheless, following the lead of Washington, California was the second state to pass such legislation.[101]

While Washington's three-strikes legislation stated that offenders had to have committed three predetermined felonies,[102] only the first two convictions had to be from a list of specific offenses in California. Any felony committed afterwards could be considered strikeable. Further, *out* in California could mean a mandatory indeterminate life sentence with no possibility of parole for at least 25 years, whereas Washington's *out* resulted in a mandatory life sentence without the possibility of parole.[103] One especially harsh aspect of California's "two-strikes" law is that a sentence handed down to a felon could be doubled if the offender had previously committed even one strikeable offense.[104]

At the turn of twenty-first century, California had more offenders sentenced under its two- and three-strike laws than any other state.[105] As of December 31, 2005, the California Department of Corrections and Rehabilitation[106] reported that there were 32,951 second- and 7,813 third-strikers in its adult institution population. The offenses for which the second-strikers were incarcerated included crimes against persons (38 percent), property crimes (28 percent), and drug crimes (24 percent). Among the third-strikers, the offenses were also crimes against persons (44 percent), property crimes (31 percent), and drug offenses (17 percent). Overall, individuals convicted of crimes against persons made up 39 percent of the second- and third-striker prison population, while 29 and 22 percent had committed property and drug offenses, respectively. As these figures suggest, nonviolent inmates are falling into the trappings of three-strikes (or two-strikes) legislation, laws that were originally designed to remove more dangerous, career offenders from the streets.

Aside from harsher sentencing laws and increases in arrests and convictions, current patterns suggest that the public is generally less forgiving of individuals who break laws. To give someone a second chance—to divert them from the formal criminal justice system—is to weaken our tough on crime stance, to forfeit our sense of control and power, and to portray the person as human rather than just another body being processed through the system.

PROBATION

Over the past two and a half decades, the rate of adults in the United States under some form of correctional supervision has increased by 180 percent.[107] With a current total correctional population of nearly seven million, and no feasible way of incapacitating all offenders, courts must seek alternatives to incarceration through probation.[108] In 2004, there were over four million adults on probation (see table 3.8),[109] half of whom were convicted of a misdemeanor and nearly a quarter who were women.[110] Probation entails a specified period during which offenders are supervised within their communities, often with strict guidelines, which if broken, may trigger a prison term. The growth that we have witnessed among prison and jail populations has been accompanied by an increasing number of offenders on probation. From 1995 to 2004, the number of individuals on probation increased by 35 percent while the number of those in prison increased by 31 percent.

Our nation's use of probation has been under considerable pressure to increase in order to contend with a rapidly growing correctional population. In some cases, violent offenders are given probation while nonviolent offenders are given prison sentences; in other situations, low-level nonviolent offenders are kept out of prison. Current probationers are 56 percent white, 30 percent black, and 12 percent Hispanic.[111] For 3 percent of this population, the most serious offense for which they received probation was

Table 3.8. Adult Correctional Populations, 1995–2004

Year	Total Estimated Correctional Population[a]	Probation
1995	5,342,900	3,077,861
2000	6,445,100	3,826,209
2001	6,581,700	3,931,731
2002	6,758,800	4,024,067
2003	6,936,600	4,144,782
2004	6,996,500	4,151,125
% Change, 1995–2004	31	35

[a]Includes individuals in prison, jail, probation, and parole.
Source: Glaze and Palla. 2005. "Probation and Parole in the United States, 2004." Washington, DC: Bureau of Justice Statistics, U.S. Department of Justice.

sexual assault. Other offenses include domestic violence (6 percent), other assaults (10 percent), battery (5 percent), larceny/theft (12 percent), fraud (5 percent), drug offenses (26 percent), driving while intoxicated (15 percent), and minor traffic offenses (7 percent).[112] For many offenders, probation is a viable alternative to incarceration, one that holds promise for nonviolent offenders and their respective families. This will be revisited in chapter 13.

SENTENCING TODAY

By 1996, sentencing was anything but homogeneous throughout the United States.[113] The strength of judicial discretion varies throughout the country as different states have adopted voluntary, presumptive, statutory, and determinate sentencing practices.[114] Discretionary parole boards were eliminated in many states where policies such as mandatory sentencing and TIS were adopted. The National Survey of State Sentencing Structures in 1996 found that the federal government and 19 states had developed sentencing commissions, and 17 states were adhering to presumptive or voluntary sentencing.[115] Moreover, the survey indicated that sentencing had become more determinate with the advent of mandatory sentencing, TIS, and three-strikes laws. Overall, however, many states seem to be returning to indeterminate sentencing, a practice originally grounded in the philosophy of rehabilitation that we have largely forgone in favor of tougher punishments. Sentencing today is still plagued with systematic injustices and disparities and continues to challenge the criminal justice community. Devising sentencing policies that are fair and impartial, yet justly implemented and not too formulaically automated, has been an overwhelming undertaking among lawmakers, academics, and prison administrators. There is unlikely to be a single solution that will yield a consensus among all of the aforementioned groups, but there *is* an emerging consensus that the practices we have adopted today are problematic and need to be amended.[116]

Overall, sentencing practices have increasingly ensured that offenders are punished to the fullest extent through incarceration rather than other forms of legal sanction, regardless of whether they have committed violent or nonviolent crimes. In many states, nonviolent offenders who would have received probation under indeterminate sentencing now have a greater chance of seeing the inside of a prison under today's mandatory sentencing policies. As seen in chapter 2, sentencing has not always been so draconian, but today's harsh statutes have changed the dynamics of the prison milieu, which is in many cases a cesspool of violent and nonviolent offenders trying to survive in harsh environments. As a result of our nation's "experiment with sentencing guidelines," there is "no single philosophy of sentencing,"[117] and those that do exist are "fractured or fracturing in most jurisdictions."[118] One certainty, however, is that our country has continued to build larger and more expensive prisons to contain a growing population of nonviolent offenders who are spending more time behind bars than their counterparts 30 years ago. By housing dangerous and predatory individuals with first-time offenders and nonviolent prisoners, prison administrators are stirring a dangerous brew—one that is increasingly making the prison experience disproportionately punitive for low-level nonviolent offenders.

NOTES

1. When one takes into account jail populations.

2. It is important to remember that conviction and incarceration rates can increase even when crime rates are static or decreasing. Conviction rates reflect the number of arrestees who are found guilty, not the number of crimes that are actually committed. Incarceration rates reflect the segment of people who are convicted and given prison/jail terms, not the number of convictions or arrests.

3. This figure of 486 per 100,000 resident population differs from the incarceration rate of 724 cited in chapter 1 (table 1.3) because the latter statistic includes jail populations, pretrial detainees, and remand prisoners.

4. The Sentencing Project 20045: 1; see Karberg and Beck 2004.

5. Hall 1999.

6. See the Administration of Criminal Justice survey 1956.

7. Ibid.

8. Tonry 1999b: 3.

9. Ibid: 3.

10. Durose and Langan 2003a.

11. Ibid: 3.

12. The Sentencing Project (website), "The Federal Prison Population: A Statistical Analysis."

13. Ibid: 1.

14. The Sentencing Project (website), "The Expanding Federal Prison Population," 1.

15. Ibid: 2.

16. Langan and Graziadei 1995.

17. Durose and Langan 2003a.

18. Langan and Graziadei 1995.

19. Durose and Langan 2003a: table 1.

20. Langan and Graziadei 1995: table 2; Durose and Langan 2003a: table 2.

21. Durose and Langan 2003a: table 2.

22. Langan and Graziadei 1995: table 4.

23. Durose and Langan 2004: table 4.

24. Lubitz and Ross 2001: 2.

25. Hall 1999.

26. Forst 1995: 376.

27. BJA 1998.
28. Lubitz and Ross 2001.
29. BJA 1998; Lubitz and Ross 2001.
30. USSC 2006: 2.
31. Ibid: 1.
32. Ibid: 3.
33. Schmalleger 2007.
34. USSC 2006: 2–3.
35. Ibid: 4.
36. Ibid: 4.
37. Tonry 1996: 98.
38. USSC 2006: 6.
39. Ibid: 6.
40. Schmalleger 2007.
41. Initially, the Supreme Court in *Blakely v. Washington*, 542 U.S. 296 (2004) "invalidated" a sentence that was given down under Washington State's sentencing guidelines. The Supreme Court stated that "the judicial application of an enhanced sentencing range under the Washington state guidelines violated the defendant's Sixth Amendment right to a jury" (USSC 2004c). Following the *Blakely* decision, the Supreme Court reviewed two additional cases focusing on the federal sentencing guidelines, *United States v. Booker* and *United States v. Fanfan*.
42. USSC 2006: iv.
43. *United States v. Booker*. 543 U.S. 220 (2005).
44. *Booker*, 543 U.S. at 264. Cited in USSC 2006: 20.
45. Schmalleger 2007.
46. USSC 2006: vi.
47. Ibid: vii.
48. BJA 1998: 6–7.
49. Ibid: xii.
50. USSC 2004b: 16–17.
51. Ibid.
52. Ibid: 136–38.
53. Ibid: 140–42.
54. BJA 1998: 4.
55. See Ditton and Wilson 1999; BJA 1998: 1.
56. FAMM 2005 (Winter): 11.
57. BJA 1998.
58. Vincent and Hofer 1994.
59. The Sentencing Project (website), "The Expanding Federal Prison Population."
60. Parent et al. 1997.
61. The Sentencing Project (website), "Crack Cocaine Sentencing Policy: Unjustified and Unreasonable": 1.
62. Ibid: 1.
63. *FAMM Primer*.
64. USSC 2006: 126.
65. King and Mauer 2006: 3.
66. Ibid: 2.

67. See foot note 41.
68. USSC 2004c: Table 34.
69. These percentages are based on 18,129 out of 18,427 offenders sentenced under USSG chapter 2, Part D (Drugs).
70. USSC 2004c: Table 35.
71. Ibid: Figure J.
72. Ibid: Table 43.
73. Ibid: Figure J.
74. Ibid: Table 43.
75. Parent et al. 1997.
76. Tonry 1987.
77. See Schulhofer 1993.
78. Vincent and Hofer 1994: 11.
79. WPA 2004.
80. WPA 2004.
81. See Vincent and Hofer 1994.
82. Vincent and Hofer 1994.
83. Vincent and Hofer 1994: statistical appendix, p. 33.
84. Vincent and Hofer 1994: 34.
85. These points are given based on prior offenses and sentence lengths.
86. Vincent and Hofer 1994: 34.
87. Vincent and Hofer 1994: 13.
88. Tonry 1996: 135, 141.
89. Parent et al. 1997.
90. Ditton and Wilson 1999.
91. Ditton and Wilson 1999: 3.
92. Hughes and Wilson 2003.
93. Ditton and Wilson 1999: 3.
94. Ditton and Wilson 1999: 1.
95. Ditton and Wilson 1999.
96. Clark, Austin, and Henry 1997: 1.
97. Clark, Austin, and Henry 1997.
98. King and Mauer 2001.
99. King and Mauer 2001: 2.
100. Walker 2006: 153.
101. The Sentencing Project.
102. Clark et al. 1997: 2.
103. Clark et al. 1997: 7–9.
104. Clark et al. 1997: 2–3.
105. See the Sentencing Project.
106. California Department of Corrections and Rehabilitation 2005: table 1.
107. From 1,132 per 100,000 adults in 1980 to 3,175 in 2004 (Glaze and Palla 2005: 2).
108. Petersilia 2002.
109. Glaze and Palla 2005.
110. Glaze and Palla 2005.
111. Glaze and Palla 2005: table 3.

112. Glaze and Palla 2005: table 3.
113. See Tonry 1999b; Lubitz and Ross 2001.
114. Tonry and Hatlestad 1997.
115. BJA 1998.
116. See Vincent and Hofer 1994.
117. Lubitz and Ross 2001: 1.
118. Tonry 1999b: 2.

4

Prison Conditions

This section explores how the conditions of confinement contribute considerably to the costs of incarceration. When offenders without histories of violence adopt disturbing survival tactics while behind bars, this should at least draw our attention to the environments in which we are expecting prisoners to adapt. Survival-oriented behavior is often turned outward and directed toward other prisoners or staff, but inmates also engage in self-destructive behavior that can disrupt the environmental stability that prison staff try to maintain. Whether prisoners are acting out against each other, injuring staff, or trying to end their own lives, the costs of these harmful behaviors accumulate as prison populations grow and more nonviolent offenders are forced to endure the hardships of prison life. While we are no longer subjecting prisoners to physical torments in order to exact confessions or to save their sinful souls from eternal damnation, "the subject and object of punishment has shifted from the body to the soul, from dead bodies to dead souls, from the maiming of bodies to the maiming of human souls."[1] We subject prisoners to inevitably unpleasant conditions that will be experienced as insufferable, but punishment is no longer intended to directly inflict pain upon the physical body.[2]

Prison costs are not merely comprised of the raw materials used to construct and maintain facilities; they also involve human costs. This section examines prison conditions that directly and inadvertently breed psychological and physical decay among vulnerable prisoners—both of which yield significant expenses. To understand to the fullest extent the impact of imprisonment on society is to acknowledge how the conditions in which both violent and nonviolent offenders are subjected—whether for one year or for life—are not only expensive to create and sustain, but are costly to the mind and body. How this affects the rest of us—the nonoffending and law-abiding population—will also be addressed.

With two million Americans behind bars, it is not surprising that maintaining a safe prison environment is an arduous and highly strategic undertaking. Accommodating the needs of hundreds or thousands of men, women, juveniles, gang members, violent offenders, nonviolent offenders, drug addicts, etc., in a single facility requires financial resources, human capital, and public support. Prison disruption and violence are virtually inevitable in any institution that attempts to force angry, sick, mentally ill, and violent beings to cohabit civilly within the restrictive confines of a total institution.[3] Even the most modern and expensive prison cannot help but encounter difficulties asserting social control and total authority over its charges. Prison conditions have improved over time, but for many vulnerable offenders who find themselves incarcerated, prison life is replete with potential dangers.

Much of our country has turned a blind eye to the abuses, deprivations, and violent circumstances that occur in prisons. We perceive inmates—whether their crimes were sadistically heinous, acts of desperation or greed, foolish relapses in judgment, or driven by mental illness—as a segment of society undeserving of our sympathy and protection. We dichotomize our deliverance of justice by creating a world defined by *us* versus *them—we* who obey and respect the boundaries law and *they* who knowingly violate it. Why should we care how criminals fare in prison? Why should we tend to their needs when there are multitudes of other pressing issues competing for our attention and financial resources, such as our current education and health care crises?

As much as we may characterize offenders as contemptible and unworthy of our concern, our society has made the conscientious, formulated, and willing decision to lock them away in institutions where they are wholly stripped of their freedom, identities, and ability to make any considerable contributions to their communities and families.[4] We have been all too willing to devise institutions of punishment without attending to the activities that take place within them. This matter should concern everyone. *Why?* Because most of these nonviolent inmates will one day return to their families and our communities only to face the inevitable difficulties of re-establishing their prior lives. Those who have experienced violence, abuse, and psychological deterioration while incarcerated will confront even greater obstacles when acclimating to life outside of prison. Their behavior and capability to adjust—which may be largely shaped by their prison experiences—inevitably affect the communities in which they return upon release. Regardless of our own personal sentiments toward inmates, we all have a stake in their welfare because they are our prospective neighbors, our future labor force, and members of our communities. In an era where we no longer banish incorrigibles indefinitely or execute individuals indiscriminately, we can only reconcile with the fact that a large segment of our current prison population will one day rejoin *our* society after they have paid their dues in prison. To fight this wave of ex-inmates is to deny this trend that the criminal justice system has generated and to ignore the inevitable return of hundreds of thousands of individuals to our neighborhoods. It is therefore in our interest to consider the welfare of prisoners who, under critical circumstances, will do whatever it takes to survive their prison experiences.

PRISON CROWDING

Prison crowding has perpetually plagued departments of correction and continues to test the skills of prison administrators and staff. In 2000, there were 1,668 federal, state, and private adult correctional facilities across the United States.[5] Among these facilities, 332 were maximum security, 522 medium security, and 814 minimum or low security. Federal prisons were at 134 percent of capacity occupied, state prisons were at 101 percent occupied, and private prisons were at 89 percent of capacity occupied in 2000, compared to 125, 104, and 89 percent, respectively, in 1995. Overall, overcrowding has decreased in state[6] and private prisons, but federal prison populations continue to expand.[7]

The overwhelming influx of prisoners can be traced to the passing of punitive sentencing policies, as discussed in chapter 3. For example, let us return to California's three-strikes law. In 2002, there were over 42,000 second- and third-strikers in California's prisons, of whom over a third had committed crimes against persons.[8] The average sentence for second-strikers was 4.9 years, whereas the average for third-strikers was 37.4 years. Much of the overcrowding in California's prisons (and elsewhere) can be attributed to the incarceration of these nonviolent second- and third-strike offenders who are utilizing resources that could otherwise be directed toward the incapacitation of violent individuals. Would we really rather incarcerate a career property offender over a rapist or murderer whose harm is physically irreparable? Apparently so, even though research has found that three-strikes laws do little to reduce crime.[9]

As more bodies enter prison facilities, administrators are faced with the daily challenges of maintaining strict control over the movement of prisoners in order to prevent minor altercations that can easily escalate into large-scale disturbances. Social control tactics practiced by prison staff and informal social control mechanisms among inmates help to maintain an orderly, predictable, and safe environment. However, officers have less control over prison populations when more inmates are processed through their gates than the number of available beds. While, as stated earlier, prison over capacity has on average decreased in state prisons, there are still numerous prisons that face the challenges of overcrowding. Prison overcrowding is particularly visible among southern states. Freeman et al.[10] examined the conditions of states[11] in the south among which there were 567,730 state inmates in 2005. Within these states that year, the capacity of their prison systems was 101 percent full. Alabama prisons, for example, were 97 percent over capacity, as were those in Arkansas by 4 percent, North Carolina by 16 percent, and Mississippi by 10 percent. States that were at capacity (100 percent) were Louisiana and Maryland.

When prisons are flooded with gang members, and when violent and nonviolent inmates are forced to cohabit, control becomes increasingly difficult to sustain and overwhelmed institutions are likely to erupt reactively in varying degrees of violence.

PRISON VIOLENCE

For anyone in prison, daily life is stressful and inevitably involves exposure to violence at some level—whether as a voluntary or involuntary participant, or as a witness. In order to avoid or contend with violent encounters and cope effectively with the realities of prison life, many prisoners acquire certain tactics or adopt attitudes that often require the willingness to commit acts of violence. Many of these behaviors would be dubbed deviant outside the prison community, but prisoners (and some prison staff) would argue that they are at least temporarily necessary for survival and adaptation to prison life. Stressors that stem from interactions with other inmates may take the shape of victimization or abuse, or they may be internalized and manifested through depression, anxiety, other psychological disorders, and suicidal tendencies.[2] Those who are vulnerable or unable to protect themselves emotionally and physically may be informally instructed by officers and other inmates to utilize preemptive violence. Without adequate protection or having physically proven oneself, many prisoners fall prey to physical and sexual abuse at the hands of other prisoners.

The Bureau of Justice Statistics (BJS) and the National Century for Injury Prevention and Control have identified three forms of sexual violence in prison: 1) nonconsensual sexual acts that have been completed; 2) attempted nonconsensual sexual acts; and 3) abusive sexual contacts.[13] The first two forms include nonconsensual contact with inmates who can neither consent nor refuse, and either 1) contact between the penis and vulva or penis and anus involving any degree of penetration, or 2) oral sexual acts, or 3) digital penetration or penetration using an object.[14] Abusive sexual contacts include contact with inmates who can neither refuse nor consent and the "intentional touching, either directly or through the clothing, of the genitalia, anus, groin, breast, inner thigh, or buttocks of an inmate."[15] Additionally, sexual violence may include sexual acts directed toward inmates by employees or staff members, completed or attempted acts among staff members and inmates, or the threat or request to engage in sexual acts, touching, and indecent exposure.[16]

The threat of rape is all too real for many prisoners—violent and nonviolent. Reporting on the prevalence of male rapes within prison, Gilligan has found evidence of a high incidence of male-on-male sexual violence and aggression.[17] He cites findings from a study of a New York state prison in which 28 percent of the inmates had been exposed to sexual aggression,[18] as well as another estimate by Nacci and Kane[19] claiming that 9 percent of state prisoners across the country have been objects of sexual assault. However, rates of rape that occur in prison are often difficult to measure and "the magnitude of sexual assault among prisoners is not currently well understood."[20] Accurately assessing the prevalence of rape in prison is especially difficult given prisoners' reluctance to report incidents. Victims rarely feel safe enough to come forward and accuse their perpetrators, and going into segregation for protection is viewed as a sign of weakness and may have even worse consequences later on. Furthermore, how does one assess consensual versus nonconsensual sex within prison? Can sex *ever* be consensual given the environment in which it takes place? Even when offenders consent to sex in return for protection or other favors, is it not coerced? The Prison Rape Elimination Act (see section 10) defines rape as:

> the carnal knowledge, oral sodomy, sexual assault with an object, or sexual fondling of a person, forcibly or against that person's will; or not forcibly or against the person's will, where the victim is incapable of giving consent because of his or her youth or his or her temporary or permanent mental or physical incapacity; or . . . the carnal knowledge, oral sodomy, sexual assault with an object, or sexual fondling of a person achieved through the exploitation of the fear or threat of physical violence or bodily injury (original italics).[21]

BJS has started to collect national data on sexual assaults in correctional facilities with the hope of examining inmate-on-inmate or staff-on-inmate assaults, how incidents of sexual violence and misconduct are recorded, what specific information is recorded, and the location in which the incidents took place.[22] In time, correctional officials might better understand the various forms of sexual violence and misconduct that take place in prison, learn how to detect and prevent such incidents, and identify individuals at risk for sexual victimization or perpetration. By methodologically collecting data from correctional institutions across the nation and bringing prison sexual violence to the forefront of administrative concerns, sexual victimization might become a more identifiable and controllable occurrence.

**Table 4.1.   Homicide Rates in
State Prisons, 1980–2003**

Year	Rate (per 100,000)
1980	54
1985	24
1990	8
1995	9
2000	5
2001	3
2002	4
2003	4

Source: BJS website. 2005c. "Key Facts at
a Glance: Suicide and Homicide Rates
in State Prisons and Jails." Washington,
DC: Bureau of Justice Statistics, U.S.
Department of Justice.

Other forms of violence and disorder manifest in prison and can be lethal. In 1990, "nearly 100 inmates were murdered; another 10,000 or so were victims of severe assaults that required medical attention."[23] The Bureau of Statistics reports homicide rates in state prisons from 1980 to 2003 (table 4.1). Homicide rates in state prisons have decreased from 54 per 100,000 inmates in 1980 to 4 in 2003, a 93 percent reduction. Homicides are generally detectible in prison for obvious reasons, but estimating the true rates of other forms of violence can be difficult given that assaults are often unreported. While rates of violence generally vary geographically and by time, all prisons face the dangers associated with inmate-on-inmate and inmate-on-staff violence. The California Department of Corrections, for example, reported that in 1993 there were 3,562 incidents of assault/battery on inmates, staff, and visitors, of which 1,766 involved weapons.[24] By 2002, the total number of assault/battery incidents had risen to 6,840, including 1,877 incidents with weapons.[25] Of these 6,840 incidents, over half were committed against other inmates and 95.5 percent perpetrated by men.

In 1995, the BJS reports that there were 25,208 assaults on inmates and 13,938 assaults on staff in state, federal, and private prisons. These figures increased to 34,355 inmate assaults and 17,952 staff assaults in 2000.[26] Freeman et al.[27] report violent incidents that occurred within sixteen southern states during fiscal year 2004/2005. States with the highest rates of inmate assaults (per 1,000 inmates) were Maryland (58.3), Oklahoma (47.3), and West Virginia (29) and states with lowest rates were Louisiana (0.4), Mississippi (0.9), and Virginia (0.7). Whether inmates have committed violent or nonviolent offenses, becoming (or facing the threat of becoming) one of these statistics should not be an acceptable component of their punishment.

Riots and other collective disturbances also threaten the order of correctional facilities, thus potentially endangering both inmates and staff. Both violent and nonviolent prisoners are susceptible to victimization, whether it originates from interpersonal relations (e.g., inmate sexual violence or abuse) or occurs during large-scale incidents, such as riots and strikes. The following review of the literature on prison violence and victimization depicts the process through which nonviolent inmates might resort to violent behavior within prison.

REVIEW OF RESEARCH ON PRISON VIOLENCE

Theories of prison misconduct, ranging from managerial practices to poor inmate coping skills,[28] indicate that the roots of violence in prison have multidimensional origins. Imprisonment not only deprives individuals of their personal freedom, but it invokes stressors such as physical and sexual victimization (as discussed above), forced inactivity, prison-life demands, and overcrowding.[29] Stress is an inevitable aspect of the prison experience, but "if a normal person is given accurate prior warnings of impending pain and discomfort, together with sufficient reassurances so that fear does not mount to a very high level, he will be less likely to develop acute emotional disturbance than a person who is not warned."[30] When inmates fail to cope with the daily routine of prison life, "loneliness, shame, and rage"[31] may set in, resulting in physiological and psychological deterioration and aggression toward staff and other inmates.

Prison misconduct takes many, often hidden, shapes, such as "physiological, economic, and social" victimizations.[32] Contraband, such as cigarettes, may be used as currency, such as in one federal prison where two cartons of cigarettes was once the "going price for a contract murder."[33] It is generally assumed that physical abuse occurs more frequently than other forms of prison misconduct, but Bowker[34] purports that psychological victimization—in the form of induced agitation, verbal extortion, and slander—occurs more often. Economic victimization, another form of abuse, may include loan sharking, gambling frauds, price fixing of prison goods, theft and robbery, protection schemes,[35] and other economic scams. Not all victimizations are reported to correctional staff for fear of retaliation or even death.

Misconduct among inmates has been attributed to prisoner characteristics,[36] environmental and physical features of prison facilities,[37] institutional structural conditions,[38] administrative and management factors,[39] and combinations of inmate characteristics with environmental features and psychological factors.[40] For example, Bottoms suggests that a prison's architectural features may increase the "'opportunity' dimension in prison violence."[41] Age,[42] boredom, ethnic and racial tension, sexual jealousy, gang rivalries, and psychological problems have also been cited as potential pre-cursors to violence among inmates,[43] as well as overcrowding,[44] institu-tional deterioration,[45] structural features of prison facilities (such as poor supervision and access to weapons),[46] disciplinary policies,[47] prison secu-rity levels, and how much time an inmate has served of his or her sen-tence.[48]

One perspective on prison violence involves importation, which occurs when inmates—usually those among the lower socioeconomic class—bring into the prison remnants of their selves outside of prison, such as values, norms, social beliefs, prejudices, gender-role perceptions, homophobia, drug use and addictions, violent subcultures,[49] personal characteristics, criminal history, and previous prison terms.[50] Other theories seeking to ex-plain prison misconduct have instead focused on the characteristics of the prisons and their conditions, such as prisoner-staff ratios, budget con-straints, poorly trained correctional staff, blind spots where victimization goes undetected, and classification practices where victimizers and vulnera-ble inmates cohabit.[51] Ultimately, imported characteristics of the inmate, in conjunction with various aspects of the prison's environment, may be a dangerous formula for prison violence. An alternative perspective on prison violence focuses on deprivation[52] and inmates' reactions to what Sykes calls the "pains of imprisonment,"[53] which include the lack of "liberty, goods, and services; personal autonomy; personal security; and heterosexual rela-tionships."[54]

Prison environments are susceptible and conducive to all forms of vio-lence and collective action. Assaults against prison and other inmates, sexual victimization, riots, and gang violence often threaten the social order and control of the prison. Prison misconduct, which usually occurs at the indi-vidual level, may also erupt collectively. Violent uprisings and other distur-bances can be prevented through a carefully balanced equilibrium among staff and inmates.[55] Sykes[56] describes a "cohesively-oriented prisoner" as "committed to the values of inmate loyalty, generosity, endurance, and the curbing of frictions who does much to maintain the prison's equilibrium."[57] When inmate privileges or informal social controls are disrupted by prison staff, and when a peaceful environment becomes tenuous, "the stage has been set for insurrection."[58] When one inmate engages in misconduct and endangers the prison's equilibrium, stress among other inmates may multi-ply and magnify,[59] thus jeopardizing the entire prison community. Bowker describes an "insane feedback system through which prison victimization rates are under constant pressure to increase."[60] Prison violence is a cyclical process in which prison victimization incites other forms of victimization, thus complicating the search for the etiology of prison disorder. Within a single episode a victimizer can easily become a victim, and vice versa.[61] Mo-tives for victimizing may include the alleviation of tension and stress through sex, economic profit, status and power, and self-defense. Violence may serve other roles within prisons, according to Lockwood,[62] such as exerting sexual preferences, demonstrating belief in prisoner norms and subculture, elevating social status, and deterring other forms of violence.

In his exploration of prisons as a "subculture of violence," Lockwood lists distrust and fear as reactions to the violent environments in which many men find themselves.[63] Intimidation through sexual aggression and violent defensive responses characterize many interpersonal encounters within male prisons. Non-violent offenders who are serving short prison sentences may attempt to avoid violent situations in order to maximize the possibility of early release through parole. While the majority of these inmates tend to stay to themselves as a way to avoid trouble,[64] other inmates experiencing severe emotional pain and trauma may cope by withdrawing, abusing drugs, seeking protective custody, engaging in recreational activities, and participating in nonviolent collective action,[65] or they may seek to voice their grievances through formal channels.

While each inmate copes with prison life differently, Johnson observes that many seek a "niche," which is "a functional subsetting containing objects, space, resources, people, and relationships between people" and "is perceived as ameliorative after," within which prisoners can find security, routinized consistency, familiarity, and most importantly, means of adaptation.[66] When prison environments are overcrowded, inmates are often displaced from their niches and forced into the general prison population where once again, they face tension and stress. When administrative practices disturb niches, and when inmates fail to utilize successful coping mechanisms, the potential for violence magnifies. Inmates also utilize "personal protection strategies"[67] to survive the prison experience. In addition to withdrawing from the prison community, they may seek support from inmates they already know or from prison staff; they may alter their self-presentation to appear tougher; they may take advantage of their skill sets; they may obtain weapons; or they may preemptively strike out at other inmates.[68]

Prison staff have been known to allow violence to occur and may even participate in certain forms of victimization and abuse. Bowker reports excessive use of violence by prison guards during prison fights and other incidents.[69] He also identifies ways in which guards participate in sexual aggression toward inmates: by perpetrating the aggression, by watching an attack on an inmate by another prisoner, or by neglecting to provide precautionary measures in high-risk areas of a facility. In addition, prison guards may engage in psychological abuse, such as stimulating anxiety, making threats, or by abusively flaunting their positions of power. Guards can also victimize inmates economically by consuming their food, or they may engage in social victimization (e.g., racial discrimination or granting certain prisoners abusive authority over other inmates). These forms of abuse undoubtedly generate mistrust of authority among inmates—a sentiment not likely to dissipate once the inmates are released into the community. Often the evidence of any abuse that might have been sustained is invisible,[70] providing little leverage for legal action and therefore leaving inmates with nothing more than an empty sense of injustice, victimization, and anger.

Ultimately, prison misconduct reflects more than individual inmate personalities and characteristics; collective action is often a mechanism through which inmates can voice their grievances over bureaucratic matters or reduce stress, and can indicate a "significant breakdown in the normal patterns of social order in the institution."[71] Violence, which is often used as a last resort, may therefore be embraced by violent and nonviolent offenders alike. When administrative procedures are perceived as empty gestures, inmates may turn to semidisruptive or violent methods of coping even if it means harming the larger prison population.[72]

Given the traumatic and disturbing experiences that many inmates experience while in the custody of the state or federal criminal justice system, it is likely that upon reentry into the community, they will continue to harbor fear, suspicion, and mistrust toward others and especially toward agents of the criminal justice system. Inmates who emerge from prison traumatized, humiliated, and distrustful may react through episodes of aggression, isolation, substance abuse, probation failure, and recidivism. By exposing inmates to violence on a daily basis, it becomes a ritualized part of their everyday functioning,[73] and learned violence may be difficult to unlearn once the inmate is released. The cost of prison violence therefore not only includes the victimizations that occur within prison walls, but the violence that may be perpetrated by otherwise nonviolent inmates after their release.

SUPERMAX PRISONS

One of society's most expensive and "perhaps the most troubling"[74] contributions to the field of corrections is the supermaximum prison, of which there are at least 57[75] in over 40 states.[76] (The financial costs of these facilities will be discussed in greater detail in chapter 5.) These high security facilities—often referred to as "special housing unit, maxi-maxi, maximum control facility, secured housing unit, intensive housing unit, intensive management unit, and administrative maximum penitentiary"[77]—are designed to house inmates who exhibit uncontrollable behavioral problems within the general prison population. Other purposes of supermax prisons, according to Mears and Watson, include reducing gang activity and increasing the safety of the public by preventing escapes.[78]

According to a National Institute of Corrections survey, a supermax prison is a free-standing facility, or a distinct unit within a facility that provides for the management and secure control of inmates who have been officially designated as exhibiting violent or serious and disruptive behavior while incarcerated. Such inmates have been determined to be a threat to safety and security in traditional high-security facilities, and their behavior can be controlled only by separation, restricted movement, and limited direct access to staff and other inmates.[79]

In short, these prisons are designed to house the worst behaved inmates—those who are security risks to the general prison population and staff, unmanageable, and consistently disruptive to daily prison operations. They can be thought of as modern, institutionalized forms of "the hole"[80] for incorrigibles, routinely violent inmates, inmates who have attempted to escape repeatedly, and inmates who incite institutional disturbances.[81] Such individuals can tax the resources of the prison staff and disrupt the regular operations of a prison facility, thus jeopardizing the safety of everybody in the institution.

On the other hand, Mears and Watson have also identified several benefits of supermax prisons.[82] For example, the use of supermax facilities to remove disruptive inmates from the general prison population may increase the quality of life for other inmates who are subjected to multiple lockdowns when an unruly inmate acts out. Further, inmates in these facilities may experience an increase in comfort levels, for supermax prisons afford prisoners more privacy than other facilities, require less program participation, may alleviate fears of being injured by other inmates, and may allow inmates to bypass the negative stigma associated with being in protective custody.[83] However, Mears and Watson also recognize that supermax prisons may play a role in facilitating disruptions among inmates, are possibly conductive to mental disorders and other physical ailments, and may also impose disproportionate punishments on prisoners who commit minor infractions.[84]

The decision to place disruptive inmates into supermax prisons is usually based on ambiguous guidelines. At the discretion of prison authorities, inmates ranging from being slightly disruptive to those exhibiting relentless patterns of violent and predatory behavior may be sent to supermax facilities. While the length of time that the inmate spends in a supermax facility is indeterminate and rests largely on his or her subsequent behavior,[85] the decision to send an inmate to a supermax prison is often clouded and complicated by limited resources and problems of overcrowding rather than based on major security threats.

A National Institute of Corrections survey found that twelve departments of correction have utilized supermax prisons due to a "shortage of segregation beds."[86] Inmates in need of psychological care may also be sent to supermax facilities despite already preexisting mental illnesses, as well as those in need of protective custody.[87] Housing inmates who require protective custody in supermax facilities, who act out due to psychological conditions, or who are at minimum occasionally disruptive, Riveland argues, is "overkill," a misuse of the expensive facilities, and bears "little overall operational impact."[88] Today, 2 percent of state and federal prisoners who are serving at least one year in prison are in supermax prisons.[89]

By filling our nation's prisons with 1.2 million nonviolent offenders, disciplinary problems are being mishandled by sending lower-custody inmates, or inmates who engage in minor misconduct, to supermax prisons where incarceration has been described as "living in a tomb."[90] Inmates are entirely isolated from all other prisoners and may be locked in a cell for 23 hours a day. Exercise generally takes place indoors where the inmate, who is handcuffed and heavily guarded, is allowed to pace the hallways. Privileges are generally restricted and may be granted to inmates based on behavioral modification plans. However, an inmate who demonstrates long-term good behavior may lose all privileges as punishment for a single minor infraction,[91] which may result in the loss of reading and writing materials, radios, visits, and other privileges that would otherwise enable them to maintain contact with other inmates or family members.

The consequence of prolonged isolation and lack of emotional or physical stimulus can lead to an inmate's deterioration into states of psychosis, depression, anxiety, and confusion.[92] Within the supermax environment, monotony and immobility become the day-to-day routine. Stripped of their humanity, inmates are exposed to what has been described as "pointless suffering and humiliation"[93] and are caged like animals. In Lawrence and Mears's discussion on calculating the costs and benefits of supermax prisons,[94] they present Haney's review[95] of the physical and psychological ramifications of spending time in a supermax prison. These include not only indicators of extreme psychological damage, but

> an impaired sense of identity; hypersensitivity to stimuli; cognitive dysfunction (confusion, memory loss, ruminations); irritability, anger, aggression, and/or rage; other-directed violence, such as stabbing, attacks on staff, property destruction, and collective violence; lethargy, helplessness, and hopelessness; chronic depression; self-mutilation and/or suicidal ideation, impulses, and behavior; anxiety and panic attacks; emotional breakdowns and/or loss of control; hallucinations, psychosis, and/or paranoia; and overall deterioration of mental and physical health.[96]

Haney's study of the Pelican Bay "security housing unit" indicates a prevalence of psychopathological characteristics among the 100 prisoners who were studied. These prisoners experienced irrational anger (88 percent), confused thought processes (84), social withdrawal (83), chronic depression

(77), mood swings (71), overall deterioration (67), talking to self (63), violent fantasies (61), hallucinations (41), and suicidal thoughts (27).[97] Indeed, these are not the intended effects of supermax prisons, but when human beings are extendedly confined for 23 hours a day and have only enough human contact to support their bare existence, these are the consequences.

With prison crowding and limited budgets, more prisons are sending less dangerous inmates to these "unduly severe" institutions that some view as "disproportionate to security needs."[98] In Wisconsin Secure Program Facility—in essence, a supermax—over 20 percent of the inmates have been described as "not true Supermax inmates";[99] rather, they are transfers from another prison whose segregation unit is overcrowded. In mid-October 2001, the Department of Corrections reported that of the 323 inmates housed in this supermax prsion, nearly one-third were initially sent to prison for nonviolent crimes.[100]

Reducing the number of nonviolent, low threat inmates in prison can alleviate prison expenses, can increase prison resources directed toward housing violent offenders, and can ultimately assuage some of the prison violence that stems from the tension of overcrowding. Many nonviolent inmates and first-time offenders cope poorly when they are incarcerated and may adapt to their new environments by acting out or engaging in violent behavior. This places them at risk for future misconduct or disciplinary problems, which in turn increases their chances of being sent to supermax prisons. This chain of events could be altered by keeping nonviolent offenders out of prison, and by doing so, valuable correctional resources could be used more appropriately and effectively to incapacitate whose who pose physical threats to society.

As stressed by the Human Rights Watch regarding the use of supermax prisons, we pay a "high price in terms of the misery and suffering it inflicts, and the likelihood that it reduces an inmate's ability to make a successful transition to society upon release."[101] Psychological instability, the lack of educational or treatment programs,[102] and the lack of human contact and interaction create environments that are anything but conducive to rehabilitation, stability, and adaptability. Since the environment of the supermax is not conducive to treatment or visitations by family members, inmates—especially those who are mentally ill—are susceptible to rapid decomposition. When inmates are subjected to the austere conditions of supermax prisons, and when isolation and mental deterioration render inmates prone to violence, physical injuries among inmates and officers increase, as well as medical costs. Thus, the conditions that prisons have created—in which acting out in the general prison population may enable susceptible inmates to successfully fend off sexual and physical attacks, and therefore survive their prison terms—only adds to the costs of incarceration by necessitating the creation and use of supermax facilities.

MENTAL HEALTH

Mentally ill individuals—those with conditions ranging from clinical depression to schizophrenia—can be found in great numbers behind prison walls. With waves of inmates streaming through our nation's prison systems, tending to those who need mental health care becomes a difficult goal, one that is nearly impossible given the paucity of resources and staff.

Not unexpectedly, inmates who are disturbed (or bored) may engage in self-mutilation; others with more severe pathologies may exhibit suicidal behavior. The loss of life through suicide or psychological deterioration is a substantial cost, yet it is often seen as a small price to pay for maintaining our correctional system. Why should we express concern over the well-being of prisoners given their deviant behaviors and apparent disregard for the law? As discussed earlier, society tends to portray prisoners as violent superpredators who are persistent threats to our communities and families. While most individuals in prison may have made poor decisions throughout their lifetimes, most are not the villainous sociopaths that we envision. Many are single mothers or young adults who will someday return to society to restart their lives. Do we want thousands of individuals reentering society who are emotionally and psychologically ill-equipped to resume their lives, or do we want healthy individuals who can handle the obstacles that await them upon their release? We all have a stake in the mental well-being of prisoners. Their success or failure upon release from prison impacts the level of community resources that they will utilize, much of which comes from programs that we, as taxpayers, fund.

CONCLUSION

The conditions in which prisoners live affect us all. As a society, we have decided upon incarceration as a primary form of punishment in order to deter, protect, and exact just deserts. Forcing offenders to live in dangerous conditions, however, has never been the main goal of incarceration, yet it has become one of the most striking aspects of our correctional system. Much of the world, including our nation, has moved away from primitive modes of punishment, and while we no longer seek to exact physical pain,[103] the conditions of modern prisons in the United States do take a physical toll on the inmates who suffer from physiological attenuation, mental deterioration, and abuse. It is tempting to lock away criminals and metaphorically throw away the keys, but as incarceration rates rise, so too does the likelihood that someone *you* know will be (or is) incarcerated. As such, we must ask ourselves whether we would want to subject a family member or friend to these conditions, regardless of their crimes. It is all too easy to ignore issues regarding prisons and inmates, especially when we do not know anyone who is incarcerated, but imagine yourself wrongfully convicted. Would prison conditions matter *then*?

NOTES

1. Gilligan 1996: 145.
2. See Foucault 1979 for a discussion on the transition of punishment from the body to the mind.
3. See Goffman 1961 for a thorough discussion on "total institutions."
4. See Sykes 1958.
5. Stephan and Karberg 2003: iv.
6. Although the mean percentage of sentences expected to be served has increased.
7. Ibid: iv.
8. CDC 2001.
9. Ehlers et al. 2004.
10. Freeman et al. 2005: 11.
11. These states include: Alabama, Arkansas, Florida, Georgia, Kentucky, Louisiana, Maryland, Mississippi, Missouri, North Carolina, Oklahoma, South Carolina, Tennessee, Texas, Virginia, West Virginia.
12. See chapter 5 for a discussion on prison suicide.
13. BJS 2004h: 2.
14. Ibid: 2.
15. Ibid: 2.
16. Ibid: 2.
17. Gilligan 1996.
18. See Lockwood 1978 (cited in Gilligan 1996: 176).
19. See Nacci and Kane 1983 (cited in Gilligan 1996: 176).
20. BJS 2004h: 1.
21. Ibid: 2.
22. Ibid: 3.
23. Camp and Camp (cited in McCorkle et al. 1995: 317).
24. California Department of Corrections 2003.
25. CDC 2003: 4.
26. Stephan and Karberg 2003: v.
27. Freeman et al. 2005: 24.
28. Johnson 2002.
29. Sykes 1958; Toch 1988, 1992; Johnson 2002.
30. Janis 1969: 196.
31. Toch 1988: 29.
32. Bowker 1988: 63.
33. Bowker 1980: 29.
34. Bowker 1988.
35. Johnson and Toch 1988; see Bowker 1980.

36. Bowker 1980; McCorkle et al. 1995.
37. Smith 1988; Bowker 1980, 1988; Parisi 1982.
38. Gottfredson and McConville 1987.
39. Fleiser 1989; Reisig 1998; Useem and Reisig 1991.
40. Fleiser 1989; Toch 1992.
41. Bottoms 1999: 242.
42. Bottoms 1999.
43. Fleiser 1989.
44. Parisi 1982; Smith 1982; Zimmerman and Miller 1981.
45. Gottfredson and McConville 1987.
46. Bowker 1988.
47. Fleiser 1989.
48. Bottoms 1999: 232.
49. Bowker 1980: 150–151; McCorkle et al. 1995.
50. Bowker 1980: 152; Bottoms 1999.
51. Bowker 1980; Johnson 2002.
52. Bottoms 1999.
53. Sykes 1958.
54. Bottoms 1999: 245.
55. Reisig 1998; see DiIulio 1987.
56. Sykes 1958: 126.
57. Cited in DiIulio 1987: 23.
58. DiIulio 1987: 23.
59. Parisi 1982.
60. Bowker 1980: 31.
61. Bowker 1980.
62. Lockwood 1991.
63. Ibid.
64. Johnson 2002.
65. Parisi 1982.
66. Johnson 2002: 172–73.
67. Bottoms 1999: 271.
68. Ibid. See McCorkle 1992.
69. Bowker 1991.
70. Hall et al. 2002.
71. Bottoms 1999: 206.
72. Ostrom 1998.
73. See Bottoms 1999: 205–81.
74. Human Rights Watch [HRW] 1990. See Haney 2006.
75. NIC 1997.
76. Mears and Watson 2006.
77. Riveland 1999: 5.
78. Mears and Watson 2006: table 1.
79. National Institute of Corrections [NIC] Prison Division and Information Center survey 1997: 1.
80. Riveland 1999: 5.
81. Ibid: 6.

82. Mears and Watson 2006.
83. Ibid: 245–47.
84. Ibid: 249–51.
85. HRW 2000.
86. NIC 1997: 3.
87. NIC 1997.
88. Riveland 1999: 6.
89. Mears and Watson 2006.
90. HRW 2000.
91. Ibid.
92. Ibid.
93. Ibid.
94. Lawrence and Mears 2004.
95. Haney 2003.
96. Ibid: 53 (cited in Lawrence and Mears 2004: 28).
97. See Haney 2006: table 2.
98. HRW 2000.
99. Jones 2001.
100. *Milwaukee Journal Sentinel* 2001.
101. HRW 2000.
102. Ibid.
103. See Foucault 1979; Johnson 2002.

III

FINANCIAL AND SOCIAL COSTS OF INCARCERATION

5

The Financial Costs of Incarceration

Our nation now spends more than $160 billion per year on our criminal justice system. In this chapter, the more visible and easily measured financial costs of incarceration are discussed, while those explored in chapter 7 are more latent yet equally significant. At the expense of taxpayers, today's sentencing policies and our penchant to incarcerate nonviolent offenders yields few tangible benefits, only enormous financial consequences. Only when the gravity of our general correctional spending is revealed to the fullest extent will the potential cost savings of using prison less for nonviolent offenders become more apparent.

A thorough analysis of the costs of incarceration would not be complete without addressing the costs that are saved by incarcerating individuals who would otherwise continue their criminal enterprises were they not incapacitated. The costs of incarceration should ideally counterbalance the overall social costs of crime that are saved through the incapacitating function of prisons.[1] This will be addressed in more detail in chapter 12. The remainder of this chapter will focus on the overall expenditures involved in building and maintaining our correctional system.

Prison construction is an expensive and challenging endeavor. In no other industry is there an attempt (or need) to build facilities that can house hundreds, perhaps thousands, of bodies in close quarters for long durations, all the while feeding and providing them with the amenities necessary to exist (these may range from toilet paper to expensive medical procedures). Not many institutions are designed to sustain basic human life and also contain and control it, and most other institutions do not have to strategize around the possibility that riots may erupt, that staff may be held hostage, and that potentially lethal violence may break out without warning. Perhaps psychiatric hospitals come close, but in these closed institutions there are some patients who elect to be hospitalized, who recognize the need for treatment, and who work *with* the doctors and staff toward recovery.

According to the Real Cost of Prisons Project,[2] some unseen financial costs that are generated from building prisons include environmental degradation, increased law enforcement needs, and strains on social and medical services.[3] These costs are borne and shouldered by taxpayers and the communities in which the prisons are built. This chapter takes a look at general correctional expenditures at the local, state, and federal levels; expenditures on prisons; and the costs of supermax prisons.

GENERAL EXPENDITURES

The two million bodies housed in modern correctional facilities present taxpayers with an exorbitant bill for obtaining and securing land, food, health care, construction equipment, staff salaries, mental health care, and utilities. Prisons throughout the United States are currently under court orders to provide certain legal rights and services to prisoners, so compliance with these mandates generates additional costs. Enormous resources are therefore required to build and sustain a single prison. Cook, Slawson, and Gries suggest that costs per prisoner may range from $16,000 to $23,000.[4] Ambrosio and Schiraldi estimate that on average, each new prison cell costs $54,000.[5] When interest is figured into the costs, the estimated spending on each new prison cell may reach nearly $100,000, culminating to an approximate $40 billion spent each year on building and maintaining prisons.[6] The North Carolina Department of Corrections, for example, reported that the construction cost of a medium-custody prison with 208 beds is approximately $5 million.[7] That equates to $24,000 per bed during initial construction.

The resources needed to build prisons vary by their intended security-levels. Constructing a maximum-custody prison may be more expensive that a medium-custody prison, reaching upwards of tens of millions of dollars for a single facility. To meet the needs of rising prison populations, the expansion and construction of additional prisons continues. As a result, the enormous magnitude of these construction projects places pressure on the system to *use these* facilities, thus justifying the increased use of prison for all types of offenders.

Unarguably, prisons are expensive to build, but why are prisons so expensive to operate? Table 5.1 shows the breakdown of state prison operational costs. In 2001, state prisons spent over $28 billion on operations and another $1.1 billion in capital costs. While total expenditures in the South reached $10 billion in 2001, states in the Northeast had the highest per pris-

Table 5.1. Operating and Capital Costs and Annual Operating Costs Per Inmate and State Resident, 2001

Region	Total Operating and Capital Costs	Operating (in 1,000s of dollars)			Capital Costs (in 1,000s of dollars)			Annual Operating Costs	
		Total Operation Costs	Salaries, Wages, and Benefits	Other Operating Costs	Capital Costs	Total Construction	Equipment	Per Inmate	Per U.S. Resident
Total	$29,488,474	$28,374,273	$18,583,923	$9,790,350	$1,114,201	$860,954	$253,247	$22,650	$100
Northeast	6,056,762	5,712,994	4,014,190	1,698,803	343,768	310,770	32,998	33,037	106
Midwest	6,327,236	5,952,214	3,960,772	1,991,442	375,022	299,321	75,701	24,779	92
South	10,000,641	9,750,580	6,017,146	3,733,434	250,061	147,512	102,549	16,479	91
West	7,103,835	6,958,485	4,591,814	2,366,671	145,350	103,351	41,999	25,231	108

Source: Stephan. 2004. "State Prison Expenditures 2001." Washington, DC: Bureau of Justice Statistics Special Report, U.S. Department of Justice: tables 2, 3, 4, pages 3–5.

Table 5.2. State Prison Expenditures, 2001

	Costs in 1,000s of Dollars			Cost per Inmate		
Region	Medical Care	Food Service	Utilities	Medical Care	Food Service	Utilities
Total	$3,288,200	$1,195,854	$996,027	$2,625	$955	$795
Northeast	590,935	210,400	203,294	3,417	1,217	1,176
Midwest	543,001	290,949	198,432	2,260	1,211	826
South	1,141,489	411,988	377,792	2,025	731	670
West	1,012,775	282,516	216,508	3,672	1,024	785

Source: Stephan. 2004: table 5, page 6.

oner operating costs that amounted to $33,000 per inmate, on average. With over 1.2 million inmates in state and federal institutions, and a 149 percent increase in the number of people employed by the correctional industry between 1980 and 2001,[8] salary expenditures have also been on the rise. In 2001, the salaries of the 2.3 million individuals who worked in the criminal justice system reached $18.5 billion (see Table 5.1).[9]

Personal Services	$567,712,907
Regular Operation	62,875,636
Travel	1,640,819
Motor Vehicle Purchases	1,083,265
Equipment	3,837,249
Computer Charges	5,252,463
Real Estate Rentals	7,862,898
Telecommunications	7,894,025
Per Diem, Fees & Contracts	258,120
Capital Outlay	12,052,301
Utilities	25,843,796
Health Services Purchases	133,951,974
Court Costs	1,278,260
County Subsidy	36,737,700
County Subsidy for Jails	11,621,740
Central Repair Fund	893,624
Meal Payments (Central State Hospital)	4,268,024
Utility Payments (Central State Hospital)	1,627,149
Meal Payments—Public Safety	577,160
Inmate Release Fund	4,356,487
Contracts	46,1824
Minor Construction Fund	752,998
Total	$975,444,054

Figure 5.1. George Department of Corrections' 2003 Fiscal Year Budget

State expenditures on prison medical care, food, and utilities in 2001 are shown on table 5.2. Medical costs reached $3.3 billion, amounting to $2,625 per inmate each year. States also spent $1.2 billion on food services ($955 per inmate) and nearly $1 billion on utility costs ($795 per inmate) in 2001. Altogether, an average $4,375 was spent on each inmate in 2001 for food, health services, and utility costs alone. There are of course less obvious expenses involved in the correctional industry. For example, Georgia's Department of Corrections spent $97.5 million during fiscal year 2003 on the items shown in figure 5.1.[10] Another example of expenditure distribution is seen within Virginia's Department of Corrections. During fiscal year 2004, expenditures on the Division of Operation alone reached slightly over $763 million; an additional $46.8 million was spent on the Division of Administrationas shown in figure 5.2[11]

Virginia's cost of operation, while steep compared to North Dakota, South Dakota, and Wyoming who each spent less than $50 million in 2001,[12] pales in comparison to spending in other states. Florida's Department of Corrections, for example, spent $1.8 billion in operating funds during fiscal year 2003–2004 (see figure 5.3).[13]

Board of Corrections	$12,554
Director's Office	1,432,961
Communications Unit	355,105
Inspector General	2,861,747
Compliance and Accreditation	909,487
Ctr. for Information Technologies	14,196,305
Controller's Office	6,495,749
Research and Management Serv.	465,794
Architect. & Engr. Services	4,687,109
Procurement/Risk Management	7,544,251
Employee Relations & Training	7,556,322
Total	$46,817,384

Figure 5.2

Department Administration	$54,852,108
Security and Institutional Operations	1,144,147,508
Health Services	307,400,119
Community Corrections	221,208,055
Information Technology	24,562,233
Programs	39,621,718
Total	$1,791,791,741

Figure 5.3

The expenses listed above are only the visible and more easily calculable costs of corrections. While we hasten our efforts to support harsh sentencing laws, we tend to forget that processing offenders through our criminal justice system involves all levels of the government. Local governments spend $83.3 billion on their criminal justice systems each year, which is 32 percent more than state governments and over 2.5 times the amount spent by the federal government. In 2001, state prisons spent $51 billion more on judicial expenditures than they did in 1993.[14] As table 5.3 indicates, spending on criminal justice functions has uniformly increased over the last 25 years at every level of government. Altogether, our nation spends nearly $167 billion each year to maintain our entire criminal justice system, over four times what it cost in the early 1980s (table 5.3).[15] From 1982 to 2001, the federal system experienced the highest growth (583 percent) in criminal justice expenditures, followed by state (446 percent) and local (298 percent) governments.

Is it worth the cost? Austin and Fabelo estimate that approximately 95 percent of costs (both financial and emotional) to victims of crime can be attributed to violent crime.[16] They argue:

> continuing to increase incarceration rates and incarceration costs for property and drug offenders, particularly in light of the fiscal crises in the states, may divert resources from prevention, incapacitation, and re-entry policies that can more effectively combat violent crime. Effective alternatives to incarceration for property and drug offenders can also reduce cost while reducing the victimization costs accounted by these offenders.[17]

As a nation, we are using a tremendous amount of capital on a substantially large group of offenders who pose very little physical threat to the public.[18] We have to wonder whether this is the most effective and efficient approach to crime control and punishment, and if not, why we continue this spending.

Table 5.3. Justice Expenditures (in Millions) and Percent Change by Level of Government, 1982–2001

Year	Total Justice	Federal	State	Local
1982	$35,842	$4,458	$11,602	$20,968
1987	58,871	7,496	20,157	33,265
1992	93,777	17,423	33,265	50,115
1997	129,793	27,065	46,444	67,083
2000	155,722	27,820	58,165	78,995
2001	167,113	30,443	63,372	83,377
% Change, 1982-2001	366.2	582.9	446.2	297.6

Source: Austin and Fabelo. 2004. "The Diminishing Returns of Increased Incarceration." Washington, DC: JFA Institute: table 3.

CORRECTIONAL EXPENDITURES

With such monumental budgets allocated to criminal justice functions, one might expect to see large budget increases on crime prevention and policing functions. Didn't the great sociologist and intellectual W. E. B. Dubois once advise, "The chief problem in any community cursed with crime is not the punishment of the criminals, but the preventing of the young from being trained to crime"?[19] We have not heeded his warning well. Corrections, as a percent of spending in our overall justice system, is increasing at a rate that is surpassing spending in any other area of the criminal justice system.

Table 5.4 compares correctional, judicial, and police expenditures from 1982 to 2001 at all levels of government.[20] Expenditures on *corrections* alone surged from under $10 billion in 1982 to an alarming $57 billion in 2001, an increase of 529 percent. From 1982 to 1999, the highest percent increase in per capita spending among the various judicial functions has been in corrections (table 5.5). During this period, per capita spending on corrections grew by 346 percent, from $39.06 to $174.17, whereas spending per capita

Table 5.4. Combined Local, State, and Federal Criminal Justice Expenses, 1982–2001

	Police	Judicial	Corrections
1982	$19,022,184,000	$7,770,785,000	$9,048,947,000
1983	20,648,200,000	8,620,604,000	10,411,363,000
1984	22,685,766,000	9,463,180,000	11,793,744,000
1985	24,399,355,000	10,628,816,000	13,534,897,000
1986	26,254,993,000	11,485,446,000	15,759,366,000
1987	28,767,553,000	12,555,026,000	14,548,769,000
1988	30,960,824,000	13,970,563,000	20,299,155,000
1989	32,794,182,000	15,588,664,000	22,566,622,000
1990	35,923,479,000	17,356,826,000	26,153,654,000
1991	38,971,240,000	19,298,379,000	29,297,200,000
1992	41,326,531,000	20,988,888,000	31,461,433,000
1993	44,036,756,000	21,558,403,000	31,946,667,000
1994	46,004,536,000	22,601,706,000	34,864,322,000
1995	48,644,529,000	24,471,689,000	39,752,230,000
1996	52,007,425,000	26,157,907,000	41,028,843,000
1997	57,753,530,000	25,828,774,000	43,511,148,000
1998	20,828,213,000	29,901,380,000	45,169,860,000
1999	65,364,070,000	32,184,560,000	49,006,871,000
2000	68,911,071,000	34,298,180,000	52,512,439,000
2001	72,406,000,000	37,571,000,000	56,956,871,000
% Change, 1982–2001	281	383	529

Source: Bureau of Justice Statistics website. 2004b. "Key Facts at a Glance: Direct Expenditures by Criminal Justice Function, 1982–2001." (http://www.ojp.usdoj.gov/bjs/glance/tables/exptyptab.htm).

Table 5.5.   Per Capita Expenditures on Justice System Functions, 1982–1999

Fiscal Year	U.S. Population (millions)[a]	Total Justice System	Corrections	Police Protection	Judicial and Legal
1982	2.31	$154.72	$39.06	$82.11	$33.54
1983	2.33	169.72	44.53	88.32	36.87
1984	2.35	186.34	50.01	96.20	40.13
1985	2.37	204.11	56.89	102.55	44.67
1986	2.40	222.79	65.63	109.34	47.83
1987	2.42	242.98	72.43	118.73	51.82
1988	2.44	266.79	83.02	126.63	57.14
1989	2.46	287.46	91.43	132.87	63.16
1990	2.49	318.50	104.87	144.04	69.59
1991	2.52	347.31	116.20	154.57	76.54
1992	2.55	367.71	123.36	162.05	82.30
1993	2.57	378.39	123.93	170.83	83.63
1994	2.60	397.44	133.92	176.71	86.82
1995	2.62	429.56	151.29	185.13	93.14
1996	2.64	454.01	154.98	200.22	98.81
1997	2.67	485.66	162.81	216.10	103.75
1998	2.67	503.75	167.44	225.48	110.81
1999	2.81	520.85	174.17	232.30	114.38
% Change, 1982–1999	21.6	237	346	183	241

[a]Based on U.S. Census Bureau, Current Population Reports.
Sources: Sourcebook of Criminal Justice Statistics [Online], Pastore and Maguire, eds. 2002c: page 11, table 1.6; BJS 2002b.

on police protection and legal/judicial functions only increased by 183 and 241 percent, respectively. Table 5.6 shows spending on corrections per different levels of government. State and local governments increased their spending on corrections by 571 and 474 percent, respectively, while the federal government increased its spending by well over 800 percent. We are seeing tremendous spending on prisons and jails in an effort to simultaneously deter, incapacitate, mete out "just deserts," and rehabilitate offenders. In later chapters we will see that our prison system is instead failing those who had hoped to use incarceration as an effective method of crime control, when all the while we have been increasingly incapacitating those who are the most unlikely to recidivate.

Our spending habit is the foremost symptom of our increasing dependence on prisons as places to dump troubled individuals whose recovery requires more than just a cell, three square meals per day, and an occasional prescription. But we have taken the easy route by herding masses of offenders into custodial settings, regardless of whether their crimes are violent or not, and we have done so by building more expansive and expensive

Table 5.6. Correctional Expenditures (Billions) and Percent Change, 1981–1999

| | Government Level | | |
	Federal	State	Local
1981	$0.436	$5.17	$2.63
1982	0.541	6.01	3.01
1983	0.606	6.87	3.54
1984	0.687	7.76	4.01
1985	0.792	9.14	4.52
1986	0.862	10.80	5.13
1987	0.994	11.69	5.94
1988	1.25	13.41	6.90
1999	1.41	15.04	7.47
1990	1.73	17.21	8.78
1991	2.12	19.22	9.63
1992	2.64	20.43	10.40
1993	2.69	20.80	10.54
1994	2.84	23.13	11.12
1995	4.16	16.06	11.89
1996	3.76	25.29	12.28
1997	3.89	27.11	12.86
1998	3.16	30.59	13.96
1999	4.08	34.68	15.09
% Change, 1981–1999	836	571	474

Source: *Sourcebook of Criminal Justice Statistics.* 2002b. "Justice System Direct and Intergovernmental Expenditures. Table 1.2, page 3. Maguire and Rastore, eds. Retrieved June 6, 2006 (http://www.albany.edu/sourcebook/pdf/sb2002/sb2002-section1.pdf).

prisons. As table 5.6 indicates, state, local, and the federal government increased their spending in correctional expenditures alone from $8.23 billion in 1981 to $53.3 billion in 1999, a total increase of 533 percent.

STATE EXPENDITURES

Though the percentage of increase in the federal government's spending on corrections from 1981 to 1999 surpassed that of state and local governments (table 5.6), states spent over eight times the dollar amount spent by the federal system in 1994. In 2001, prison expenditures were the smallest in North Dakota ($26.8 million), South Dakota ($37.5 million), Vermont ($46.1 million), and Wyoming ($56.2 million).[21] States with the largest expenditures on prisons were New York ($2.8 billion), Texas ($2.3 billion), Michigan ($1.6 billion), and California ($4.2 billion). By 2003, the California

Department of Corrections' annual budget had grown to $5.7 billion.[22] Geographically, the South spends more per inmate than any other region in the United Stated.[23] Virginia's operating and capital expenditures, which reached approximately $723.7 million in 2002, was the fifth highest in the South after Texas ($2.32 billion), Florida ($1.48 billion), Georgia ($923.5 million), and North Carolina ($863.9 million).[24]

In an analysis of 16 southeastern states from 1992/1993 to 2002/2003, Freeman, Hainkel, and DeWitt[25] reported that prison expenditures increased by slightly over 79 percent. Florida experienced a 120.5 percent increase over the span of one decade, whereas Missouri increased its prison expenditures by 151.7 percent and West Virginia by 239.6 percent.[26] Within these 16 states, inmates cost anywhere from $9,837 (in Alabama) to $22,845 (in North Carolina) per year. With a total of 32,253 inmates at year-end 2001 and 23,451 new admissions in that year alone, the North Carolina Department of Corrections' authorized budget for fiscal year 2000–2001 (not including capital expenditures) reached over $960 million.[27]

Have these enormous costs paid off? Among states with the highest increases in incarceration rates from 1984 to 1991, crime increased by 15 percent, whereas other states experienced a 17 percent increase—a mere 2 percent difference.[28] In essence, "the estimated cost for additional prison construction and housing for this 2% gain was $9.5 billion,"[29] an alarming price tag for states to pay, especially when an overwhelming majority of crime is nonviolent. These figures reflect our unprecedented commitment to incapacitation, a stance that has promulgated enormous and costly changes in both prison demographics and correctional facilities. A $50 billion correctional system is a steep price to pay for prisons and jails in a period during which crime rates are falling, yet the spending carries on.

Should we continue to spend at our current rates when projections for federal discretionary and mandatory criminal justice spending are as alarming as the estimates in table 5.7? These expenditures include federal law enforcement activities, federal litigative and judicial activities, correctional activities, and criminal justice assistance. By 2009, the federal government alone is expected to spend over $47 billion toward our criminal justice system. With this type of predicted growth in the federal system, we can only imagine the projected criminal justice budgets at the state and local levels.

WHY ARE WE SPENDING SO MUCH?

There are several factors contributing toward our nation's spending on corrections, two of which are inherently intertwined—the increased use of prison for nonviolent offenders and large prison populations that have inevitably followed. These two elements, in conjunction with harsher sen-

Table 5.7. Federal Criminal Justice Budget (in millions) in fiscal year 2003, and projected 2004–2009

Fiscal Year	Total	Discretionary	Mandatory
2003 (actual)	$39,689	$35,741	$3,948
2004	42,719	36,993	5,726
2005	41,958	38,146	3,812
2006	42,202	39,304	2,898
2007	43,573	40,602	2,971
2008	44,904	41,918	2,986
2009	47,189	44,188	3,001

Source: *Sourcebook of Criminal Justice Statistics.* 2003. "Federal Criminal Justice Budget Authorities." Table 1.12, page 15. Maguire and Pastore, eds. Retrieved June 6, 2006 (h t t p : / / www.albany.edu/sourcebook/pdf/t112.pdf).

tences, have given rise to extensive medical and mental health care costs during an era when the entire nation is struggling with surging health care costs. To make matters even worse, inmates are unable to contribute significantly to the costs of their incarceration. Furthermore, many states have elected to build supermax prisons and to utilize them to incarcerate inmates from general prison populations when overcrowding becomes too overwhelming to handle, a practice that has potentially costly consequences. To better clarify the costs of corrections, each of these aforementioned components will be discussed in greater detail.

Prison Population Growth

Calculating the full costs of incarcerating non-violent inmates would be incomplete without recognizing the impact that mass incarceration has had on our economy. Were our prison population not the largest in the world, the expenses we allocate to prisons would be unlikely to raise any eyebrows, yet in 2003 our nation's state and federal prisons housed 1,470,045 million adults.[30] When jails, Immigration and Naturalization Service facilities, military prisons, juvenile institutions, and facilities in Indian country are figured into this calculation, the population reached approximately 2,212,475.[31] Table 5.8 shows the average annual percent change in state and federal prison populations from 1995 to 2003. The average annual rate of growth in the federal system (7.7 percent) has been more than twice that of state prisons (2.9 percent). Among the states, the largest annual percent changes occurred in the West (3.9 percent), followed by the Midwest (3.1), the South (3.0), and the Northeast (0.7). In all states but Massachusetts, New York, and Ohio, prison populations have increased since 1995. More prisoners means more costs, and thus perhaps fewer resources available for social or educational programs.

Table 5.8. Percentage of Average Annual Change in Prisoners under State or Federal correctional Authorities, 1995–2003

U.S. Total	3.3	Delaware	4.0
Federal	7.7	Florida	2.8
State	2.9	Georgia	4.1
Northeast	0.7	Kentucky	3.7
Connecticut	3.4	Louisiana	4.6
Maine	4.9	Maryland	1.6
Massachusetts	−2.1	Mississippi	7.7
New Hampshire	2.4	North Carolina	0.6
New Jersey	0.1	Oklahoma	2.7
New York	−0.6	South Carolina	2.4
Pennsylvania	2.9	Tennessee	6.6
Rhode Island	1.0	Texas	2.6
Vermont	3.7	Virginia	3.2
Midwest	3.1	West Virginia	8.3
Illinois	1.8	West	3.9
Indiana	4.6	Alaska	3.2
Iowa	4.7	Arizona	4.9
Kansas	3.3	California	2.7
Michigan	2.3	Colorado	7.5
Minnesota	6.2	Hawaii	6.1
Missouri	5.9	Idaho	7.4
Nebraska	3.6	Montana	7.7
North Dakota	9.8	Nevada	4.0
Ohio	0	New Mexico	5.3
South Dakota	6.1	Oregon	8.7
Wisconsin[a]	—	Utah	6.4
South	3.0	Washington	4.1
Alabama	4.5	Wyoming	3.7
Arkansas	5.4		

[a]Data not provided.
Source: Harrison and Beck. 2004. "Prisoners in 2003." Washington, DC: Bureau of Justice Statistics Bulletin, U.S. Department of Justice: Table 4.

In 2001, Maine spent the most per prisoner in operation costs, followed by Rhode Island, Massachusetts, Minnesota, and New York (see table 5.9).[32] Over the next decade, southern states—where incarceration rates are generally higher than the national average[33]—are expected to continue experiencing immense population growths in their prisons.[34] Alabama will likely face a 25.2 percent increase in its prison population from 2002 to 2007, and a 45.5 percent increase by year 2012.[35] Similarly, Tennessee's prison population is projected to expand by 58.5 percent from 2002 to 2007, and 70.6 percent by 2012. With these figures in mind, the estimated cost of our future prison population is a forewarning of an inevitable financial nightmare.

Table 5.9. Prison Populations and Annual Operating Costs by Inmate by State and Region, 2001

	Prison Population	Annual Operation Costs per Inmate
All states	1,252,743	$22,650
Northeast	166,632	33,037
Connecticut	13,155	26,856
Maine	1,635	44,379
Massachusetts	9,479	37,718
New Hampshire	2,257	25,949
New Jersey	29,784	27,347
New York	70,199	36,836
Pennsylvania	36,844	31,900
Rhode Island	1,966	38,503
Vermont	1,313	24,178
Midwest	236,458	24,779
Illinois	45,281	21,844
Indiana	19,811	21,841
Iowa	7,955	22,997
Kansas	8,344	21,381
Michigan	47,718	32,525
Minnesota	6,238	36,836
Missouri	27,519	12,867
Nebraska	3,816	25,321
North Dakota	994	22,425
Ohio	45,833	26,295
South Dakota	2,613	13,853
Wisconsin	20,336	28,622
South	53,7086	16,479
Alabama	24,123	8,128
Arkansas	11,851	15,619
Delaware	3,937	22,802
D.C.	5,008	26,670
Florida	71,318	20,190
Georgia	44,141	19,860
Kentucky	14,919	17,818
Louisiana	35,207	12,951
Maryland	22,490	26,398
Mississippi	19,239	12,795
North Carolina	27,043	26,984
Oklahoma	23,181	16,309
South Carolina	21,017	16,762
Tennessee	22,166	18,206
Texas	158,008	13,808
Virginia	29,643	22,942
West Virginia	3,795	14,817

(*continued*)

Table 5.9.   (*continued*)

	Prison Population	Annual Operation Costs per Inmate
West	264,147	25,231
Alaska	2,128	36,730
Arizona	25,412	22,476
California	160,412	25,053
Colorado	16,833	25,408
Hawaii	3,553	21,637
Idaho	5,535	16,319
Montana	3,105	21,898
Nevada	10,063	17,572
New Mexico	4,666	28,035
Oregon	10,553	36,060
Utah	5,541	24,574
Washington	14,666	30,168
Wyoming	1,680	28,845

Sources: Stephan. 2004; Beck and Harrison. 2001: Table 4; Harrison and Karberg. 2003: Table 7; U.S. Department of Justice, Bureau of Justice Statistics. 2003. Compendium of Federal Justice Statistics, 2001. NCJ 201627. Washington, DC: Department of Justice: 104. Downloaded from Sourcebook of Criminal Justice Statistics online.

Lack of Prisoner Contributions

At the turn of the new millennium, a state or federal inmate cost an approximate $62 per day in operating costs.[36] Given such high expenses per inmate, the public often wonders why inmates are not required to earn their keep, thus reducing overall expenses that taxpayers must front. It has been estimated that 66 percent of inmates participate in some form of work,[37] but the average pay they receive falls anywhere between $2.17 to $8.94 per day.[38] At most, inmates earning $2.17 daily would make less than $800 per year if they worked *every single day*, and if inmates worked full-time for $8.94 daily (excluding weekends), they would earn less than $2,400 annually. Prisoners working for private prison industries may earn $26.35 to $35.62 daily by producing items such as baked goods, clothing, tires, traffic signs, paint, and milk,[39] but a significant percentage of their earnings go toward restitution, child support, and personal purchases. Even if prisoners who earned a daily wage of $35.62 (excluding weekends) paid for their upkeep, they could only contribute up to $9,300 annually toward the annual cost of their incarceration, which ranges anywhere from $16,000 to $23,000 and perhaps more for inmates with special needs.

Even at the current federal minimum wage of $5.15 per hour, an individual working part-time at 20 hours a week in the "outside world" could earn $10,000 per year.[40] The loss of income and taxes incurred by removing nonviolent offenders from their original places of employment comprises a substantial portion of the overall costs of incarceration. States spent $22,650 per inmate in operation costs in 2001, yet the returns on this investment are disproportionately small.

Increasing Use of Incarceration for Nonviolent Offenders

To incarcerate any type of offender is expensive, but is this spending warranted on nonviolent offenders? From 1978 to 1996, the number of incarcerated drug offenders increased by 700 percent, from 14,241 to 114,071, and by 1998 there were approximately one million nonviolent offenders in our nation's prisons and jails.[41] Compared to the 126 percent increase in violent offenders during the same time period, the rising number of nonviolent offenders filling our nation's jails and prisons has left many departments of corrections in a state of financial disarray. Not only have the last few decades ushered an unprecedented number of bodies into our correctional facilities, but states have designed more laws to keep them behind bars for longer periods.

According to Morris and Tonry, the "marginal savings of removing a few from prison may not be great; until a section or a wing of a prison can be emptied there will be no substantial savings"[42] in diverting offenders from prison. In that spirit, one could also argue that the marginal costs of each additional prison bed—once a prison has been built—are also diminishing. However, when crowding occurs with each additional bed, when the demand to build a new prison eventually arises, and when $20 million is spent to construct a new facility that holds fewer than 200 individuals, the cumulative cost savings of diverting even a few handful of offenders from prison could become quite significant over time (see chapter 7).

Harsh Prison Sentences for Nonviolent Offenses

Sentencing policies, designed to increase the proportion of sentences that are actually served by offenders, have also contributed toward surging correctional costs over the last several decades. Today, because of our drug laws, many offenders are receiving prison terms in lieu of probation, and many are expected to serve a longer portion of their sentence than in earlier years (see chapter 3). Despite efforts at all governmental levels to remain "tough on crime," Austin and Fabelo suggest that increasing sentence lengths by a few months has shown no marginal effects on recidivism rates in some states.[43] In fact, they estimate that the extra cost of increasing the average time served in prison by one month throughout the country would amount to $1.5 billion and "would probably only achieve marginal returns or no returns in term of new crime reductions."[44] Our nation has clearly established an expensive tough on crime initiative, yet we cannot logistically or financially afford to follow through on our plan to demonstrate this tough stance, and many future offenders know this as well. On average, it is expected that state offenders (violent and nonviolent) sentenced in 2002 will only serve half of their original prison sentences. Without the funds to fulfill promises off harsher sentences, it is questionable as to whether we are even actualizing our tough on crime agenda and effectively deterring future offenders.

Medical Costs

Since the 1980s, rising health care costs have been sweeping the nation and are currently at the forefront of political agendas and public forums. Prisons have not been immune to these concerns and are as affected by rising costs as much as any other segment of society, for millions of bodies requiring medical care continue to flood our prisons. The milieu of prison life is inherently violent, an atmosphere where injuries—whether accidental or inflicted by other inmates—are frequent.

In 1997, 20.1 percent of state inmates and nearly 22 percent of federal inmates were in accidents while in prison.[45] In state and federal prisons, where approximately 25 percent of violent offenders were injured in accidents, the same was true of almost 15 and 23.2 percent of state and federal drug offenders, respectively, and 14.3 and 21.2 percent of state and federal public-order offenders. Since 1997, 10.1 and 3.2 percent of state and federal inmates, respectively, have been injured in fights since their admission to prison.[46] Violent offenders were more likely to be injured in a fight in state (14.4 percent) and federal (9.4 percent) prisons than inmates in other offense categories. In state prisons, 8.5 percent of property offenders, 4.1 percent of drug offenders, and 5.9 percent of public-order offenders were hurt in a fight. The percent of property, drug, and public-order offenders in federal prisons injured in fights was 2.6, 1.7, and 3.8 percents, respectively. With ever-increasing health care costs, and with an historically large prison population, providing adequate medical attention to prisoners and retaining qualified medical staff have been expensive challenges.

The American public decries providing inmates with medical care when 15.6 percent of the U.S. population[47] is without health insurance.[48] When the stereotypical image of a prison inmate is that of a predatory, violent sociopath—a generalization that is far from accurate—we loathe affording offenders access to the medical services that many hard-working Americans are unable to obtain. It is only within the last few decades, however, that inmates have been afforded minimally adequate health care. Prior to the 1970s, prison health care was atrocious. Prisoners received medical attention under isolated, "negligent" and often "brutal" conditions.[49] It was not uncommon for an untrained inmate to medicate and perform medical procedures on other inmates, such as surgery and dental extractions. The standards of medical care within prisons changed however, following several court cases, such as *Newman v. State* (1972),[50] which found these medical conditions in violation of prisoners' Eighth Amendment rights. In *Estelle v. Gamble* (1976),[51] the Supreme Court ruled that inmates have a constitutional right to medical care, which must be provided by the state;[52] in 1976 the American Public Health Association published the first national standards of care for prisoners;[53] and in *Fernandez v. United States* (1991),[54] the courts determined that health care should be "reasonably commensurate with modern medical science" and "acceptable within prudent professional standards."[55]

Spending on health care in prison varies per state, as do the actual providers of medical care. The estimated annual cost of health care per prisoner increased by 70 percent from 1982 ($883) to 1996 ($2,387).[56] Altogether, prisons forked out approximately $2.45 billion toward prison medical care in 1996. Those that rely on "community health care providers," and thus the "larger health care market," face stiffer prices.[57] In fiscal year 2003, the Georgia Department of Corrections[58] spent $143 million on health and mental health care. Florida's Department of Corrections[59] spent $307 million on health services during fiscal year 2003/2004, and Virginia's Department of Corrections[60] spent $35.5 million on their Office of Health Service in 2004, which only reflected 36.6 percent of their entire health care costs.[61] Like players in any other industry, many prisons are turning to the managed care market as a response to rising costs of health care.[62] While this is a highly debatable and complex topic, one that is beyond the scope of this chapter,[63] it is certain that delivering quality health care to prisoners is an expensive task that receives very little political and public support.

Today, prisons are faced with the medical costs associated with treating and managing inmates with conditions such as HIV/AIDS and tuberculosis. Since 1991, the number of AIDS cases in prisons have increased by an estimated 248 percent,[64] although the percent of prisoners with HIV has been decreasing since 1999.[65] Nonetheless, at year-end 2002, approximately 1.1 percent of federal inmates and 2 percent of state prisoners were HIV positive (see table 5.10). Though the percent of state and federal inmates with HIV is decreasing, the average rate of AIDS is more than three times higher in prison than in the general United States population (see table 5.11).[66] Medical care for HIV/AIDS can range from $14,000 to $34,000 annually.[67] Given that there were over 34,000 inmates with HIV and nearly 10,000 with AIDS in 1999, the costs of treatment are enormous.[68] For example, New York state prisons housed approximately 7,000 inmates with HIV in 1999. While the death rate of inmates with AIDS has decreased—258 deaths in 1995 to 39 deaths in 1998—New York has had to make extensive changes in their medical policies regarding HIV positive inmates. As a

Table 5.10.   Percent of State and
Federal Prisoners Who Are HIV
Positive, 1998–2002

	State	
Federal		
1998	2.3	1.0
1999	2.3	0.9
2000	2.2	1.0
2001	2.0	1.2
2002	2.0	1.1

Source: Maruschak. 2004. "HIV in Prisons
and Jails, 2002." Washington, DC: Bureau
of Justice Statistics, U.S. Department of Justice: pg. 3; Centers for Disease Control and
Prevention. 2001. "Providing Services to

result, the state now provides HIV positive inmates with "antiretroviral
medications and medications for opportunistic infections,"[69] uses satellite
video teleconferencing to enable medical providers in prison to receive
training and education, and has made changes regarding medical record
and pharmaceutical procedures.[70] Some prisons are also adopting procedures to screen inmates for medical and psychosocial problems and provide treatment, case management services, and hospice care.[71] While these
services are necessary, they are undoubtedly costly. With so many inmates
to care for, prisoners are "dying preventable deaths."[72]

Delivering adequate health care is met with criticism by the public at large,
for as McDonald points out, "incarcerated criminal offenders are the only
persons in the United States who have a constitutional right to health

Table 5.11.   Percent of Population with Confirmed
AIDS by U.S. Population and State/Federal Prisoners,
1995–2002

	U.S. Population	State and Federal Prison Population
1995	0.08	0.51
1996	0.09	0.54
1997	0.10	0.55
1998	0.11	0.53
1999	0.12	0.60
2000	0.13	0.53
2001	0.14	0.52
2002	0.14	0.48

Source: Maruschak. 2004. "HIV in Prisons and Jails, 2002." Washington, DC: Bureau of Justice Statistics, U.S. Department of Justice: 5
(http://www.ojp.usdoj.gov/bjs/pub/pdf/hivpj02.pdf).

care."[73] But in many institutions, health care is still far from adequate and acceptable. Finding qualified medical professionals to work within prison environments for little pay is difficult, resulting in shortages of prison health care staff across the nation. Further, many prisons are still ill-equipped to provide care to prisoners with severe medical problems.[74] In 1997, over 7 percent of state and nearly 10 percent of federal inmates reported medical conditions that required surgery.[75] That same year, 16.7 and 16 percent of state and federal inmates, respectively, reported "specific medical problems," categorized by Maruschak and Beck as: HIV/AIDS, heart, circulatory, cancer, kidney/liver, respiratory, neurological, skeletal, and diabetes.[76] Within state prisons, 31 percent of inmates reported conditions labeled as learning, speech, hearing, vision, mental, and physical, whereas the same was true for 23.4 percent of federal inmates.[77] Overall, 21 and 18 percent of state and federal prisoners, respectively, were unable to work due to various physical or mental conditions.[78]

Female inmates are one of the most rapidly growing prison populations with their own unique health care needs. There are over 100,000 women in state and federal prisons[79] and nearly 82,000 women in jail.[80] Naturally, female inmates who are pregnant require special medical care and thus also require specialized health care not necessary in male prisons, such as obstetric and gynecological services. In 1997, female offenders reported more medical problems (excluding injuries), physical impairments—such as hearing and vision—and mental disorders than male inmates in both state and federal prisons.[81] A higher percentage of female state inmates also required surgery (7.9 percent) in state prison than their male counterparts (7.5 percent).[82] Similarly, within the federal system, more female inmates (11.3 percent) required surgery than did males (9.5 percent).[83] Chapter 6 discusses issues that are specific to female inmates in greater detail.

By increasing the number of nonviolent offenders who are sentenced to prison, states are forced to increase their spending on correctional health care and perhaps even sacrifice the overall quality of services provided to each individual prisoners. With the world's largest penal population, it is no surprise that American prisons are facing steep health care costs. Along with incarceration comes the responsibility of medical, an expense that will only grow as more offenders—especially inmates—continue to enter the correctional system.

Supermax Prisons

Many states are boasting about their newly constructed multimillion dollar supermax prisons, proudly showing off the latest technological advances they have implemented in order to cage difficult inmates for 23 hours a day. As we saw in chapter 4, however, we have been abusing the functions for

which supermax prisons were designed, which was originally to incapacitate the "worst of the worst."[84]

The purpose of building supermax prisons, and the psychological and
physiological effects they often have on inmates, were discussed in chapter
4. In this section, I turn to the expenses associated with building these massive yet increasingly popular facilities.

Lawrence and Mears have reviewed the various costs and benefits associated with supermax prisons.[85] In one example, they list several benefits to
society and prison administrators, such as better prison management, fewer
assaults in prison, and reduced recidivism among general population inmates.[86] While potentially a cost to prison administrators, communities
might also benefit from the additional jobs that supermax prisons may bring
to their areas, as well as their property taxes. Lawrence and Mears also list potential costs, such as damaged relationships between inmates and family
members, higher recidivism rates among supermax inmates, and increased
mental health problems within the prison. Though supermax prisons vary in
annual budgets, operating costs, inmate populations, and administrative issues, each one is contributing toward the facilitation of prison growth and
adding to the costs. As reiterated by Mears and Watson,

> supermax prisons may adversely affect state and local communities through the costs
> associated with them and the corresponding diminished investment in public services
> [original italics]. Additional costs accrue if supermaxes increase the mental and
> physical health or court processing caseloads communities face. These costs
> then translate into tax burdens for businesses and residents and fewer state-
> funded programs and services.[87]

(The costs of mental illness will be discussed further in chapter 6.) Supermax
prisons are more expensive than traditional prisons because they require a
higher inmate-to-guard ratio and depend on advanced and expensive technology.[88] Additional training is also required among correctional officers
who work within supermaxes. As previously mentioned, supermax prisons
are used to house inmates from other prisons that are overcapacity. Ohio's
Youngstown supermax prison, built in 1998, cost $65 million and was de-
signed to hold 500 inmates, which initially equaled $130,000 per inmate
just to build. The Wisconsin Secure Program Facility in Boscobel is a $47.5
million supermax designed to house 509 inmates, and according to the Wisconsin Department of Corrections, operates on a budget of over $14 million
per year. Employed in what has been described as "the most expensive, state-
of-the-art, high-tech, outdated eighteenth-century dungeon ever considered"[89] are 180 security-staff and 72 nonsecurity staff. The current population in this supermax is only 288 even though it was designed to house 509
inmates. This is what McNally refers to as a "Superwaste." Regarding Wis-

consin's Boscobel supermax prison, McNally skeptically asks "why [build] a prison for people already in prison"?

NOTES

1. See Forst 2004.
2. Supported by a grant from the Community Advocacy Project of the Open Society Institute.
3. Pyle and Gilmore 2005.
4. Cook et al. 1993: 2.
5. Ambrosio and Schiraldi 1997.
6. Gainsborough and Mauer 2000.
7. North Carolina Department of Corrections [NCDOC] 2002.
8. Bauer and Owens 2004: 6.
9. Ibid: 5.
10. Georgia Department of Corrections 2004: 20.
11. Virginia Department of Corrections [VDOC] 2005.
12. Stephan 2004.
13. Florida Department of Corrections 2005.
14. Stephan 2004: 2.
15. See Bauer and Owens 2004.
16. Austin and Fabelo 2004: 9.
17. Ibid.
18. See Fukuyama's (1999) discussion on different forms of capital in *The Great Disruption*.
19. Dubois 1903.
20. Bureau of Justice Statistics 2004b.
21. Stephan 2004: 2.
22. CDC 2004b.
23. Stephan 2004: 3.
24. Ibid: table 2.
25. Freeman et al. 2002.
26. Freeman et al. 2002: 16.
27. NCDOC 2002.
28. Gainsborough and Mauer 2000: 4.
29. Ibid.
30. Harrison and Beck 2004.
31. Harrison and Beck 2003: 1.
32. Stephan 2004.
33. In 2003, states with the highest incarceration rates (per 100,000 residents) were Louisiana (801), Mississippi (768), Texas (702), Oklahoma (636), and Alabama (635) (Harrison and Beck 2004).
34. Freeman et al. 2002.
35. Freeman et al. 2002: 7.
36. Stephan 2004: 1.

37. Stephan 1997 (cited in Cullen 2002: 268).
38. Cullen 2002: 269.
39. Ibid.
40. Economic Policy Institute 2005.
41. Irwin et al. 1999.
42. Morris and Tonry 1990: 234.
43. Austin and Fabelo 2004. For related studies, see McGinnis and Austin 2001; Kentucky Department of Corrections 2001.
44. Austin and Fabelo 2004: 13.
45. Maruschak and Beck 2001.
46. Ibid: 4.
47. Approximately 45 million Americans.
48. National Coalition on Health Care 2004.
49. McDonald 1999: 427.
50. *Newman v. State*, 12 Crim. L. Rptr. 2113 [M.D. Ala. 1972].
51. *Estelle v. Gamble*, 97 S. Ct. 285, 291 (1976).
52. Pollock 1997.
53. McDonald 1999: 437. See American Public Health Association 1976.
54. *Fernandez v. United States* (941 F. 2d 1488 [11th Cir. 1991].
55. McDonald 1999: 428.
56. Ibid: 452; Stephan 1999: v.
57. McDonald 1999: 453.
58. Georgia Department of Corrections 2004.
59. FDOC 2005.
60. VDOC 2005.
61. The rest is paid by specific correctional facilities.
62. McDonald 1999.
63. For more detailed reading, see McDonald's "Medical Care in Prisons" (1999).
64. McDonald 1999: 449.
65. Maruschak 2004.
66. CDC 2001.
67. Feig 2002.
67. CDC 2001.
67. Ibid.
70. Ibid: 1.
71. Ibid: 1–2.
72. *Birmingham News* 2003.
73. McDonald 1999: 471.
74. McDonald 1999.
75. Maruschak and Beck 2001: 1.
76. Ibid: 9.
77. Ibid: 1.
78. Ibid: 2.
79. BJS 2004k.
80. BJS 2004j.
81. Maruschak and Beck 2001.
82. Ibid: 8.

83. Ibid: 8.
84. NIC 2004a.
85. Lawrence and Mears 2004.
86. Ibid: 10.
87. Mears and Watson 2006: 252.
88. Lawrence and Mears 2004.
89. McNally 1999.

6

Expensive Prisoners

Because of our nation's affinity for punishment, we must understand the potential long term effects of this wave of imprisonment as well as *who* is being affected by current sentencing practices and *how*. Prison communities possess a certain fluidity that shifts with social and political changes.[1] For example, the growing number of prisoners during the mid-1900s largely reflected the widespread activism during the civil rights movement,[2] and the composition of prison populations during the 1980's war on crime reflected heated political pressure to exert more severe punishments against drug offenders. It is among these more recent prisoners who are ushered into our contemporary "warehouse[s] of violence"[3] that we see a significant number of "Million Dollar Inmates."

As a result of today's incarceration rates, the increased institutionalization of nonviolent offenders,[4] the overuse of prison for drug offenders, the widespread abolition of discretionary parole, and increases in the number of women behind bars, the correctional industry has been deluged with waves of young African American men, drug offenders, and women. The traditional convicts of the earlier "Big House"[5] are being replaced by a new breed of prisoner who is reshaping prison cultures and communities and thereby posing new challenges to the field of corrections. This chapter identifies the offenders who have been disproportionately affected by the changes described above; they are African American men, women, nonviolent offenders (e.g., property and drug offenders), lifers, aging prisoners, and the mentally ill.

AFRICAN AMERICAN MEN

The mid-twentieth century ushered in an era of political turmoil but one of great historical social transformation. While African Americans were in the process of gaining their civil rights and achieving unprecedented levels of equality, they were also streaming into the criminal justice system's grasp.[6] Despite the overall gains made during the Civil Rights era, the African American community could not fully traverse the racial divide. As Mauer points out, discrimination still lingered in urban areas and was accompanied by high levels of poverty, unemployment, and crime.[7] As such, the segregation that was losing momentum within the general population was reemerging within prison walls and causing intense racial strife among prisoners.

The more recent wave of young African American males flooding our criminal justice system was largely a reflection of our nation's social and political attack on drug offenders during the 1980s. One tragic event that bolstered support for the implementation of severe mandatory sentences for crack cocaine-related offenses was the death of 22-year-old Len Bias, a University of Maryland basketball star who overdosed on crack cocaine. His death was followed by a Congressional bill that would make mandatory sentences for the possession of crack cocaine—the drug of choice among many urban African American cocaine users—up to 100 times more punishable than offenses involving the same amount of powder cocaine.[8, 9] Perhaps the most tragic outcome of the war launched against drugs has been its toll among African Americans who now represent about 12 percent of the U.S. population and 12 percent of drug users,[10] but 38 percent of drug arrests, 59 percent of convicted drug offenders, and by 2002, slightly more than 40 percent of state prisoners.[11] Today, African American males have a greater chance of being imprisoned than any other group.

The incarceration rate of African Americans per 100,000 resident population increased each year from 1980 to 1992 by an average of 138.4.[12] In 1989, close to 25 percent of African American men in their twenties were in prison, on probation, or on parole,[13] and in the mid-1990s it was estimated that "one in fourteen adult black males was locked up in a prison or jail on any given day."[14] By 2002, African American men were being sent to prison or jail at a rate of 4,810 per 100,000 resident population, over seven times that of white males.[15] The number of African American women in state and federal prisons has also swelled, increasing 204 percent between 1985 and 1995.[16]

Many of the gains made by the African American community during the mid-1900s have been overshadowed by the range of draconian sentencing laws implemented as a response to the war on drugs. Table 6.1 provides state prison and jail incarceration rates by state and race in 2005, as well as the ratios of black-to-white incarceration rates.[17] For example, the incarceration rate among whites in Alabama was 542 per 100,000 population and 1,916

Table 6.1. State Prison and Jail Incarceration Rates (per 100,000 Population) and Ratios by Race, 2005

States	White	Black	Ratio (white:black)
All States	412	2,290	5.6
Northeast	225	2,060	9.2
Midwest	351	2,278	6.5
South	536	2,156	4.0
West	500	3,014	6.0
Alabama	542	1,916	3.5
Alaska	500	2,163	4.3
Arizona	590	3,294	5.6
Arkansas	478	1,846	3.9
California	460	2,992	6.5
Colorado	525	3,491	6.6
Connecticut	211	2,532	12.0
D.C.a	56	1,065	19.0
Delaware	396	2,517	6.4
Florida	588	2,615	4.4
Georgia	623	2,068	3.3
Hawaii	453	851	1.9
Idaho	675	2,869	4.3
Illinois	223	2,020	9.1
Indiana	463	2,526	5.5
Iowa	309	4,200	13.6
Kansas	443	3,096	7.0
Kentucky	561	2,793	5.0
Louisiana	523	2,452	4.7
Maine	262	1,992	7.6
Maryland	288	1,579	5.5
Massachusetts	201	1,635	8.1
Michigan	412	2,262	5.5
Minnesota	212	1,937	9.1
Mississippi	503	1,742	3.5
Missouri	487	2,556	5.2
Montana	433	3,569	8.2
Nebraska	290	2,418	8.3
Nevada	627	2,916	4.7
New Hampshire	289	2,666	9.2
New Jersey	190	2,352	12.4
New Mexico	*	*	*
New York	174	1,627	9.4
North Carolina	320	1,727	5.4
North Dakota	267	2,683	10.0
Ohio	344	2,196	6.4
Oklahoma	740	3,252	4.4

(continued)

Table 6.1. (*continued*)

States	White	Black	Ratio (white:black)
Oregon	502	2,930	5.8
Pennsylvania	305	2,792	9.2
Rhode Island	191	1,838	9.6
South Carolina	415	1,856	4.5
South Dakota	470	4,710	10.0
Tennessee	487	2,006	4.1
Texas	667	3,162	4.7
Utah	392	3,588	9.2
Vermont	304	3,797	12.5
Virginia	396	2,331	5.9
Washington	393	2,522	6.4
West Virginia	392	2,188	5.6
Wisconsin	415	4,416	10.6
Wyoming	*	*	*

*Indicates data unavailable.
ªExcludes all inmates with sentences of more than one year who are held by the Federal Bureau of Prisons.
Source: Adapted from Harrison and Beck. 2006. "Prison and Jail Inmates at Midyear 2005." Washington, DC: Bureau of Justice Statistics, U.S. Department of Justice.

among blacks. The white-to-black ratio was 3.5, indicating that for every 1 out of 100,000 whites incarcerated in state prisons or jails, there were 3.5 per every 100,000 black residents. Racial disparities in incarceration rates are prevalent throughout the entire country; in no state was the incarceration rate of whites higher than blacks in 2005. The white-to-black incarceration rate ratio was the highest in the Northeast (9.2) and lowest in the South (4.0). The District of Columbia had the largest white-to-black ratio (19.0), followed by Iowa (13.6), Vermont (12.5), New Jersey (12.4), and Connecticut (12.0). States with the lowest white-to-black incarceration rate ratios included Hawaii (1.9), Georgia (3.3), Mississippi (3.5), and Alabama (3.5). The extent to which the African American community has been affected by increasing incarcerating rates can also be seen by the number of African American men in college and universities versus prison. From 1980 to 2000, the number of African American men entering the prison system was over three times the number entering college, and in 2000 more African American men could be found in jails and prisons than in institutions of higher education.[18] States where the number of incarcerated African American men (in 2000) exceeded those in college or universities (in 1999) included Alaska, Connecticut, Delaware, Indiana, Louisiana, Michigan, Missouri, New Jersey, Ohio, Oklahoma, Pennsylvania, Texas, and Wisconsin.[19]

Racial disparities throughout all domains of the criminal justice have generated considerable concerns regarding issues of justice, fairness, and equality. When the public hears statistics such as the 1989 finding that "one in four black males in the age group 20 to 29 was under some form of criminal justice supervision on any given day,"[20] this undoubtedly triggers heightened levels of fear and distrust. With African Americans disproportionately processed through the criminal justice system and the media's excessive coverage of crime stories involving black perpetrators, the fear that has been directed toward young African American men continues to perpetuate racial stereotypes among the majority population. Even individuals who are least vulnerable and minimally affected by crime harbor intense fears of victimization, due in part to the overgeneralized and stereotyped depictions of crime and offenders in the media.[21] The cycle we have started—one that perpetuates social fear and institutionalized bias—has the potential to cease, but only when we as a society are willing to confront these issues head-on.

WOMEN AND MOTHERS IN PRISON

Much of the expanding prison population can also be attributed to increasing rates at which women are being incarcerated. Women, who are "the fastest growing category of prisoners nationwide,"[22] have felt the sting of mandatory sentencing laws, especially women of color. Between 1980 and 1998, the female prison population in state and federal prisons combined increased by over 500 percent.[23] While the number of women as a percent of *arrests* has not increased significantly, the rates at which they are *incarcerated* has risen sharply. Table 6.2 shows the number and rate of sentenced prisoners under federal and state jurisdiction by sex from 1925 to 2001. From 1925 to 2001, the rate of sentenced males under state and federal jurisdiction increased by 501 percent, from 149 per 100,000 resident population in 1925 to a rate of 896 in 2001. Among women, the same rate increased by 900 percent. The rate of growth among females is clearly outpacing the rate among males.

In 1999, Ditton and Wilson estimated that the chance of a women being sent to a federal or state prison in her lifetime is 11 out of 1,000 (compared to 90 out of 1,000 for males).[24] This phenomenon can be understood by examining sentencing policies—especially those mandating prison terms for drug offenses—that are continuing to disproportionately affect women, especially mothers, and that are unique to the United States. The female prison and jail population in our nation is ten times that in Western Europe,[25] and 1 in 109 women in the United States is under the control of the criminal justice system in some manner.[26] The crimes for which women are in prison are largely nonviolent, yet their plight with the law is comparable to those who are convicted of violent offenses and are dangerous to society. According to

Table 6.2. Number and Rate (per 100,000 Resident Population) of Sentenced Males and Females under State and Federal Jurisdiction on December 31, 1925–2001

	Male		Female	
	Number	*Rate*	*Number*	*Rate*
1925	88,231	149	3,438	6
1930	124,785	200	4,668	8
1935	139,278	217	4,902	8
1940	167,345	252	6,361	10
1945	127,609	193	6,040	9
1950	160,309	211	5,814	8
1955	178,655	217	7,128	8
1960	205,265	230	7,688	8
1965	203,327	213	7,568	8
1970	190,794	191	5,635	5
1975	231,918	220	8,675	8
1980	303,643	275	12,331	11
1985	459,223	397	21,345	17
1990	699,416	575	40,564	32
1995	1,021,059	789	63,963	47
2000	1,246,234	915	85,044	59
2001	1,260,033	896	85,184	60
% Change, 1925–2001		501		900

Sources: BJS. 1982; Beck and Mumola. 1999; Beck and Harrison. 2001; Harrison and Beck. 2002; Harrison and Beck. 2003; Brown et al. 1996; BJS. 2000b; cited in Sourcebook of Criminal Justice Statistics 2000.

the Women's Prison Association (WPA), "women are 33% more likely than men to be in prison for drug-related crimes."[27] In New York in 2003, for example, half of the women in prison were convicted of offenses involving drugs.[28]

Among the women in state and federal prison, over 60 percent are African American or Hispanic[29] and nearly half (47 percent) are in their thirties. Because women in prison generally tend to be older than male inmates, they may also require more health care associated with the aging process. (The section on geriatric inmates later in this chapter addresses the needs of aging inmates.) It is often overlooked that female prisoners generally require more medical attention than women within the general population.[30] Because women in prison have a much greater likelihood of having experienced sexual or physical abuse than men,[31] they are susceptible to drug use, which also places them at high risk for transmittable diseases. While 69 percent of male prison inmates report the regular use of drugs before their incarceration, the same is true of 74 percent of women.[32] Conditions that are disproportionately found among female prisoners include HIV, mental illnesses, drug abuse related inflictions, and Hepatitis C.[33] Approximately 15 percent of male and female inmates incarcerated in jails and prisons test positive for Hepatitis C, compared to the national rate of 1.3 percent. The WPA reports that 25 percent of women in California's prisons test positive for Hepatitis C.[34] Additionally, 3.6 percent of women in state and federal prisons have HIV, which is three times the rate among their male counterparts and twelve times the national rate (0.3 percent) among women in the general U.S. population. Among female prisoners who are HIV positive, half report histories of sexual abuse, whereas the same is true among 23 percent of women without HIV in prison. Some regions have disturbingly high rates of women with HIV,[35] such as New York, whose state prisons once reported that 18 percent of their female inmates were HIV positive.[36]

Physical health is not the only issue that disproportionately affects women in prison. In 1991, over 900,000 minor children had parents in prison.[37] Women who are incarcerated are often torn from their children, many of whom have no other caretakers (see chapter 7 for more on the effects of incarceration on children). In 1997, 65.3 and 54.7 percent of female and male state prisoners, respectively, had minor children,[38] as did 63.4 percent of males and 58.8 percent of females in federal prison. However, among female prisoners, 64.3 percent of state and 84.0 percent of federal inmates lived with their children at the time of their incarceration, compared to 43.8 and 55.2 percent of male inmates in state and federal prisons, respectively.[39] Though a significant number of men in prison have children,[40] the female prison population has been increasing by approximately 8.5 percent each year since 1990, whereas the male prison population has been increasing by approximately 6.6 percent annually.[41] During the 1990s, the number of incarcerated mothers increased by 87 percent, whereas the number of incarcerated fathers increased by 61 percent,[42] and in 1999 there were an estimated 250,000 children with mothers in jail or prison, of whom 50,000 were less than five years old.[43] On average, state female prisoners have 2.4 minor children.[44]

African American inmates are more likely to have children than their Hispanic or Caucasian counterparts. Approximately 48 percent of state and federal African American inmates have children, whereas the same is true for 29 percent of state and 22 percent of federal inmates who are Caucasian and 19 percent of state and 30 percent of Hispanic federal inmates.[45] Ultimately, 7 percent of black children, 3 percent of Hispanic children, and 1 percent of Caucasian children have a parent who is incarcerated.[46]

Once incarcerated, maintaining meaningful contact with children is extremely difficult. Over 60 percent of parents in state prisons and over 80 percent of parents in federal institutions are incarcerated at least 100 miles from their last residence.[47] The WPA reports that 38 percent of women who are incarcerated over 100 away miles from their children will never see their children throughout the duration of their incarceration.[48] In a study by the National Council on Crime and Delinquency, researchers found that over 50 percent of the female inmates had not seen their children since entering prison.[49] A 2000 survey in Oregon reported that 57 percent of women expected to be reunited with their children after their release, yet half of the women had received no visits, 15 percent had no telephone calls, and 8 percent had absolutely no contact with their children in the three months preceding the survey.[50] As Chesney-Lind argues, our nation can continue to incarcerate "women guilty of petty drug and property crimes, or we can seek other solutions to the problems of economically marginalized, abused, and often drug-dependent women."[51] Additionally, she argues that reducing the number of women in jail and prison would not pose a threat to society given the nature of the crimes for which they have been convicted.

DRUG OFFENDERS

Harsh drug laws are intended to reduce drug abuse, drive up the costs of illegal substances on the streets, preclude offenders from committing crimes indirectly related to drug use, and to mete out just deserts upon drug offenders.[52] Thus, drug offenders (especially low-level offenders) have been hit the hardest by changes in sentencing laws. In 1996, the state and federal incarceration rate for drug offenses was 148 per 100,000 resident population, a nine-fold increase since 1980 when the rate was 15 per 100,000 resident population.[53] By 1998, over half of federal prisoners (58 percent) and 21 percent of state prisoners were incarcerated for drug-related crimes.[54] An overwhelming number of these individuals are users, low-level dealers, or those peripherally connected to conspiracies, and not those who are high up in the drug trafficking chain.

Not only is it expensive to house nonviolent drug offenders, but many of these inmates (namely, addicts) require special treatment facilities, services, and programming, all of which are additionally expensive. In 1997, 83 percent of inmates in state and federal prisons had used drugs prior to their incarceration, and nearly 70 percent had used drugs on a regular basis.[55] Furthermore, 52.5 percent of state and 34 percent of federal prisoners in 1997 had been under the influence of drugs or alcohol at the time of their offense.[56] Among those who had used alcohol at the time of their offense, 14 percent were treated for alcohol abuse since their admission to prison and 33 percent had participated in other forms of alcohol abuse programs. There is clearly a great need for effective drug and alcohol programs within prison, and not all prisoners who need such services receive them.

LIFERS AND AGING PRISONERS

The prisoners who are often the most overlooked and disregarded are the geriatric inmates who are aging and dying in prison. Greco writes, "Aging in prison has been virtually ignored by the medical staff and rehabilitative apparatus of the criminal justice system."[57] As our prison populations continue to grow and sentences continue to increase, concerns regarding lifers and geriatric inmates will no longer be ignorable as they will inevitably tax the resources and capacities of correctional facilities. New York State, for example, experienced a 54 percent increase in the number of elderly inmates from 1994 to 1999. If we as a nation are going to impose upon offenders an increasing number of lengthy and life sentences, we must be prepared for the costs required to keep them alive—both in the short- and long-run. Given today's trends, prisons will need to accommodate larger populations of elderly inmates, which in turn requires medical supplies, staff, and physical space.

Lifers

While many inmates are fairly young and healthy when they enter prison, we must remember that those who receive sentences of life (or long sentences) will age within the prison system and inevitably experience medical problems and conditions as they deteriorate physically and mentally. The National Institute of Corrections (NIC) observes, "several important factors seem to speed the aging process for those in prison,"[58] such as the amount of stress experienced by new inmates trying to survive the prison experience unharmed; efforts to avoid confrontations with correctional staff and fellow inmates; financial stress related to inmates' legal, family, and personal circumstances; withdrawal from chronic substance abuse; and a lack of access to adequate medical care prior to incarceration. All contribute to inmate stress, which, in turn, accelerates the aging process.[59]

By 2004, almost 10 percent of prisoners in the United States were serving life sentences.[60] The number of lifers increased by 83 percent from 1992 to mid-2004, reaching an exorbitant 127,000. In 2003, states with the highest percent of inmates sentenced to life without parole were Louisiana (10.6 percent), Pennsylvania (9.7), Iowa (6.6), Florida (5.8), and Alabama (4.8).[61] Today, there are 2,225 inmates serving life sentences without the possibility of parole for offenses they committed as juveniles.[62] Most of these offenders are products of mandatory sentencing statutes. States with the largest populations of juvenile offenders serving life sentences are Pennsylvania, Louisiana, Michigan, and Florida. Yen reports that in 2000, 9 percent of juveniles who were convicted of murder were given life sentences without the possibility of parole.[62]

Today, lifers serve an average of 29 years in prison, a 37 percent increase from 1991 when they served 21.2 years.[63] In many states, inmates receiving life sentences are not eligible for parole.[64] Mauer et al. assert "the increase in prison time for lifers is a result of changes in state policy and not continuous increases in violent crime."[65] Our prison populations have exceeded capacity levels in many states[66] that are now being forced to reconsider their sentencing statutes for nonviolent offenders. The use of alternative sentencing options, however, requires the capability to identify offenders by weighing public safety concerns against the costs of incarceration. Increasing the selectivity of prison admissions can ensure that violent and nonviolent offenders are sensibly placed in the most rational environments, but it also demands a certain amount of flexibility among the public and a willingness to shed many of our draconian attitudes toward offenders. The costs of our current policies—those that mandate long prison terms for offenders who would be more suitable for community-based sanctions—quickly come to light when we examine the expenses of sustaining a population of geriatric inmates serving long and life sentences.

Elderly Inmates

Currently, our prisons house an estimated 60,300 inmates who are ages 55 or older.[67] Table 6.3 show state and federal prisoners by age group in 1995 and 2003. In table 6.3, the percentage change in the number of inmates in each age category from 1995 to 2003 was greatest among inmates who were 55 years or older (an 85 percent increase) and second highest among inmates ages 45 to 54 (a 76.5 percent increase). Elderly inmates have been classified into three groups.[68] First-time offenders are those who

Table 6.3. Sentenced State and Federal Inmates by Age Group, 1995 and 2003

	1995	2003	*Percent Change (1995–2003)*
Total	1,085,022	1,409,280	−29.9
17 or younger	4,800	2,800	−41.5
18–19	30,000	26,400	−12.2
20–24	177,400	219,400	23.7
25–29	203,700	245,300	20.4
30–34	210,200	238,200	13.3
35–39	190,200	228,100	20.0
40–44	127,900	197,900	54.7
45–54	108,100	190,800	76.5
55 or older	32,600	60,300	85.0

Source: Harrison and Beck. 2004. "Prisoners in 2003," table 10. Washington, DC: Bureau of Justice Statistics, U.S. Department of Justice.

were incarcerated for the first time after they turned 50; they generally have problems adjusting to prison life and experience high rates of stress.[69] Reasons that the elderly commit crimes later in their lives include desperate attempts to receive medical care for various ailments, dementia, or other mental health problems.[70] Recidivists are those who have repeatedly been sent to prison over the course of their lives. Many of these individuals have histories of substance abuse, which can result in "asthma, heart problems, circulatory problems, and kidney or liver problems."[71] Finally, long-termers are those who have been serving extensive prison sentences and have inevitably aged while in prison. Because most inmates in this latter category have been in prison for decades, many are well-adjusted to their prison environments.[72] A study in 2000 found that among inmates age 55 and over, 45.6 percent were repeat offenders, 41.4 percent were first-time offenders, and 13 percent had aged while serving long prison sentences.[73]

A survey conducted by the National Center on Institutions and Alternatives [NCIA] of state correctional departments and the Federal Bureau of Prison indicated that slightly more than half of older inmates were serving time for nonviolent offenses, although the Federal Bureau of Prisons reports that over 97 percent of its aging inmate population is serving time for nonviolent offenses.[74] States with elderly inmates who comprised a large percentage of the total prison population in 2001 included New Hampshire (12.1), Massachusetts (11.1), Wyoming (10.9), Nevada (10.8), Maine (10.3), and Pennsylvania (9.9).[75] Elderly inmates generally pose little threats to the safety of the prison population, yet are expensive to house. For example, in 2003 54.7 percent of elderly inmates in Pennsylvania's prison system had no criminal history. Those who were 50 or older, in comparison to those age 49 and under, were more likely to have been incarcerated for "rape, murder 1, and sexual offense," yet they were also more likely to commit fewer infractions, be perceived as a low institutional risk, have lengthier sentences, experience mental health problems, and be in lower custody settings.[76]

The natural process of aging, as well as the medical care required when individuals are struck by diseases or serious medical conditions, is expensive. In 1997, nearly 40 percent of inmates who were age 45 or older experienced medical problems, 47.6 percent had some physical impairment or mental disorder,[77] and 12 and 11 percent of state and federal inmates, respectively, reported "an overall physically impairing condition."[78] Younger inmates were less likely to have medical problems or other impairments. Federal inmates age 45 or older had a higher percentage of hearing, vision, and physical conditions than any other age group, as was the case among state prisoners. Federal (17.7 percent) and state (15.7 percent) inmates in the oldest age group (45 or older) were also more likely to require surgery, whereas inmates who were 24 years or younger were the least likely to require surgery in both state and federal prisons. In 2000, approximately 18.5 percent of federal inmates were receiving medical attention for a chronic illness, including diabetes, asthma, and hypertension.[79]

Mauer and his colleagues estimate that incarceration costs per inmate range from $20,000 to $69,000 each year, depending on the age of the inmate. Based on their conservative estimations, they write "an average life sentence imposed by a judge costs taxpayers about $1 million."[80] Elderly inmates in New York who experience chronic illnesses, for example, may ultimately cost anywhere from $50,000 to $75,000 per year.[81] In Texas, elderly inmates cost the state $14.36 per day (or $5,241 per year), while Georgian inmates cost their state $27 each day (or $9,855 per year).[82] In Virginia, Madden et al.'s study indicates that the number of elderly inmates has risen significantly.[83] In 1991, there were 851 inmates in Virginia's prisons who were age 50 or older; by 2004, the number had risen to 3,515, an increase of 313 percent. In their study, the age category consisting of inmates 65 or older made up the smallest percentage of the inmate population, yet accounted for over 30 percent of medical costs from 2002 to 2003.

While inmates are constitutionally guaranteed the right to health care, they are ineligible for Medicaid or Medicare benefits. Thus, according to Madden et al., Virginia prisons are paying not only for many medical visits, but for provisions such as dentures, wheelchairs, and prosthetics. The most prevalent conditions within the elderly inmate populations include heart disease, hypertension, osteoarthritis, ulcers, inflammatory bowel disease, diabetes, hearing impairments, prostate diseases, asthma, vision problems, and hepatitis.[84] Other common medical conditions among elderly inmates include "incontinence, sensory impairment, impaired flexibility, respiratory illnesses, cardiovascular disease, and cancer."[85] Chronic illnesses include "arthritis, hypertension, ulcer disease, prostate problems, and myocardial infarction."[86] Maruschak and Beck reported that

> approximately 17 percent of inmates housed in state facilities self-reported specific conditions, including HIV/AIDS (1.7 percent), heart disease (1.1 percent), circulatory problems other than heart disease (2.4 percent), respiratory problems (1.4 percent), cancer (0.2 percent), neurological problems (0.7 percent), skeletal problems (2.6 percent), kidney/liver problems (0.9 percent), and diabetes (0.9 percent).[87]

Elderly inmates who are chronically or seriously ill generally pose little or no threat to society and are unlikely to recidivate, but they can cost up to $69,000 per year to incarcerate.[88] The NCIA estimates that elderly state and federal inmates cost over $2 billion annually.[89] Within the federal system, they cost $409 million, or 12.7 percent of its annual budget. Between 1992 and 2000, daily medical care costs per inmate increased by 31.5 percent—

from \$5.62 to \$7.39—and from 1997 to 2001, prisons increased their spending on health care from \$2.75 billion to nearly \$3.5 billion.[90]

In certain circumstances, elderly inmates with severe medical problems may be released on geriatric parole. The United States Parole Commission specifies conditions under which these geriatric inmates may be released, stating that if an inmate is 65 years or older, he or she is eligible for parole if there has been a documented identification of a "chronic infirmity, illness, or disease related to aging."[91] Inmates may be released under geriatric parole if there is a low risk of recidivism and if the inmate poses little threat to society. Factors such as the severity of the inmate's offense and the age at which the offense was committed are also considered, as well as the inmate's current age, the severity of the illness or disease, health evaluations, criminal record, and the inmate's risk for violence. Geriatric parole does not apply, however, to individuals who have been "convicted of first degree murder or who [have] been sentenced for a crime committed while armed"[92] under specific D.C. codes, or who had the medical condition at the time of the original sentencing. This practice could potentially be adopted in other regions to reduce prison crowding.

Despite the costs and resources needed to house elderly inmates, our sentencing policies are inevitably leading to geriatric health issues among prisoners serving long/life sentences for both violent and nonviolent offenses. Prison medical staff are often inexperienced in treating geriatric patients, warns Greco, who argues that health care within prisons "is not designed to serve the large number of prisoners who are chronically, acutely, or terminally ill."[93]

As communities tackle rising health care costs, so too do prisons, which are fully responsible—physically and psychologically—for each inmate in their custody. By committing offenders to prison for life, states are also committing to support and treat the elderly who are within their care. Yet, this type of responsibility requires a tremendous amount of resources that are expensive, burdensome, and often difficult to provide to even the general public.

MENTALLY ILL PRISONERS

In addition to providing adequate housing for the general inmate population, prison administrators are faced with the monumental task of caring for mentally ill inmates. In 1999, approximately 30 percent of state and federal inmates currently had or had previously been treated for a mental problem.[94] Due to the chaotic and unpredictable nature of the prison milieu, mental health is expensive and difficult to sustain in prison environments. Nonetheless, many of the nonviolent inmates who are sucked into the whirlwind of incarceration suffer from mental illnesses—minor or severe. While mental health costs are accrued by the needs of both violent and nonviolent inmates, we must remember that the resources directed toward nonviolent inmates are those that could otherwise be used to treat violent inmates.

Overall, 10 percent of state inmates and 4.8 percent of federal inmates have some form of mental illness,[95] a rate that is disproportionately greater than in the general public. In 1997, 30 percent of both state and federal inmates had or were previously treated for a mental problem[96] and in 1998, 179,000 state and 7,900 federal prisoners had mental illnesses.[97] The Sentencing Project describes jails and prisons as "institutions most likely to house the mentally ill."[98] For example, there are five times more mentally ill inmates in Florida's prisons and jails than in their state mental hospitals. Within state and federal prisons, female offenders have a higher rate of mental illnesses than male offenders.[99] Among the female prison population, approximately 24 percent of state offenders and 12.5 percent of federal offenders have mental illnesses, compared to 15.8 and 7 percent of state and federal male inmates, respectively. Compared to women in the general population, female prisoners are 16 times more likely to have been diagnosed with a psychiatric illness.[100]

Providing mental health services to prisoners yields benefits to inmates and their families, communities, yet it also incurs many expenses. A large percentage of property, drug, and public-order offenders in state and federal prisons have mental illnesses[101] that require treatment, often in the form of psychotropic drugs. McCarthy et al. report the percent of inmates with mental illnesses by offense type. While violent offenders have a higher percentage of mental illnesses, property and drug offenders make up a significant proportion of the mentally ill prison population. In state prisons, 24.4 percent of property offenders and 12.8 percent of drug offenders have mental illnesses, and within federal prisons over 40 percent of drug offenders and 17 percent of public-order offenders have mental illnesses. By incarcerating these nonviolent mentally ill inmates, prisons are incurring significant costs from medication, mental health workers' salaries, hospital visits, and policies and practices directed toward individuals who are mentally ill, suicidal, or self-mutilating.

Nearly all state prisons provide some form of mental health care to prisoners, yet only 13 percent of prisoners receive therapy and counseling and only 10 percent receive medication.[102] In 2000, Beck and Maruschak found that 12.5 percent of all state inmates received some mental health treatment and 10 percent received psychotropic medication.[103] Approximately 78 percent of facilities designed to confine (rather than those that are community-based) actually screened inmates as they entered the system, yet only 63

Table 6.4. Suicide Rates in State Prisons, 1980–2003

Year	Suicide Rate (per 100,000 Inmates)
1980	34
1985	26
1990	16
1995	16
2000	16
2001	14
2002	14
2003	16

Source: BJS website. 2005c. "Key Facts at a Glance: Suicide and Homicide Rates in State Prisons and Jails." Washington, DC: Bureau of Justice Statistics, U.S. Department of Justice.

percent provided 24-hour care.[104] Only 63 percent of the Midwest's 301 state prisons screened inmates during intake and only 55.5 percent conducted psychiatric assessments.[105] In the South, 72.2 percent of the 730 state prisons screened inmates during the intake process, and 68 percent conducted psychiatric evaluations. While the amount of resources directed toward mental health varies by prison, mental illness is pervasive among prisoners. This adds layers of complexities to the functions of prisons; not only must they confine, control, and protect the general prison population, but they are also responsible for the safe-keeping of inmates who require constant monitoring, treatment, and special services.

Upon taking individuals into custody and therefore assuming responsibility for their health, prisons must be assured that inmates are not only physically safe, but that they do not hurt others or themselves. While the overwhelming majority of inmates survive their prison experience, a significant number attempt to or actually commit suicide while in the care of state or federal authorities (table 6.4). Suicide rates have decreased over time within prison, but the inmates who do commit suicide must not be discounted, for their deaths represent not just liabilities to prison administrators, but losses to families and communities.

Many studies attribute prison suicidality to inmate characteristics, but the environment in which a person is imprisoned has a significant effect on their ability to cope with the stressors of incarceration. Inmates who are at risk for attempting or committing suicide are generally those who are emotionally vulnerable and who respond poorly to the stressors they encounter in prison. As we continue to incarcerate at mass levels, prison environments remain in constant flux and transience. Prison violence, isolation, the lack of quality mental health care, and inmate abuse are only a handful of stressors that emerge within overcrowded prisons where inmates are being constantly processed in and out of facilities. Prison life is not easy, but to certain inmates with mental health problems and poor coping techniques, suicide may be the only escape they can find.

COSTS OF INCARCERATING NONVIOLENT OFFENDERS

Though Americans are often reluctant to channel funds into federal or state welfare policies or prevention programs, they are willing to scrape together the financial resources to place prisoners in institutions where they have limited opportunities to support their families and to contribute financially to our economy. We have become tolerant of the absence of millions of individuals from our communities while not fully recognizing the toll that this is taking on society. Considering how many nonviolent offenders are in prison and the contributions that they will not make to society while incapacitated, the costs of their incarceration to states, the federal government, and to communities are colossal.

To incarcerate these "million dollar" inmates places a monumental strain on our available resources. In 1998, approximately 630,000 nonviolent inmates were housed in state prisons, each costing the state $19,800 per year.[106] Each of the 106,090 nonviolent inmates in federal prisons cost the country an additional $23,500 per year. Overall, our country spent nearly $15 billion in 1998 to keep 736,090 state and federal nonviolent inmates to prison. By 2000, we spent $23.74 billion to incarcerate over one million nonviolent offenders.[107] Today's spending on corrections, let alone the entire criminal justice system, has reached an unexpected magnitude that has long-term financial and social consequences. We can see now that the level of spending in corrections has become incredulous, but we persist in incarcerating nonviolent inmates despite the lack of tangible benefits.

As much as prisons are intended to punish offenders, they are also designed to make our world safer by removing dangerous elements from society. In essence, prisons provide an incapacitating function through highly controlled environments in which violent individuals are isolated, micromanaged, and disconnected from the law-abiding community. As we have seen, however, there are more nonviolent offenders in state prisons than there are violent offenders. By locking up men and women who pose little or no physical threat to society, our system is depleting the resources that could otherwise be used to arrest, convict, and imprison individuals for whom prisons were originally meant to incapacitate.

NOTES

1. See Ahn-Redding 2005.
2. See Johnson 2002.
3. Fleiser 1989.
4. Donziger 1996.
5. Johnson 2002.
6. Ibid.
7. Mauer 1999.
8. Donziger 1996: 118–19.
9. In *United States v. Booker* 543 U.S. 220 (2005), the United States Supreme Court ruled that the mandatory aspect of the federal sentencing guidelines violated defendants' Sixth Amendment rights to trial by jury, "thereby converting the mandatory system that had existed for almost 20 years into an advisory one" (USSC 2006: iv).
10. FAMM 2002a.
11. Harrison and Beck 2005: table 12. This statistic reflects the number of black prisoners with state sentences of at least one year.
12. JPI 2001.
13. Mauer 1999: 124.
14. Ibid.
15. Harrison and Karberg 2003.
16. Mauer 1999.
17. The Sentencing Project 2004b.
18. Justice Policy Institute 2002b.
19. JPI 2002: table 5, pages 10–11.
20. Mauer 1999: 124.
21. See Glassner 1999.
22. Donziger 1996: 146.
23. FAMM 2002c.
24. Ditton and Wilson 1999.
25. Chesney-Lind 2002: 81.
26. Women's Prison Association (WPA) 2003b: 1.
27. WPA 2003c: 4. Also see Greenfeld and Snell 1999.
28. WPA 2003a.
29. WPA 2003c: 1.
30. Ibid: 2.
31. Within state prisons, over half of women have histories of sexual or physical abuse.
32. WPA 2003c.
33. Ibid.
34. Ibid.
35. Maruschak 2002.
36. WPA 2003b.
37. Parke and Clarke-Stewart 2002.
38. *Sourcebook 2002*: page 504; BJS 2000a.
39. Ibid.

40. Senate Bill 133 2002: 3.
41. FAMM 2002c.
42. Parke and Clarke-Stewart 2002: 1.
43. Honderich 2003: 1.
44. WPA 2003c.
45. Parke and Clarke-Stewart 2002:1–2.
46. Ibid: 2.
47. Honderich 2003: 16.
48. WPA 2003c: 3.
49. Mauer 1999.
50. Senate Bill 133 2002: 4.
51. Chesney-Lind 2002: 94.
52. Kleiman 2004.
53. Blumstein 2002: 452.
54. Blumstein 2002.
55. Mumola 1999: table 6.
56. Ibid: page 1.
57. Greco in Project 2015: *The Future of Aging in New York State* (http://aging
.state.ny.us/explore/project2015/briefOP.pdf).
58. NIC 2004b: 8.
59. Ibid: 8–9.
60. Mauer et al. 2004a: 19.
61. Mauer et al. 2004b: table 2, page 10.
62. Yen 2005.
63. Mauer et al. 2004b: 3.
64. Mauer et al. 2004b.
65. Mauer et al. 2004a: 3.
66. Lavine et al. 2001.
67. Pennsylvania Department of Corrections (DOC). See http://www.hawaii.edu/
hivandaids/PA_DOC_Elderly_Inmate_Profile.pdf.
68. NIC 2004b.
69. Ibid: 10.
70. Gallagher 2001.
71. NIC 2004b: 10.
72. Ibid: 10.
73. Dunlop et al. 2001: 289.
74. NCIA's 2004b: 2.
75. Pennsylvania Department of Corrections (DOC).
76. Ibid.
77. Maruschak and Beck 2001.
78. NIC 2004b: 11.
79. Ibid: 12.
80. Mauer et al. 2004b: 25
81. Greco in Project 2015: *The Future of Aging in New York State.*
82. Madden et al. 2003.
83. Ibid.
84. Madden et al. 2003.

85. NIC 2004b: 10.
86. NIC 2004b: 10.
87. Maruschak and Beck 2001 (cited in NIC 2004b: 12.)
88. National Center on Institutions and Alternatives (NCIA) 2003.
89. NCIA 2003: 2.
90. NIC 2004b: 11.
91. U.S. Parole Commission 2003: § 2.78a.
92. U.S. Parole Commission 2003: § 2.78g1.
93. Greco in Project 2015: *The Future of Aging in New York State.*
94. McCarthy et al. 2001: 311.
95. Maruschak and Beck 2001.
96. McCarthy et al. 2001.
97. Ibid: 313.
98. Sentencing Project 2002: 3.
99. McCarthy et al. 2001.
100. WPA 2003c.
101. McCarthy et al. 2001.
102. Beck and Maruschak 2001: 1.
103. Beck and Maruschak 2001.
104. Beck et al. 2002: 1.
105. Ibid: 5.
106. Irwin et al. 1999.
107. JPI 2000.

7

The Social Costs of Incarceration: The Hidden Yet Expensive Side of Prison

This chapter might be more appropriately labeled *The Hidden Costs of Prison [That We Choose to Ignore]*. Chapter 5 addressed the financial costs associated with current incarceration practices, focusing specifically on the expenses incurred from incarcerating nonviolent offenders. However, much of society fails to recognize the indirect and less easily calculable costs of incarceration that are just as significant as the tangible costs. These "collateral consequences"[1] are the "invisible punishments"[2] that affect "parents, spouses, children, friends, and communities who have committed no crimes but must suffer the largely invisible punishments"[3] and are products of our increasing reliance on incarceration as a method of punishment.

For each man, woman, and juvenile in prison today, there are many more individuals in the community who are affected by their incarceration in unique and often ambiguous ways. For example, the separation of mothers from their children not only takes a toll on families, but it taxes the resources of the child welfare systems. Children with parents in prison are at risk for psychological and behavioral problems (which will be addressed later), both of which are costly to their families and to all of society. Communities themselves also suffer the backlash of losing members to prisons. The political disenfranchisement of ex-inmates, for example, can take a large toll on regions that have a disproportionate number of residents in prison. In the end, incarceration impacts more than the person being imprisoned, and the resulting social consequences ultimately transform into visible financial costs that are borne by everyone. This chapter examines some of the micro- and macrolevel social costs of incarceration, many of which are obfuscated by our traditional focus on the pure pecuniary consequences of incarceration.

113

FAMILY COSTS

When crimes are committed and people wronged, the principle individuals involved are, as we might expect, the perpetrator and victim. Victims, of course, are deserving of some legal recourse through which they might receive a judicious response, whether through restitution or the offender's incarceration.[4] Perpetrators, from a retributive perspective, are equally deserving—they are deserving of punishment, thus warranting a swift response by our judicial system. Despite the injuries sustained by the victim, and regardless of the offender's culpability, there are others who are marginally affected by the legal outcomes of each case. This population is less visible and often recognized only tangentially as being affected by judicial outcomes and decisions. These are the families of individuals who are incarcerated; more specifically, the children who are separated from their parents who, as low-level offenders, are subjected to harsh sanctions.

This section draws on the earlier discussion of imprisoned women and mothers in chapter 6. Most adult women involved in the criminal justice system have never been married, and as such there is a plethora of incarcerated mothers who have no spouses or partners to care for or support their children. In 1999, an estimated 6 percent of women who were sent to prison were pregnant.[5] Many of these children are placed into the child welfare system after they are born if they are unable to live with their biological fathers or relatives. In 90 percent of cases where fathers are incarcerated in state or federal prisons, the mother continues to care for the child(ren).[6] However, fathers become the primary caretakers in only 30 percent of cases where mothers are incarcerated. In the majority of these situations, grandparents become the primary caretakers, followed by kin, friends, and the child welfare system.[7]

For over two million children with parents in prison or jail,[8] the experience of having a parent incarcerated is traumatic (assuming the parent was neither neglectful nor abusive), leading to drastic life changes that are often uphill battles.[9] Over half of the children with incarcerated parents are under the age of ten years.[10] Being separated from a parent can create an atmosphere of distress, or it can exacerbate any previous family or social problems that existed before the parent's incarceration, such as "family instability, poverty, child abuse or neglect, marital discord and conflict, or father absence,"[11] and thus contribute toward family conflicts and struggles that were already compromising the family's stability.

Children who have incarcerated parents are initially faced with the trauma of being uprooted from their neighborhoods and placed in foster care or with other relatives. The experience of witnessing a parent being arrested,[12] in addition to the absence or lack of contact with a parent for an extended period, can leave a child facing the hardships associated with "low self-esteem, anxiety, low achievement motivation, poor conscience development, poor social adjustment and peer relations, depression, juvenile delinquency, aggression, drug abuse and other problems."[13] Furthermore, children of incarcerated individuals are at a greater risk of being incarcerated themselves,[14] thus perpetuating a destructive cycle of delinquency and incarceration. Other difficulties that children face include nightmares and flashbacks of the parent's arrest,[15] poor or no emotional attachments to parents which often leads to behavioral problems,[16] unstable friendships, psychological problems,[17] problems at school,[18] and ostracization.[19] Children may internalize their emotions, which can lead to "anxiety, withdrawal, hypervigilance, depression, shame and guilt,"[20] or they may exhibit aggression and anger toward others. Children may also be humiliated when a parent is incarcerated.[21] Additionally, they may display behavioral problems at school, exhibit distrust toward law enforcement officials, or find themselves in foster care. Teaching and reinforcing positive values to children and sustaining meaningful familial relationships may be near impossible when their parents are incarcerated. When children fail to form attachments to caregivers, they often exhibit violent and aggressive behaviors, as well as other antisocial tendencies. Children with psychological or emotional problems may perform poorly in school or drop out altogether. The psychological, financial, social, and academic problems experienced by children with incarcerated parents take a monstrous toll on their futures, their family relationships, and on their communities. With over two million children who are affected by the incarceration of a parent, our society as a whole faces an enormous task of providing them with care, housing, emotional support, and financial assistance. Friends, family members, and the child welfare system absorb the social and financial costs of children who often have little or no opportunity to visit and maintain contact with their incarcerated parents.

With 1 out of every 109 adult females under some type of criminal justice control, it is not surprising that many families find it difficult to remain intact. The Vera Institute of Justice reports that family members are crucial to the successful reentry of inmates into the community.[22] The support that a family is able to provide an ex-inmate "can help make or break a successful transition from prison to community."[23] By providing food, shelter, and emotional support, inmates with strong family networks have a higher chance of refraining from falling into patterns of illegal and harmful behaviors once they are released. All too often, though, families are unable to sustain their stability after years of separation. When the imprisoned parent is incarcerated hundreds of miles away, when children are unable to visit their parents regularly, when marriages or relationships disintegrate, maintaining a strong family support structure becomes an enormous task that many families are unable to handle or unwilling to attempt. Upon release, many prisoners have difficulty reestablishing ties with their estranged children who may be in the custody of the state or kin.

If our country is to continue incarcerating nonviolent offenders, fully realizing that the experience may be permanently life altering, we must recognize the toll it takes on the families of prisoners. To cope with the distresses and economic hardships resulting from incarceration, prisoners are forced to turn to others for assistance. However, in areas marked by weak ties, low levels of trust, or economic hardships such as poverty, families in crisis may not find adequate resources, and thus remain vulnerable to even worse social conditions that generate additional alienation and familial disintegration, such as substance abuse and crime. This in turn can be financially disastrous to families and damaging to the structural stability of communities.

Family disruption is one hidden cost of incarceration. The effects of these struggles are not isolated behind closed doors, however, but permeate into the larger community and therefore accumulate over time. The next section examines the fear and mistrust that mass incarceration may produce and the potential for the subsequent depletion of social capital, a vital community resource.

COMMUNITY COSTS

Punishment has not always been wholly disruptive to families and communities. The American institution of justice originally gave birth to a system that took into consideration an offender's status within the surrounding community when determining appropriate punishments. During colonial times when communities were small and neighbors connected, offenders were often publicly shamed and embarrassed rather than incarcerated,[24] and calculated punishments served to strengthen communities. Punishments within colonial communities with labor have been described as "swift and certain"[25] so as not to disrupt the community's productivity. However, the justice system has since shifted its focus to the complete removal of individuals from their families and communities, and society continues to rely upon institutionalization as a preferred response to crime.[26] *How has this approach affected the health and stability of communities?* In this section, I shall explore the effect of mass incarceration on community stability, with a particular focus on the consequences of large-scale social fear and its potential effect on the generation and maintenance of social capital. The next section describes the concept of social capital and its relevance to fear, crime, and mass incarceration.

Social Capital

Social capital has been defined as the connectivity flowing among individuals—a resource that is stronger when utilized within communities where reciprocity flourishes among citizens[27]—and the World Bank has described it as "the institutions, relationship, and norms that shape the quality and quantity of a society's social interactions."[28] Social capital exists in many forms, all of which involve social structures and the facilitation of action.[29] It allows "the achievement of certain ends that in its absence would not be possible"[30] and is thereby comparable to human and physical capital in its ability to generate productivity. For social capital to foster reciprocal behavior, social environments must sustain both trustworthiness and obligations. Social norms and effective sanctions are necessary as well, for they inhibit or generate certain behaviors.

Coleman's earlier work on social capital illustrates how it might be used as a resource to "facilitate action"[31] within a community. Coleman maintains that social capital can exist both within and outside of families; within families, it appears between children and parents and helps foster intellectual development,[32] whereas outside of the family, it surfaces "in the community consisting of the social relationships that exist among parents, in the closure exhibited by this structure of relations, and in the parents' relations with the institutions of the community."[33] Thus, for social capital to function as a community resource, trust must flourish within families and between community members. In areas that are affected by high incarceration rates and fear of crime, and where neighborhood and familial cohesion have been tenuous, it is difficult to imagine high levels of social trust.

Communities thrive on capital, both human and social.[34] When large numbers of individuals from a given region are incarcerated, the loss of residents reverberates strongly throughout their communities. There is not only a loss in human capital within the labor force, but a hindrance in a community's capacity to draw upon the benefits that social capital can provide in strengthening networks of relationships and facilitating community action. Even intellectual resources available to community members can be hindered. For example, when educational institutions suffer financially because funding is directed elsewhere, such as to the construction of new prisons, their capability to pass on "knowledge and skills to students"[35] diminishes.

Social capital research is not limited to large communities but has also been measured in smaller residential areas. Over the past two decades, there have been several applications of social capital to studies of crime.[36] Sociologists and economists have directed much of their research toward describing social action in their attempts to understand both individual and collective behavior. Empirical studies of inner cities have found that collective action or components of social capital are instrumental in reducing violent crime and increasing neighborhood connections.

Little research, however, has examined the role of mass incarceration in the depletion of social capital. *How might mass incarceration affect this community resource and valuable asset?* During the 1960s, reforms within the prison system led to a "wave of building and filling prisons virtually unprecedented in human history"[37] and from 1972 to 1997, the number of prisoners in the United States increased by approximately one million.[38] The consequences that have resulted from the increased incarceration of nonviolent offenders—especially in areas where significant proportions of communities or neighborhoods are behind bars[39]—are vast. These include limiting the number of marriageable men in certain communities, increases in crime rates, joblessness, social disorganization, and frequent residential relocation. Moreover, high incarceration rates may alter levels of political participation and voting and lead to a decreased respect for the criminal justice system. Community trust, a critical component of social capital, has been undermined by mass incarceration practices that shake the foundation of families and communities. As noted by Stone, "[T]he culture of the prison . . . is rapidly becoming the culture of the streets."[40] This change can potentially bring about an erosion of social capital, a resource that provides "a basis for action."[41]

In neighborhoods disrupted by violence, crime, and family disintegration, decreasing levels of trust undermine the potential for social capital to accumulate or flourish. In *Trust*, Fukuyama explores the many benefits reaped by societies where mutual trust flourishes.[42] Overall, he associates the health of a nation with the level of trust existing within its boundaries, which enables and encourages individuals to operate and associate beyond their immediate families and kinship circles. For this trust to exist, however, a certain level of social capital must be present within the broader community. Social capital, according to Fukuyama, is crucial for societies who desire to accomplish joint goals, yet the building blocks of social capital, which include association, shared values, customs, and common norms, are ultimately a function of the level of trust dispersed throughout a community.[43] Similar to one assertion that the "density and 'connectivity' of local friendship and acquaintanceship networks"[44] can curb criminal behavior, social capital relies upon the idea of closure, through which close relationships can utilize informal "norms and sanctions"[45] to reinforce appropriate behaviors.

To achieve healthy economic development, low rates of criminal behavior and delinquency, and even decreases in teen pregnancy rates, social capital has been deemed critical because it leads to community cooperation.[46] However, "interpersonal trust,"[47] which stems from civic participation, repeated interaction, and extended cooperation,[48] is a crucial element in the creation of social capital. Trust may be strengthened through the use of consistent norms but may also deteriorate from rampant poverty or high divorce rates. In addition, victimization, minority status, and discrimination may also arouse mistrust, although education may help to counteract these disruptive forces and restore trust. Trust is also influenced by "collective experiences,"[49] whereas income disparities, unemployment, and individual characterological differences may serve to reduce trust. Certain social conditions are therefore critical to generating social capital, which ultimately may be used to resolve crucial community problems that also threaten to weaken existing social capital. Such social dilemmas or collective action problems range from pollution problems to "exchanges of threats and violent confrontations."[50]

Crucial elements of social capital cannot be strengthened merely through rational utilitarian behavior;[51] ultimately, they must be consistently fortified through culture, community, and family. Today, our levels of trust have seemingly withered as social capital dissipates, due in part to the shifting composition of our country and fragmented communities. Accordingly, we have reached the point where our current level of spontaneous sociability is fueled by reserves of social capital rather than recently accrued and replenished levels, implicating a lingering element of unhealthy individualism.[52] In examining social capital, it is necessary to explore the role that the criminal justice system has played in disrupting families, neighborhoods, and communities, and in fostering mistrust rather than trust.

While each community needs to identify its own unique crime problems, assess its current level of fear, and generate appropriate responses through collective action, it is also crucial that each community works closely with broader formal institutions that play key roles in shaping individual conceptions of fairness, justice, and equality within the community. It is important to build on the capabilities of institutions such as law enforcement agencies and other criminal justice bodies in order for them to restore sentiments of distrust and help build or strengthen pools of social capital. With mutual collaboration between formal and informal social controls, communities can begin to reverse the tide of damage brought about by mass incarceration and ultimately restore trust among their residents.

Social Fear

As was discussed in the previous section, trust is a crucial component of social capital. Yet, fear pervades the American public. Fear is generated not only by crime rates, but also by public perception. People are largely afraid of each other for reasons that are both warranted and exaggerated. Certainly there are members of society who are violent, who have yet to commit violent offenses, and who are deserving of cautious appraisal. However, in communities where residents are being uprooted, incarcerated, released, and reuprooted in a perpetual cycle of incarceration, and where social connectedness is difficult to maintain, people become afraid and distrusting of their neighbors. Much of this fear is a product of actual crime and personal experiences of victimization, but a great deal stems from perceptions about crime and offenders. This is especially prevalent when released prisoners, who seek lawful lifestyles after incarceration, are given few opportunities to establish healthy lifestyles.

When offenders reenter the community, they are at high risk for recidivating, violating conditions of their release, and subsequently returning to prison. Recidivism rates are high for individuals on probation and parole, especially during the first year after sentencing or release.[53] In 1990, 17 percent of those arrested for felony crimes were on probation at the time of their offense and 8 percent were on parole.[54] It is no wonder that ex-prisoners have become the target of much fear and apprehension among law-abiding citizens. With such high recidivism rates and with the public's (mis)perception of violent superpredators roaming the streets, of rampant and wild juveniles, and of high levels of random violence, it is becoming increasingly difficult to generate or sustain feelings of trust, cooperation, social participation, and social capital within communities that are disproportionately affected by the criminal justice system.[55]

Certainly the mass incarceration of violent and nonviolent offenders has generated grave concern within the public regarding personal safety and crime, and "the more TV people watch, the more fearful they are of the world."[56] This fear has not only been generated by the media and pop culture, but also by politicians who often reinforce and capitalize upon these stereotypes. When individuals are afraid of crime, they view criminals as less than human, especially because "fear and hate often go hand in hand,"[57] and are likely to support "tough on crime" initiatives and prison construction. Further, it is not above reason to argue that many people expect inmates to recidivate or to fail. Johnson describes the problems associated with these expectations and attitudes, where

> if [inmates] have high rates of revocation, that might be seen as effective uses of parole resources. It often goes back to the assumption that we often think of offenders as damaged goods, as really not worthwhile people. We run prisons as if we have a prejudice against the people in them, as if we expect them to fail. We act as if they're going to fail and we're just ready for them. So we really can't create social capital in that type of a system. We have to be willing to not only talk about corrections but act on it, and also take risks to protect people from their failures if they're generally improving. We know that when people are improving behavior, it's often a matter of two or three steps forward and a few back. But we don't allow people to go back. As soon as they slip, we send them right back into the prison system.[58]

Only when the public feels safe or realizes the potential for many individuals to change their lifestyles will it relax its assumption that all ex-inmates are dangerous recidivists and begin to replace suspicion with trust.

While this section has suggested that correctional practices can disrupt the creation and preservation of trust within communities and have ultimately contributed toward the declining efficacy of many informal social controls, it is also important to question whether fear of crime itself can help *generate* civic action, community participation, and reductions in crime. We generally perceive fear to be a disruptive emotion that triggers retaliatory reactions, stereotypes and assumptions, and punitive policies, but can fear promote social solidarity by facilitating social action?

In responding to crime among communities, individuals are motivated not only out of pure self-interest, but out of a sense of duty or responsibility toward the community.[59] This is demonstrated through certain collective actions and public-oriented responses designed to not only serve the interests of the individual, but strengthen the larger community. Some research suggests that the fear of crime can be divisive and destructive while other evidence indicates that fear can serve to unite communities.[60] On the one hand, individuals may choose private-minded responses to crime and withdraw into their homes, thus precluding communities from solving collective problems.[61] On the other hand, fear may bring together the members of a community and provide them with a common goal, thus inciting interaction and community mobility.[62]

Two community approaches embrace collective responses to crime.[63] In the opportunity-reduction approach, communities work together to encourage self-interested behaviors that promote social responsibility and thereby increase levels of safety. Through neighborhood watches, surveillance activities, and crime reporting, communities work to deter crime and strengthen informal social controls. The second approach, the social-problems strategy, also seeks to increase the efficacy of informal social controls, but from this perspective the community is seen as a network of institutions that can play active roles in preventing crime and reducing fear of crime. Through this approach, communities and public service workers jointly attack the roots from which crime stems. Through actions such as community policing, neighborhoods can tackle the conditions fostering criminal activity, such as unemployment, lack of education, cultural differences, and youth misbehavior. The community hypothesis suggests that individuals who are offered the chance to participate in collective actions will draw upon a "moral commitment to the safety of the community,"[64] acting in ways that encompass not only their own interests but that also contribute to their communities. As a result of this social cohesion, crime rates and fear of crime will dissipate.

Other research examining the effects of collective action strategies on fear of crime has yielded mixed conclusions. One study of neighborhoods in

Chicago found that "where collective crime prevention programs were implemented, respondents reported being more fearful of personal and property crimes."[65] Another study, however, reported no change in the levels of fear of crime but also no increases in crime within communities engaging in collective programs.[66] These mixed results suggest that each neighborhood may experience and implement collective responses with different intentions, strategies, and motivations. For example, middle-class and upper-class communities, homeowners, and families who have settled down with children are more likely to participate in collective action responses than are low-income communities.[67] Those who do participate in collective responses generally do so out of a sense of responsibility and commitment to their communities and are already socially active within their communities. Thus, those participating may be drawing upon already existing social capital in communities where crime rates are already low and levels of trust generally high. Many families may engage in a combination of public-minded and private-minded responses to crime, such as possessing a firearm and joining a community watch program. This strategy should be included in future research on collective responses to crime.

Overall, it appears that certain communities with civic-minded citizens can use their fear of crime to strengthen their pool of social capital. On the other hand, the communities in which this occurs may already experience low crime rates and have large resources of social capital. Other communities may respond to crime through individual private-minded actions, such as buying security alarms or purchasing handguns. If the fear of crime can restore social capital and promote collective action, it is important to recognize ways in which communities can draw upon this fear to not only protect themselves, but to strengthen their uses of various informal social controls and intervene on behalf of individuals at risk for offending and incarceration. If the fear of crime drives individuals to engage in self-preserving behavior without consideration of the whole of the community, it would be in our interest to explore how fear can derail the generation of social capital and affect the cohesion and productivity of communities.

REENTRY BARRIERS

When inmates are released back into society, as are an overwhelming majority, they are expected to assume legitimate lifestyles by finding housing or returning to their families; seeking, gaining, and maintaining employment; and sustaining this new lifestyle despite numerous social and financial obstacles. Drug users, for example, make up a significant and increasing percentage of our prison population, yet they are expected to stay fully substance-free after their release with little tolerance for relapse. However, not all offenders receive adequate treatment while in prison and are thus still in need of support. The individuals who could use the most assistance in maintaining the lifestyles expected of them, at least until they are able to find employment, may be barred from receiving welfare benefits, public housing assistance, and financial aid for education.[68] In a *Wall Street Journal* article,[69] the original intention of laws banning ex-felons from obtaining student financial aid, accessing public welfare, and from entering certain sectors or the workforce was recognized as a way to convey society's intolerance of crime. However, as the article states, "there is an emerging belief that the larger price is being borne by society"[70] due to the high risk of recidivism among ex-felons who are faced with enduring social and economic marginalization. Confronted with these obstacles and stressors, do we really need to ask why so many drug offenders return to prison? With limited social support, fragmented families, and a widespread stigmatization of offenders, it is foreseeable that many ex-inmates will turn to drugs and alcohol and thus violate the conditions of their probation or place themselves at risk for rearrest.

DENIED WELFARE BENEFITS

The difficulties associated with being an ex-inmate, whether the offense is violent or not, are eternal in many regards. When individuals are uprooted from society through incarceration, and then returned to society after the completion of their sentences, many have little or no financial resources with which to create law-abiding lifestyles. However, the *Personal Responsibility and Work Opportunity Reconciliation Act*, which was signed by President Bill Clinton in 1996, imposes a lifetime ban on TANF (Temporary Assistance to Needy Families) and food stamp benefits on persons who are convicted of drug-related felonies.[71] Interestingly, this ban does not apply to individuals convicted of homicide, sex offenses, or any other felony offense (aside from welfare fraud).[72] As Rubinstein and Mukamal explain, "No one is exempt from the drug felony ban, not even pregnant women, individuals in treatment or recovery, or people with HIV/AIDS."[73] Ex-inmates can also be barred from public housing. Under President Clinton's "one-strike" policy, people using illegal drugs are banned for life from federal public housing, even if they have never been convicted of a drug-related offense.[74] According to the Human Rights Watch, public housing authorities (PHA) can also choose to ban applicants who

> have been evicted from public housing because of drug-related criminal activity for a period of three years following eviction . . . those who have in the past engaged in a pattern of disruptive alcohol consumption or illegal drug

use, regardless of how long ago such conduct occurred . . . those who have en-
gaged in any drug-related criminal activity, any violent criminal activity, or
any other criminal activity, if the PHA deems them a safety risk.[75]

Unsurprisingly, ex-drug offenders fall into the category of individuals who
could benefit the most from public housing and TANF, yet the government
continues to marginalize offenders who have served their sentences and are
trying to establish healthy lifestyles. By incarcerating low-level nonviolent
offenders and then barring them from access to social services, we are making it increasingly difficult for ex-inmates to stay clear of the criminal justice system. If, instead, we were to keep these individuals in the community
where they could work while serving community-based services, we could
help them avoid the financial hurdles that their counterparts in prison will
inevitably face upon release.

THE LABOR FORCE

Another latent cost of incarceration is the removal of capable and able-
bodied individuals—especially those already with lawful employment—from
the workforce. While this inevitably occurs during the period of the individual's incarceration, many offenders are unable to find legitimate employment
upon their release from prison. Bushway found that 66 percent of employers
in five large cities would not hire an individual knowing that he or she had
spent time in prison.[76] In addition, many ex-inmates cannot legally obtain
employment in certain professions, such as nursing and healthcare.[77] This is
understandable given the nature of some professions, but from a labeling theory perspective, ex-inmates have difficulty obtaining legitimate work due to
community fear or distrust.[78] A prison term can be a large detriment to an individual's financial future,[79] especially due to the "stigma attached to a criminal history record in the legal labor market"[80] that undoubtedly extends to
other areas of society, such as marriage, educational opportunities, professional organizations, and trust in interpersonal relationships. In addition,
many ex-inmates are faced with a lack of skills when seeking employment.[81]
There is also a widespread perception of prisons as jungle environments that
harden those whom its confines.[82] Thus, when individuals are released from
prison, they are largely regarded as "tainted."[83] While this may be true of
some ex-inmates, the large majority of prisoners exit their incarceration with
hopes of finding legitimate employment.

Offenders who have spent time in prison and are bound for release may
not develop appropriate social skills necessary for interviewing with potential employers. The longer they remain in prison, the more they are susceptible to psychological deterioration or physical harm, which may subse-

quently affect their ability to interact with others or perform certain work-related functions after their release. Over time, future prospects of legitimate employment erode as nonviolent offenders, who may have great amounts of determination to readjust their lifestyles, confront the aforementioned barriers. By placing them in prisons, we are subjecting them to additional unnecessary hardships that are not easily overcome.

Because our incarceration practices disproportionately affect African Americans, there is a large gap in employment rates of white and African American young males.[84] With racial disparities among nonoffenders already noticeably high in certain regions, this additional discrepancy may continue to promulgate racial inequalities. This only serves to feed lingering sentiments of fear and distrust.

By reducing the number of nonviolent prisoners who are incarcerated, and thereby subjecting them to alternative community sanctions, we can strengthen our workforce and reap the economic benefits that are produced by steady employment, income taxes, and stronger communities. As is the case for many ex-prisoners, however, postincarceration jobs are difficult to find, especially employment that pays well enough to cover everyday expenses and bills and to support a family. With few or no economic resources upon their release, and an inability to turn to the government for assistance, ex-prisoners continue to burden and drain their families and communities.

POLITICAL DISENFRANCHISEMENT

Across the nation, felons lose certain rights after their release from prison. These "civil disabilities"[85] include being barred from serving jury duty or holding public office. In addition, most prisoners are barred from voting and participating in the political arena while in prison and even after they have served their sentence.[86] Only inmates in Maine and Vermont are afforded the right to vote.[87] In over 30 states, felons on parole or probation are denied their voting rights[88] and in 14 states, felons lose their right to vote permanently.[89] Considering there were over four million probationers and approximately 775,000 parolees in 2003,[90] it is no surprise that "1.7 million disenfranchised persons are ex-inmates who have completed their sentences."[91]

The Sentencing Project estimates that 4.7 million Americans—a total exceeding that of any other nation—are disenfranchised permanently or temporarily, including 13 percent of African American men.[92] Approximately 36 percent of those who are disenfranchised have completed their sentence yet are still unable to exercise their right to vote.[93] Disenfranchised communities are alienated from the political processes that directly affect their own social and financial stability. In seven states,[94] approximately 25 percent of African American males are disenfranchised indefinitely.[95] The Sentencing Project estimates that up to 40 percent of African American males may lose their right to vote in states with disenfranchisement laws.[96]

States with disenfranchisement policies pertaining to individuals on probation or parole affect both violent and nonviolent offenders, but the latter are unnecessarily affected by these policies. By needlessly uprooting millions of nonviolent offenders from their families and communities and sending them to prisons where they are disenfranchised temporarily, if not permanently, our society is also losing vital quantities of political capital. When we incarcerate nonviolent offenders, we not only separate them from their families and disrupt opportunities for employment, but we are also marginalizing an ever-increasing group of individuals by denying them the right to participate in the political process for at least the duration of their prison terms. If these same individuals were sentenced to probation rather than prison, they could contribute to society in states that allow probationers (or those who have completed their sentences) to vote.

Society's heightened levels of punitiveness and low levels of tolerance have led us to view inmates with suspicion and mistrust.[97] Fear, in addition to the declining trust associated with recent immigration trends, has created many communities where neighbors are unknown to each other, where negative racial and ethnic stereotypes are harbored, and whose members feel largely disconnected from their communities. Ex-inmates who have difficulty transitioning back into the public may offer little in the way of fostering trust and social capital within their families and communities when they are repeatedly marginalized from society.

CONCLUSION

Having now explored the financial and social costs of incarcerating nonviolent offenders, Part IV of this book will examine the various functions of incarceration and address whether these goals are currently being met. We must ask ourselves if we should continue funneling billions of taxpayers' dollars into a system if it is not meeting its purported goals. Finally, we must question whether nonviolent inmates belong in such a system, and whether taxpayers should continue to support the incarceration of individuals who could otherwise serve their sentences in their communities while maintaining employment, contributing to society, and supporting their families.

Some may ask, *Why should we give benefits to individuals who have broken laws when scores of law-abiding citizens are in need of such assistance?* First, many ex-inmates who are barred from receiving public assistance have done their time and have made the required reparations for their offenses. Is it fair to hold their mistakes against them throughout their entire lifetimes? Second, these individuals are going to return to society whether we like it or not. Thus, we must choose whether we want to accept them back into society or make it more arduous for them to cope with postincarceration. Third, by helping ex-inmates, we can decrease rates of recidivism and prison crowding, which affect us all. And finally, by giving ex-inmates a chance to belong to their communities in the fullest sense, we are helping our own. When communities flourish, so too does society.

NOTES

1. Mauer and Chesney-Lind 2002.
2. Travis 2002: 16.
3. Mauer and Chesney-Lind 2002: 1.
4. See Hall's (1999) discussion on theories of punitive justice.
5. Senate Bill (SB) 133 2002: 1.
6. Parke and Clarke-Stewart 2002: 2.
7. Ibid.
8. SB 2002.
9. Also see Parke and Clarke-Stewart 2002.
10. Parke and Clarke-Stewart 2002: 2
11. Ibid: 5.
12. SB 2002.
13. Katz 1998 (cited in SB 2002: 1).
14. See Katz 1998: 1.
15. Parke and Clarke-Stewart 2002: 3.
16. See Myers et al. 1999 (cited in Parke and Clarke-Stewart 2002).
17. See Baunach 1985 (cited in Parke and Clarke-Stewart 2002).
18. See Sack et al. 1976 (cited in Parke and Clarke-Stewart 2002).
19. Parke and Clarke-Stewart 2002: 4–5.
20. Ibid: 5.
21. Clear 1996.
22. Bobbitt and Nelson 2004.
23. Ibid: 1
24. Mauer 1999.
25. Ibid: 3.
26. Mauer 1999.
27. Putnam 2000 (cited in Smith 2001).
28. The World Bank Project 1999.
29. Coleman 1988: S98.
30. Ibid: S98.
31. Coleman 1988: 100.
32. Ibid: 110.
33. Ibid: 113.
34. Hagan and Dinovitzer 1999.

35. Ibid: 131.

36. See Taylor et al. 1984 (cited in Morenoff et al. 2001); Taylor 2000 (cited in Faggins 2001); Bursik and Grasmick 1993; Saegart et al. 2002; Sampson et al. 1997; Morenoff et al. 2001; Lederman et al. 2000.

37. Mauer 1999: 9.

38. Ibid: 9.

39. Ibid: 183.

40. Schlosser 2003: 15.

41. Coleman 1988: S98.

42. Fukuyama 1995.

43. Ibid: 26-27.

44. Sampson 2002.

45. Ibid: 232.

46. Brehm and Rahn 1997.

47. Ibid: 1001.

48. Ibid: 1002.

49. Ibid: 1009.

50. Ostrom 1998: 2.

51. Fukuyama 1995.

52. Ibid.

53. Petersilia 2002.

54. Ibid: 491.

55. See Glassner 1999 and Mauer 1999.

56. Johnson interview 2002.

57. Ibid.

58. Ibid.

59. Fisher 1993.

60. Ibid.

61. Fisher 1993: 181.

62. Fisher 1993.

63. Ibid.

64. Ibid: 182.

65. Rosenbaum et al. 1986 (cited in Fisher 1993: 183).

66. Bennett 1984.

67. Fisher 1993.

68. Rubenstein and Mukamal 2002: 37.

69. Fields 2005a.

70. Ibid: A1.

71. Department of Health and Human Services 1997; Rubenstein and Mukamal 2002.

72. Rubenstein and Mukamal 2002: 41.

73. Ibid: 41.

74. Human Right's Watch (HRW) 2004.

75. Ibid: 11.

76. Bushway 2000 (cited in Travis et al. 2001).

77. WPA 2003b.

78. Bushway and Reuter 2002.

79. Mauer 1999.
80. Bushway and Reuter 2002: 208.
81. Western et al. 2002: 176–77.
82. Interview with Robert Johnson, American University 2002.
83. Ibid.
84. Western et al. 2002: 170.
85. Fellner and Mauer 1998.
86. The Sentencing Project 2004.
87. Ibid.
88. Ibid.
89. Mauer 1999: 186.
90. BJS 2004i.
91. The Sentencing Project (website) 2004.
92. Ibid.
93. Ibid.
94. Alabama, Iowa, Mississippi, New Mexico, Virginia, Wyoming (see Mauer 1999).
95. Fellner and Mauer 1998.
96. The Sentencing Project 2004.
97. Johnson interview 2002.

IV

GOALS OF INCARCERATION

8

Retribution: Can We Have Our "Just Desert" and Eat It Too?

This chapter poses the question of whether our courts and prisons are exacting retributive justice through sentences that are *too* tough. *Related questions include:*

- *Is a system that incarcerates two million adults and juveniles maintaining principles of rationality and proportionality?*
- *Are we meting out appropriate sentences that are reflective of the severity of their respective certain crimes?*
- *Are some crimes, such as drug offenses, excessively punished while others not punished with enough severity?*
- *Can we justify sending away first-time drug offenders to prison for more time than violent offenders?*

While there is no perfect system and no one definitive answer, we can tackle these questions by looking at what appears to be working for society today, and what seems to be ineffective.

This chapter examines the extent to which we have gone in order to incarcerate nonviolent offenders. Here the question is asked: *is it worth incarcerating nonviolent offenders in the name of retribution in light of the costs that will inevitably follow?* When one considers the impact of incarceration on nonviolent individuals, the elements that must be examined transcend the day-to-day experiences that individual offenders face. We must frame Sykes's description of deprivations in prison[1] within a modern context that takes into account the correctional changes that have occurred over the last five decades since his seminal work. Discussions of deprivations would benefit from recognizing the transformations we have witnessed within the infrastructure of modern prisons and the peripheral sociopolitical climate.

For some first-time nonviolent offenders, incarceration results in not only the loss of personal freedom, but of family, relationships, financial stability, and prospects for future lucrative employment. Recidivists may have already lost family members or employment, but first-timers must contend with these drastic changes for the first time and thus may have a more difficult time adjusting to prison life. While these deprivations are often a part of the punitive aspect of imprisonment, each of these losses takes an enormous toll on the individual's potential for familial and financial success after prison.

GOALS

Retribution has always been sought and justified by the logic of its imposition. In a formulaic manner, retribution involves counteracting a wrong through a just and reasonably weighed punishment. Under this model of justice, "punishment is justified simply because it is deserved."[2] It therefore encapsulates the expression "just deserts"[3] in which the punishment imposed is directly proportionate to the severity of the offense. Therefore, the victim and society receive compensation through retribution. From a utilitarian perspective, the pain that is produced through punishment is warranted only if it brings about a greater good.[4] Kant's classical theory of retribution,[5] however, maintains that crime itself justifies the use of punishment, which should be proportional to the crime, and that punishment honors offenders by recognizing them as rational and worthy human beings. In general, the retributive theory of punishment is wrought with dilemmas, such as the inherent difficulty of establishing degrees of guilt, determining proportionate punishments, disregarding aggravating or mitigating circumstances, and undermining the power of mercy and emotions.[6]

The desire for retribution is a powerful emotion leading to reactionary behaviors that we have sought to tame through a just, unbiased, and equitable legal system. Retaliatory, vengeful acts carried out by angry mobs or individuals seeking personal justice threaten social order and the integrity of the law. So to prevent vigilantism and appeal to the emotions of victims of crime, our sentencing laws are designed to punish, in addition to deter and incapacitate. Inevitably, designing a system that exacts just the right amount of punishment will appear overly harsh to some while too lenient to others. Throughout time and place, the behaviors that are considered criminal fluctuate and the punishments we propose are malleable. The process of identifying punishments that are proportionate to the severity of crimes is shaped by current social values, morals, and priorities and is therefore never static.

COSTS

The losses of personal freedom, family, and employment are all tangible costs incurred by sentencing nonviolent offenders to prison. Judges should consider alternative punishments that can help preserve an offender's family and job, while at the same time exact the desired and appropriate level of retribution and impose a punitive measure of social control. This section discusses the disproportionate costs generated by the overuse of prison for non-violent offenders in the name of retribution.

Personal Freedom

As discussed in chapter 4, incarceration not only involves the loss of autonomy, but the loss of one's sense of identity. The physical and emotional stress associated with these losses place many inmates—especially those with poor coping skills—at risk for being victimized or acting out. Faced with new situations—for which there is generally no preparation[7]—unseasoned inmates, especially those who have never been exposed to violence, must develop certain survival skills. Too often, these tactics involve aggression or violence. Other inmates who have difficulty coping may experience an attenuation of psychological functioning. Depression, stress, and anxiety take a toll on one's emotional and physical state. Thus, the restriction of personal freedom through imprisonment entails a host of other significant potential damages.

Incarceration is intended to restrict the body, to limit the physical autonomy of someone who has committed a misdeed, and to subject the offender to a rigid regimen of social control. It is not, however, intended to restrict the mind and to limit mental functioning. Today, incarceration entails subjecting inmates to conditions in which they are susceptible to psychological damage, an experience has never been an expressive function of prison. Thus, those who do accrue significant mental health problems while in prison are paying a disproportionate price for their crimes.

Family

Chapter 7 discussed the prevalence of inmates who have minor children. With an increasingly large population of female prisoners, the number of dependent children with parents in jail or prison is startling. Punishing offenders—whether their crimes were violent or not—also severely penalizes their families. This begs the question: *would nonviolent offenders be better off at home with their child[ren] than incarcerated hundreds of miles away?* Asked in another way: *For offenders who are nonabusive and are competent caretakers, would remaining with their children benefit society more than any foreseeable positive outcomes of their incarceration?* The incarceration of parents, especially those who are single, may result in the removal of children from their homes, relocating them to temporary placements (whether kin or foster), and up-rooting them from their schools. Further, children with incarcerated parents fall susceptible to emotional problems that affect their behavior,[8] their schoolwork, and their relationships,[9] and children are also at high risk for acting out and encountering the criminal justice system themselves. Parents who remain at home and undergo supervision through community corrections programs, or through probation, can still provide emotional and financial support to their children while also receiving treatment for any alcohol or drug problem they themselves may have. In addition, the parent can earn money to pay court-ordered restitution to any victim(s) of the crime. However, our society appears to only equate punishment with prison—with the absence of freedom, independence, and individuality. Needless incarceration punishes not just the offending party, but those whose welfare relies upon the offender.

Employment

The financial toll that incarceration takes on a family is enormous (see chapter 7). Not only does the separation of working adults from their children disrupt familial stability, but it jeopardizes the future earnings of that individual. When we incarcerate individuals for sentences that are less than life, society expects offenders to reintegrate back into society and resume law-abiding, productive lives. We are telling offenders that their crimes are not so grave as to discount their entire futures; we are indicating that we will give them another chance by releasing them. Yet, after spending years within a prison, many individuals find few legitimate economic opportunities aside from menial, low-paying jobs with no prospects of upward mobility. When explaining a resume gap to potential employers and identifying oneself as a convicted felon leads to too many closed doors, maintaining a legitimate lifestyle becomes considerably difficult. Furthermore, as was explained in chapter 7, they may be barred from ever receiving public assistance during their entire lives, even after they have paid society back for their crimes. Considering that numerous ex-inmates who have substance abuse problems or mental illnesses, it is almost understandable that many fail after trying to succeed by themselves while living in impoverished conditions.

When nonviolent offenders are diverted from prison, they can potentially retain their current employment and continue to support their families. Many individuals *can* succeed, but they need assistance as they attempt to steer their lives in a more positive direction. Yet, as this chapter suggests, newly released offenders have highly unstable social and financial prospects.

As much as society may dislike these individuals, thousands are being released from prison each year and therefore need somewhere to go, somewhere to work legitimately, and some way to restore their families. By keeping certain nonviolent offenders out of prison in the first place, the ensuing benefits extend beyond each individual case to the whole of society—to the workforce, to communities, and to families.

When incarceration is instated to counteract the severity of an offense, a lack of employment is generally assumed throughout the duration of the individual's confinement. The essence of this punishment, however, is not intended to extend beyond the scope of the imposed sentence, yet nonviolent offenders today pay lingering costs when they are unable to make a living and support their families because of their past records. This is a great cost borne by the individual and society, one that is heavily disproportionate to the severity of many nonviolent crimes.

HAVE THE GOALS OF RETRIBUTIVE JUSTICE BEEN MET?

Returning to the original question posed at the opening of this chapter as to whether our system is exacting retribution through sentences that are overly harsh, we have seen a tremendous overhaul of our criminal justice system in a direction that suggests that we are being excessively punitive. In the words of federal prisoner Michael Santos in his book *About Prison*, "prisoners begin growing accustomed to the fences and walls" after being incarcerated for five years and the "formerly ill effects of punishment begin to subside."[10] *What is the marginal social and rehabilitative utility of an additional year past five years, ten years, or twenty years in prison? Does a prison sentence of seven years deliver the desired justice and retribution that a prison term of six years cannot?* These are questions that cannot be answered in the context of this discussion but should be the focus of future research.

Retribution is a valid and logical justification for punishment, one that provides a buffer against emotionally sparked acts of vigilantism. Retribution applies reasoning and a deliberate weighing of punishments against the severity of an offense. Based on the sheer number of nonviolent offenders entering state and federal correctional facilities, it is only inevitable that people will start to scrutinize the rationale that underlines these current practices. Other models of justice, such as restorative justice (see chapter 13), have been introduced and explored as alternatives to our current system. Perhaps it is time for us to consider these alternative approaches to sentencing and redefine what "justice" actually means to our society, or what it *should* mean.

We have created a system that exacts retribution from offenders, but perhaps *too much* retribution for certain nonviolent offenses. When people are victimized, their lust for retaliation is understandably justified, but we are no longer living in a time where vigilantism is the face of justice, where physical pain and public humiliation are state-supported functions of punishment, and where deviants are permanently exiled from society. We are also not a society that does not expect wrong-doers to take responsibility for their actions, nor are we living in a time where opportunities for treatment and rehabilitation are unavailable. Considering that we live in an era that places a high value on efficiency and rationalization,[11] we have adopted what appears to be fairly inefficient judicial practices.[12] Expanding on Ritzer's notion of "McDonaldization"[13] and Weber's description of bureaucratic practices,[14] Bohm identifies several irrational aspects of sentencing, specifically determinate sentencing.[15] He argues that determinate sentencing results in "an unusually harsh prison system,"[16] that the abandonment of parole in many states has resulted in difficulties sustaining social control within prison populations, and that determinate sentences do not "define in advance all of the factors that ought to be considered in determining a criminal sentence."[17] We have been so focused on efficiency and machinelike productivity that perhaps our judicial practices have gone to the other extreme of inefficiency.

Our legal system was founded on principles of equality, fairness, and rationality, and as long as we allow the "tough on crime" philosophy to dominate our policies and supersede our belief in personal reformation, our system will continue to bear financial and social losses that are now reaching unprecedented proportions.

NOTES

1. Sykes 1958.
2. Hall et al. 2000: 195.
3. Ibid.
4. Duff and Garland 1998.
5. Hall et al. 2000: 196–97
6. Ibid: 202.
7. Although in some cases, defendants are given time to prepare for their incarceration. Martha Stewart, for example, was sentenced to five months in prison in July 2004 for lying to federal officials about her financial activities regarding ImClone Systems (Crawford 2004), but did not begin serving her sentence until October of that year.
8. See Myers et al. 1999.
9. See Parke and Clarke-Stewart 2002
10. Santos 2004: 215.
11. See Ritzer 2006.

12. See Bohm 2006 for a discussion on the "McDonaldization" of our criminal justice system.

13. Ritzer 2004 (cited in Bohm 2006).

14. See Weber 1978.

15. Bohm 2006.

16. Ibid: 137

17. Ibid: 138. See Tonry 1996.

9

Incapacitation: If We Lock Them Up, Maybe They'll Just Go Away!

Prisons as we know them today have undergone many significant physical and philosophical transformations, from the first Quaker penitentiary in 1790 to reformatories of the late 1800s; from the Big House of the early 1900s to today's modern correctional facility and supermax prison. Prior to the creation of the American penitentiary,[1] postconviction incarceration was for the most part merely a precursor to the later execution of confined offenders, so the notion of confining criminals for long periods of time is a relatively recent concept (see chapter 2).

Despite the positive intentions of the penitentiary, the notion of redemption was eventually overshadowed by swelling prison populations and anomic prison conditions.[2] Penitentiaries were no longer institutions of reform but of custody and confinement. This surge in incarceration has not gone unabated and has instead forged an era of unprecedented prison expansion. Today, we are witnessing an explosion not in crime rates, but rather in the number of people who are being incarcerated, the severity of their sentences, and in the resources used toward erecting newer and bigger prisons. For example, California's prison population growth, which rose from slightly over 20,000 in 1980[3] to approximately 170,000 in 2006,[4] was accompanied by 21 new prisons built since 1980, all of which cost approximately $5.3 billion in building expenses and require $4.8 billion annually to operate.[5] This type of extensive growth in prison population and prison construction is not unique to California and indeed characterizes the state of corrections throughout much of the country.

GOALS

The philosophy of incapacitation rests upon the belief that criminals should be placed in the custody of the state as a preclusion to recidivism[6] and to secure the protection of the public. When society encounters serious offenders, our penal system swiftly meets force with force. And incapacitation is nothing less than a forced egress from society, albeit an expensive practice, but one that at least temporarily isolates, confines, denies offenders the right to partake in the regular functioning of society, and deprives them of future opportunities to deviate. However, the notion of incapacitation is problematic, according to Gibbons, who suggests that increasing sentence lengths to prevent future crimes is not a just practice, nor is our system's capability to predict future criminality wholly reliable.[7] Nevertheless, our nation has proven its financial commitment, organizational capacity, and public willingness to incapacitate. We demonstrate day after day the system's dedication to crime control and punishment via prisons and jails; indeed, the criminal justice system has flexed its 'tough on crime' muscle by forcibly removing millions of adults and juveniles from their families and communities—some for only a few months, others indefinitely.

COSTS

At the turn of the century, state prisons held ten times the number of drug offenders than they did in 1980.[8] Yet, there is an enormous cost to accomplishing this goal. For example, the 3,300 new prisons that were built during the 1990s most definitely expanded our system's capacity to incapacitate, but at a cost of $27 billion.[9] Prison growth within state and federal prisons has been vast. Much of the costs of incapacitation has been explored in previous chapters and need not be reiterated here, but we can attribute these expenses to the overuse of prison within the state and federal systems, both of which are responsible for the 280 percent increase in the number of people under some form of correctional supervision from 1980 and 2004.[10] Table 9.1 shows changes in these populations. During the last two decades of the twentieth century, our prison and jail population increased from 500,000 to nearly 2 million.[11]

For most individuals not directly associated with the criminal justice system, the effect of this growth may seem irrelevant, non existent, or even unworthy of consideration, but for those on the front lines of these changes—namely prisoners, their families, and prison employees—these drastic increases in prison populations pose many emotional and logistical challenges.

As stated in the introduction of this book, the federal system spent $22,632 on each inmate in 2001.[12] Federal drug offenders, on average,

Table 9.1. Correctional Populations, 1980–2003

	Probation	Jail	Prison	Parole	Total
1980	1,118,097	183,988	319,598	220,438	1,842,100
1985	1,968,712	256,615	487,593	300,203	3,013,100
1990	2,670,234	405,320	743,382	531,409	4,350,300
1995	3,077,861	507,044	1,078,542	679,421	5,342,900
2000	3,826,209	621,149	1,316,333	723,898	6,445,100[a]
2001	3,931,731	631,240	1,330,007	732,333	6,581,700[a]
2002	3,995,165	665,475	1,367,856	753,141	6,732,400[a]
2003	4,073,987	691,301	1,394,319	774,588	6,934,200[a]
2004	4,151,125	713,990	1,421,911	765,355	6,996,500[a]
% Change, 1980–2004	271	288	345	248	280

[a]These totals do not include probationers in jail or prison.
Source: BJS website. 2005a. "Key Facts at a Glance: Correctional Population." Washington, DC: Bureau of Justice Statistics, U.S. Department of Justice.

spent over three years in prison while public-order offenders spent an average of two years in prison. By incarcerating these nonviolent inmates and spending over $22,000 annually per inmate, resources that could otherwise be spent on arresting and incarcerating violent offenders are being depleted by incapacitating offenders who pose little physical threat to society for very short periods of time. Incapacitation would be efficacious and cost-effective with regards to increasing public safety if those who *should* be incarcerated are imprisoned, and those who *should* be diverted from prison are sentenced accordingly. Traditionally, judges were the agents of the justice system who made this distinction. Due to waning sentencing discretion, as discussed in chapter 2, many judges, against their professional opinions, are forced to send certain nonviolent offenders to prison. Thus, incapacitation has become the default punishment for many crimes that would have at one time been punished through probation. A penal system designed to incapacitate needs to assess and determine who is *worth* incarcerating—both socially and financially.

RESEARCH ON INCAPACITATION

In the 1970s, there was a large growth in the prison population, yet the expected downward trend in crime rates was not observed. However, in 2005, the FBI reported a "decade-long downward trend in serious offenses,"[13] proclaiming that all major violent crime offenses reached a level in 2004 that was 32 percent less than the rates in 1995. Intuitively, it would therefore seem that putting criminals behind bars is the most effective method of crime control. Yet, this is not necessarily the case, as there is little cited statistically significant evidence to suggest that rising incarceration rates directly cause declines in crime rates.[14] For two decades, research conducted by the National Academy of Science has indicated that sentencing laws have negligible effects on changes in crime rates.[15] As incarceration rates continued to climb in the late 1990s, rates of violent crime actually decreased. While many associated a deterrent and incapacitative effect of prison with this decrease in violent offenses,[16] others have maintained that incarceration rates actually had little effect on violent crime.[17]

How is it possible for incarceration rates to increase while crime rates decrease? Let's say that in City A the violent crime rate is 50 crimes per 100,000 residents. Thus, the crime rate would be 50 per 100,000. Say, out of these 50 crimes, 10 of the perpetrators are arrested. Thus, the arrest rate is 10 per 100,000. Next, let's say that 5 of 10 people who are arrested are convicted; the conviction rate is 5 per 100,000 residents. And finally, if two of those who are convicted are actually incarcerated, the incarceration rates equals 2 per 100,000 residents. Now, let's say that in City B the violent crime rates is also 50 crimes per 100,000 residents; thus the crime rate is 50 per 100,000, just like City A. However, let's say that City B has more resources than City A and is able to arrest 20 of the 50 perpetrators. Now our arrest rate is 20 per 100,000. Let's say that 10 of those who are arrested are actually convicted. We now have a conviction rate of 10 per 100,000. Now, let's imagine that City B has decided to take a more punitive approach than City A and decides to send 5 of these convicted felons to prison. Now our incarceration rate is 5 per 100,000, more than double that of City A. This little exercise demonstrates how incarceration rates largely reflect how many perpetrators are arrested, convicted, and imprisoned, rather than how many crimes actually occur. City B had a much higher incarceration rate, yet, it would be improper to conclude that City B has more crime than City A. While on the surface it would seem logical that rising incarceration rates have driven down crime rates, we must remember that correlation does not infer causation.

Gainsborough and Mauer analyzed increases in incarceration rates as well as violent and property crime rates in each state from 1991 to 1998.[18] On average, the rate of incarceration from 1991 to 1998 increased by 47 percent throughout the country, while crime rates decreased by 15 percent. Nineteen states and the District of Columbia had above average increases; Maine had the smallest percent increase in incarceration rate (2 percent) whereas Texas had the largest increase (144 percent).[19] In many of the states with the highest percent growth in incarceration rates, crime decreased less than in states with smaller increases in incarceration rates. For example, North Dakota experienced an 88 percent increase in its incarceration rate, yet only a 4 percent decline in crime rates. Rates of violent crime in North

Dakota actually increased by 37 percent whereas property offenses declined by a mere 5 percent. In Maine, however, where the incarceration rate increased by only 2 percent, crime rates declined by 19 percent, and rates of violent and property crime, respectively, decreased by 5 and 20 percent. Among the states with "above average" increases in incarceration rates, the average percent increase was 72 percent, with an average 13 percent decrease in crime rates.[20] Violent and property crime rates fell by 7 percent and 13 percent, respectively. Within the states with "below average" increases in incarceration rates, the average percent increase in incarceration rates was 30, whereas the average percent decrease in crime rates was 17. Interestingly, the decreases in violent and property crime rates were greater in these "low average" states, each declining by 16 percent. This would suggest that states with higher incarceration rates do not necessarily experience fewer crimes than their neighbors with lower incarceration rates.

A similar pattern can be found when one extends this analysis from 1980 to 2002/2003. During this period, the rate of incarceration increased by an average 268.1 percent throughout the country (table 9.2). The greatest increases were in Pennsylvania, North Dakota, Mississippi, Connecticut, and New Hampshire, all of which experienced an incarceration rate growth exceeding 400 percent. Nevada, Ohio, and North Carolina increased their incarceration rates by 100 percent or less. On a national level, index crime rates decreased by an average 25.5 percent from 1980 to 2002. Violent crime rates decreased by 2.7 percent and property crime rates fell 28.2 percent. Of the 22 states with incarceration rate changes that surpassed the national average, the average increase in incarceration rates was 385.7 percent. The rate of index crimes decreased by 24 percent; there was a 1.8 increase in the violent crime rate and a 25.7 percent decrease in the property crime rate. The 28 states with below average increases in their incarceration rates, on average, increased by 175.7 percent and index crime rates decreased by 26.6 percent. Both violent crime and property crime rates decreased, respectively, by 6.2 and 30.2 percent. It appears that states with below-average percentage increases in incarceration rates over the last 25 years actually experienced overall declines in violent and property crimes, whereas the rest of the states had an increase in violent crime and a smaller decrease in property crime rates. As Mauer observes, the increasingly large prison populations we see in state prisons can be attributed to changes within criminal justice policies, and not increases in incarceration.[21]

Of course incarcerating every criminal would eliminate crime drastically, notes Hughes, yet he suggests that there may be a tipping point at which the proportion of our population in prison induces "economic and social deterioration."[22] He continues by offering the possibility that the costs of mass incarceration might, overall, exceed the costs of high crime rates.[23] Thus, it is necessary to identify nonviolent offenders whose incarceration

Table 9.2. Percent Changes in Incarceration, Index Crime, Violent Crime, and Property Crime Rates, 1980 to 2003

	% Change in Incarceration Rate, 1980–2003[a]	% Change in Index Crime Rate, 1980–2002[b]	% Change in Violent Crime Rate, 1980–2002[b]	% Change in Property Crime Rate, 1980–2002[b]
Pennsylvania	768.4	−24.0	10.4	−27.7
North Dakota	714.3	−18.8	44.8	−20.0
Mississippi	481.8	21.7	0.4	24.1
Connecticut	472.1	−49.0	−24.6	−50.9
New Hampshire	437.1	−52.6	−10.3	−54.2
Hawaii	400.0	−19.2	−12.5	−19.5
Idaho	390.8	−33.7	−18.7	−34.7
Missouri	372.3	−15.3	−2.8	−16.7
Wisconsin	366.7	−32.2	23.2	−34.4
California	364.3	−49.7	−33.6	−51.7
Colorado	347.9	−40.7	−33.3	−41.3
South Dakota	346.6	−29.7	39.9	−32.6
Alabama	326.2	−9.5	−1.0	−10.3
Oklahoma	321.2	−6.1	20.0	−8.5
Montana	318.1	−30.1	57.9	−34.2
Massachusetts	316.1	−49.1	−19.4	−52.4
New Jersey	313.2	−52.8	−38.0	−54.3
West Virginia	306.3	−1.0	27.5	−3.7
Kentucky	296.0	−15.5	4.6	−17.2
Louisiana	279.6	−6.5	−0.4	−7.4
Utah	275.0	−24.3	−21.9	−24.4
Arkansas	271.9	9.1	26.6	7.4
Average	268.1	−25.5	−2.7	−28.2
Illinois	253.2	−35.9	−23.2	−37.8
Vermont	237.3	−49.3	−40.3	−49.6
Iowa	237.2	−27.4	42.5	−30.4
Texas	234.3	−15.5	5.1	−17.6
Wyoming	229.2	−28.2	−30.3	−28.0
Arizona	228.1	−21.8	−15.1	−22.4
Indiana	224.6	−23.9	−5.5	−25.5
Minnesota	216.3	−26.3	17.4	−28.5
Kansas	215.1	−24.0	−3.3	−25.6
Michigan	200.0	−42.0	−15.5	−94.5
New Mexico	196.2	−15.1	20.2	−19.1
Oregon	195.0	−27.2	−40.4	−26.2
Virginia	193.2	−32.0	−5.1	−33.9
Rhode Island	183.1	−39.5	−30.2	−40.2
Tennessee	183.0	11.6	56.5	6.5
Alaska	180.4	−23.7	29.2	−28.1
New York	175.6	−59.4	−51.8	−60.8
Delaware	173.8	−41.9	26.2	−47.0
Nebraska	156.2	−1.1	39.8	−3.4

	% Change in Incarceration Rate, 1980–2003[a]	% Change in Index Crime Rate, 1980–2002[b]	% Change in Violent Crime Rate, 1980–2002[b]	% Change in Property Crime Rate, 1980–2002[b]
Georgia	146.1	−19.6	−17.4	−19.8
Washington	145.3	−26.1	−25.6	−26.2
Maine	144.3	−39.2	−44.3	−39.0
South Carolina	131.5	−2.6	24.5	−6.4
Maryland	129.5	−28.4	−9.7	−31.2
Florida	122.6	−35.5	−21.7	−37.3
Nevada	100.9	−49.2	−30.1	−51.4
Ohio	44.8	−24.4	−29.5	−23.9
North Carolina	42.6	1.7	3.3	1.6

[a]1980 data from *Sourcebook of Criminal Justice Statistics Online*, table 6.23; 2003 data from Harrison and Beck. 2004.
[b]BJS 2004g. "Data for Analysis, State-Level Crime Trends Database: *Crime in 2002* and *Crime in 1980*" (data from FBI's Uniform Crime Reports).

makes financial sense and those whose incarceration could prove excessively costly.

REENTRY

Once we remove individuals from their respective communities, families, and places of employment, we innately disrupt a personal sphere of relationships, careers, family and parenting, support structures, and education. Once incarcerated, this network is difficult, if not impossible, to re-create and can easily dissipate the moment a person is sent to prison. While the transition from one's family, career, freedom, and autonomy to the life of an inmate is devastatingly traumatic, so too is the process of reentering society once released from prison. Generally speaking, ex-inmates continue to pay for their crimes even after they have served their time and paid the dues that the law required of them. The ramifications of incapacitating nonviolent offenders are monumental and continue to climb. Men and women who have been in prison face the challenges that are addressed in chapter 7, such as denied welfare benefits, lack of housing, and an inability to find lawful employment.

Women, for example, face especially difficult challenges if they have children with whom they hope to reunite. During their period of incarceration, they may have lost parental rights altogether.[24] Each year, approximately 70,000 women leave the prison setting[25] and try to reestablish lives for themselves. Well over half of them have minor children.[26] Furthermore, an overwhelming number of female state inmates have less than a high school degree, and 15 percent were homeless within the 12 months preceding their arrest. In 1997, 58 percent of the women in state prison who were without employment the month prior to their incarceration received job training while in prison.[27] One in four faced the challenges of mental illness and three in four had substance abuse problems prior to their incarceration. However, only 67 percent of those in need of mental health services and 53 percent of those in need of substance abuse counseling actually received such services.[28] These women are largely ill-prepared to reenter society. Thus, for this population, the effects of incapacitation extend well beyond one's release.

HAVE THE GOALS OF INCAPACITATION BEEN MET?

To this question one might answer both *yes* and *no*. If measured by the absolute number of people in prison, our nation's goal of removing offenders from the streets and demonstrating our intolerance of crime has been overwhelmingly victorious. We have successfully locked up a larger percentage of our resident population than any other nation. In a country with a total population of 294 million, we have incarcerated over two million[29] adults and juveniles within our jails and prisons, a rate that exceeds 700 per 100,000 national population.[30] As of 2003, China—with a national population of 1.3 billion—had a prison body of 1.5 million people; yet, this only amounted to an incarceration rate of 118 per 100,000 residents.[31] Sentencing policies have led to the overincarceration of offenders, and the public safety goals of incapacitation have been shrouded by the ideals of an excessively harsh system. This book's argument is that we are not incarcerating the *right* people, for one's level of dangerousness is no longer an overwhelming determinant of whether one is bound for prison or probation and for what duration. We have turned our prison system into one that confounds retribution with incarceration, falsely making the assumption that imprisonment is the best and only way to exact justice. In the meantime, prisons are practicing what Zimring and Hawkins have called "bait-and-switch,"[32] a process whereby politicians assuage the public's demands for more crime control by building more expensive prisons. However, rather than incarcerate the most violent and dangerous of offenders, nonviolent offenders are instead finding themselves in these new, state-of-the-art prisons. Donziger describes this as scamming the American public, and "a policy that pretends to fight violence by locking up mostly nonviolent offenders is an inefficient use of taxpayer resources."[33]

Ehrlich notes that the "incapacitative value" of incarceration is "deficient,"[34] mainly because criminals continue their deviant behavior within prison and learn the skills needed to commit future crimes while in prison.

In his economic analysis of the effectiveness of incapacitation, he suggests that incapacitation can only account for up to 25 percent of the elasticity of felony offenses. Mauer's examination of crime and incarceration rates from 1970 to 1995 show no "dramatic decline" in crime, in light of steadily increasing incarceration rates.[35] According to Santos, "Total incapacitation . . . isn't an effective response when offenders are serving decades at a time" because the lack of connection with the external world leads to prisoners who are "absorbed by the prison subculture" that "diametrically opposes the larger culture outside of prison walls."[36]

In conclusion, incapacitating offenders, especially those who are nonviolent, in the name of crime control, cannot be the sole solution to our exaggerated crime epidemic. There are certainly individuals who should be in prison due to the heinous nature of their crimes and the risks they pose to society. The incarceration of such individuals is well worth the necessary financing and resources. But to incapacitate nonviolent offenders to prove our disdain for crime is an increasingly inefficient and senseless practice, one that is both financially costly and socially anomic. The criminal justice system can still exert control over individuals who break the law without uprooting them from society and locking them away for years. Other forms of punishment are available (as discussed in chapter 8) that have the potential to preserve the just yet fair intentions of our criminal justice system.

NOTES

1. Aside from individuals incapacitated in debtor's prisons.
2. Johnson 2002.
3. Macallair and Terry 2000.
4. CDCR 2006.
5. Beiser 2001.
6. Senna and Siegel 2002.
7. Gibbons 2004: 299.
8. Beiser 2001.
9. Ibid.
10. BJS 2005a.
11. Schiraldi and Ziendenberg 2002: 4.
12. Stephan 2004: 1.
13. Frieden 2005 (see http://www.cnn.com/2005/LAW/10/17/crime.rate/index.html).
14. JPI 2000.
15. See Morris 1993; Blumstein 2001; Tonry and Hatlestad 1997.
16. See Wilson 1975; Lyons and Scheingold 2000.
17. See Lyons and Scheingold 2000.
18. Gainsborough and Mauer 2000: table 1, page 8.
19. Ibid: 8.

20. Ibid: figure 3, page 9.
21. Mauer 1999: 34.
22. Ibid: 54.
23. Ibid: 54.
24. WPA 2003b.
25. Ibid.
26. See Mumola 2000.
27. WPA 2003b.
28. Ibid.
29. This figure includes pretrial detainees and remand prisoners.
30. ICPS 2005.
31. Ibid.
32. Zimring and Hawkins 1994.
33. Donziger 1996: 18.
34. Ehrlich 1981: 315.
35. Mauer 1999: 91.
36. Santos 2004: 214.

10

Some Specifics on Deterrence, in General

If we are to continue incarcerating offenders at our current rate, our beliefs in the deterrent effects of imprisonment and harsh sanctions should be empirically substantiated. From a pure rational choice perspective, individuals are believed to be endowed with free will and are portrayed as seekers of maximum utility who determine their actions based on pain and pleasure, costs and benefits.[1] Therefore, why not raise the stakes of offending and make punishments more painful? Our intuitive logic might suggest that increasing prison terms would deter individuals from engaging in criminal behavior or reoffending, but our bare assumptions should not fuel our reliance on the philosophy of deterrence. Studies on the deterrent effects of arrest, conviction, and imprisonment have indicated that individuals are not the rational beings they were previously described as, and to a certain degree, may be unresponsive to various deterrence initiatives while responsive to less-calculable forces.[2] With that in mind, we need to evaluate our policies that are based on the philosophy of deterrence to determine whether they are able to carry out this function.

GOALS

The roots of punishment as a means of deterrence are grounded in the classical school of criminology. Cesare Beccaria, an Italian philosopher whose voice emerged during the Enlightenment, believed that deterrence should be the ultimate rationale behind punishment.[3] Just the right degree of punishment would prevent rational risk-calculating individuals from choosing to engage in criminal activity. He also expanded his utilitarian argument by suggesting that effective crime control can only be achieved through "severity, certainty, and immediacy of punishment, all in the proper degree."[4] This argument ultimately relied on the assumption that offenders calculate the risks and gains involved in criminal undertakings and formulate their course of action by deciding if the final gains outweigh the risks of being caught. If punishments are not delivered in a swift and consistent manner, then the risks associated with illegal activities are perceived as less severe and the deterrent effect of the sanction diminishes.

There are two main forms of deterrence: specific and general. Policies founded on the idea of general deterrence attempt to deter the general public from committing crimes, whereas specific deterrence refers to punishing an individual to prevent said person from committing another crime. Some deterrence literature suggests that the certainty of punishment is important in deterring crime but "when certainty of arrest drops below 30%, severity and certainty both fail to correlate significantly with crime rates."[5] But as Ellis and Ellis warn, "one can hardly regard deterrence *by itself* as a promising approach, regardless of what moral-theoretical justifications might be predicated on the erroneous assumption that it does work."[6]

COSTS

We would certainly hope that the harsh conditions and deprivations of prison life, as well as the threat of probable severe sanctions, would serve to deter individuals from recidivating or engaging in criminal activities in the first place. Yet, it is not uncommon for prisoners to expand their criminal repertoire while in prison via exposure to seasoned offenders. Sutherland's theory of differential association, which is one among several learning theories of crime, suggests that criminal behavior is a product of a learning process that takes place among people with whom an individual is intimate and closely associated.[7] When individuals are exposed to people or groups who have unfavorable perceptions of the law and who can school the individual in the ways of criminality, they learn the techniques, norms, and beliefs associated with deviant behavior. Differential association is not necessarily limited to the world of the free. One can apply Sutherland's principles to prison cultures to understand how certain offenders who exit the prison system may be more hardened than upon their initial arrival. The physical or emotional survival of many inmates often relies upon their ability to resort to violence or obtain protection through gangs.[8] Once prisoners have intimate associations with gangs, who certainly favor the use of violent dispute tactics over the less violent strategies that would make them appear weak, the learning process commences.

The costs of sending individuals to prison under the philosophy of specific deterrence runs the risk of transforming nonviolent offenders into hardened inmates who may resort to criminal behavior within the prison or who, upon their release, may have adopted a new code of deviant behavior. If their unfavorable perceptions of the legal system are exported with them, any deterrent effect of incarceration could be irreparably mitigated. Ahn-Redding also examined inmate surveys in 1991 and 1997 and found that nonviolent inmates are susceptible to violence while incarcerated and demonstrate the same infractions as do violent offenders.[9] Whether these nonviolent offenders engage in violent behavior in prison as a reactive means of self-protection and self-preservation, or as a proactive means of preying upon others, they are still learning a code of behavior, one that bears potentially harmful ramifications.

Perspectives and policies founded on the logic of general deterrence focus on how punishments might send a general moral message to the public. General deterrence, therefore, is based on the idea that the public will see what happens to law-violators—they will learn what punishments the government is capable of employing and therefore be deterred from committing crimes. If, however, our current system of punishment does not deter future offenders from engaging in illegal behaviors because it fails to effectively convey the intended warning to the public, or it is applied unequally and unpredictably, or for any other reason, then the practice of mass incarceration is an unnecessarily expensive mechanism of crime prevention, one that should be reconsidered.

DETERRENCE RESEARCH

While Becarria's earlier stance on deterrence dominated much of the classical perspectives on crime control, Becker's more recently constructed economic model of crime offered the "first formal mathematical model of deterrence."[10] From a neoclassical position, Becker claims that criminals are "rational utility maximizers"[11] who have access to complete information regarding the probability of capture, conviction, and potential sanction. Only when the gains of criminal behavior are greater than those obtained through legitimate venues will they engage in criminal acts. While Becker's model makes some bold assumptions regarding rational choices and information availability, his model instigated a wave of research that furthered the exploration of the risks and benefits associated with illegitimate behavior. Many researchers seized upon the chance to expand Becker's economic approach;[12] however, this framework is limited by the difficulties of measuring the elements involved in decision-making and also undermines the strength of other drives that are not directed toward maximizing tangible gains.[13] Some researchers have considered elements such as the psychological or emotional dispositions of criminals[14] and other "extra-legal" factors, such as moral beliefs, peer pressure, impulsivity, and unemployment.[15] Additionally, impulsivity, adolescent rebellion, and other circumstances also compete with rational decisions.

A plethora of studies has emerged over the past 50 years, with researchers using a mixed array of methodologies, measurements, and suppositions. Von Hirsch et al.[16] have extensively reviewed the empirical literature on deterrence, which has taken various twists and turns as researchers differentially address the calculating nature of criminals and attempt to address the methodological issues that have plagued past research.[17] A 1978 report by the National Academy of Sciences' Panel on Research on Deterrent and Incapacitative Effects[18] marked the first of many that were commissioned in the United States and Great Britain during the 1970s. According to von Hirsch et al., the panel found many problems involved in association research. These obstacles include:

> (1) the possible existence of "common third causes" that might influence both crime rates and sanction levels; (2) possible errors in the measurement of the dependent variable, crime rates; (3) possible confounding effects of incapacitation with those of deterrence; and (4) the possibility of simultaneous (two-way) relationships between crimes and sanctions, such that a negative statistical association between crimes and sanctions might exist because higher crime rates produce lower sanctions, rather than the converse . . . effect.[19]

Overall, von Hirsch et al. describe major studies during the late 1970s as having "defects when subjected to stringent evaluation, although none of [the] reviews doubted the existence of deterrent effects in some circumstances."[20]

Von Hirsch and his colleagues also describe several recent associational studies to illustrate some of the methodological and measurement problems that still occur.[21] For example, Murray's attempt to link a high probability of incarceration with declining crime rates in the United States failed to distinguish *certainty* from *severity*.[22] Other studies[23] that have compared crime rates in England and the United States have failed to disaggregate crime data by jurisdiction in the United States and instead "treat[ed] the United States as a single unit."[24] In order for strong inferences to be drawn from empirical studies, researchers must adhere to the methodological rigor of social science research. Von Hirsch et al. have identified several problem areas that persist in deterrence research, such as confusing correlation with causation, not identifying independent variables with high degrees of specificity, and failing to employ the use of appropriate statistical controls to eliminate the effects of other variables.[25]

Certainly our attempts to implement harsh sentences in hopes of deterring existing and potential offenders have good intentions, logical foundations, and principled origins. Undoubtedly, some would-be criminals have thought twice about engaging in some illegitimate undertaking after considering the potential sentences that await them if captured. But more knowledge on the deterrent effects of punishments on *potential* offenders, not just those who are ex-inmates or from at-risk populations, is needed.[26] Rather than wait until individuals have been convicted of crimes or incarcerated, researchers should also interview at-risk noncriminals to help understand events that may inhibit criminal activity. While the thought processes that occur prior to and during the commission of a crime are unmeasurable among nonoffending populations, data can be gathered to understand why these nonoffenders have elected not to commit crimes and what mechanisms have deterred any criminal consideration. Additional areas that need further research include the deterrent effect of punishments on individuals who do not fall within the typical "at-risk" categories but who find themselves incarcerated, as well as juveniles.

Today, juveniles who are ages 16 or 17 can be tried as adults in 12 states.[27] However, it is unlikely that the cognitive processes utilized by adults to formulate decisions to act are identical to the processes employed by juveniles, whose neurological development may not be entirely complete. Additionally, juveniles may not possess the maturity or the capability to accurately or rationally weigh the costs and benefits of their behavior. Nonetheless, they are increasingly treated as adults within the criminal justice system and are assumed to respond to deterrence efforts in the same manner as adults.

Overall, theories of deterrence and studies on the effectiveness of sentencing laws to deter and reduce crime have been met with mixed evidence. Some would argue that by ensuring offenses are met with severe penalties, deterrence is an effective means of reducing crime. Others, however, maintain that criminals are not fully rational beings, arguing instead that harsh sanctions have an overall negligible impact on criminal behavior.

HOW KNOWLEDGEABLE ARE CRIMINALS?

The philosophy of deterrence has been used to justify the implementation of severe sentencing practices, yet it rests on the assumption that laws are accurately communicated to the public at large, and that potential offenders have an adequate understanding of sentencing policies within their respective states of residence and can use this knowledge in a calculable fashion. Intuitively, one might surmise that convicts are self-educated, that offenders inform family members, peers, associates, or other inmates of their personal experiences, and that Sutherland's process of differential association would lead to the diffusion of this knowledge throughout criminal circles. Yet, the existence of this hypothesized informal instructive system remains uncertain.

Sentencing practices throughout the country are continuously undergoing extensive and complex changes, thus obscuring the public's understanding of the legal system itself and what consequences are associated with what specific offenses. One of Walker's main assumptions underlying the basis of deterrence is that potential offenders must be knowledgeable of the punishments for certain crimes.[28] For harsh sentencing laws to effectively deter, offenders must comprehend new "statutory penalties."[29] Though researchers are improving methodological designs used to determine the efficacy of deterrence policies, von Hirsch et al. maintain that many studies neglect to take into account the extent to which new sentencing policies are conveyed to their target audiences.[30] With so many recent changes in our justice systems, however, it is unlikely that the average individual has a sufficient understanding of sentencing practices in his/her own state.

Ultimately, future empirical research needs to take into consideration the manner in which potential offenders perceive risks and how such risk assessments affect their behavioral decision-making processes.[31] Von Hirsch et al. suggest that studies of "sanction risk perceptions should be extended to examine how knowledge of *changes* in the probability of conviction or in the severities of punishment is disseminated to the public and to potential offenders."[32] Some studies have indeed considered the ways in which future criminals obtain information,[33] but it is a far more complex process than previously assumed and theories describing how this occurs remain largely absent. As Nagin observes, we have only a slight understanding of the process through which offenders calculate risk.[34]

HAVE THE GOALS OF DETERRENCE BEEN MET?

Lyons and Scheingold express widespread agreement that the decline in crime during the 1990s can be attributed to deterrence or incapacitation.[35] However, they recognize that deterrence theory is based on the assumption that "would-be offenders [make] rational cost-benefit calculations before deciding to commit a crime."[36] Hughes, on the other hand, argues that there is little empirical support of the notion that harsh sanctions have a deterrent effect "on the overall incidence of the kinds of criminality at which they aim."[37] While offenders may respond to harsh sanctions in crime categories such as drinking-and-driving, tax fraud, and domestic violence, Hughes suggests that "we have surely reached or passed the point at which increasing sanctions yields an efficient return."[38] Piliavin et al. also find little evidence in support of deterrence theories.[39] In a longitudinal study of individuals from populations at risk for offending, they determined that individuals react to the opportunity and reward components of rational-choice theories of crime, but claim that the threat of punishment does little to deter potential criminals who are "less committed to conventional morality."[40] On the other hand, von Hirsch et al. conclude that "criminal punishment has by now been shown capable of having deterrent effects."[41]

Among the goals of the federal sentencing guidelines is deterrence, but in a list of "substantially" and "partially" achieved goals of the Sentencing Reform Act, there is no mention of deterrence.[42] From the 1967 President's Commission on Law Enforcement and Administrative Justice and the 1978 National Academy of Sciences Panel on Research on Deterrent and Incapacitative Effects to the more recent 1993 study by the National Academy of Sciences Panel on the Understanding and Control of Violent Behavior, researchers have continuously rendered deterrence ineffective in crime control.[43] In conclusion, it appears that deterrence has a marginal effect on certain crimes, a negligible effect on other offenses, and a stronger impact on crimes such as drinking-and-driving and tax evasion. For example, a 1992 study by Loftin and Wiersema found evidence that mandatory sentencing enhancements used to target crimes involving handguns had a deterrent effect on homicide but no effect on other violent crimes.[44] Ultimately, it appears that other factors influence changes in crime rates, which suggests that only a specific handful of offenders under very specific circumstances may respond to deterrence efforts.

Despite a history of deterrence studies using poor methodology and yielding mixed results, our nation still pursues harsh sentences for a range of offenses in hopes that they will deter. These sentencing policies, however, do not come without a stiff price. With prison populations swelling, and with many overcrowded correctional facilities operating under tight budget constraints, the prison environment continues to sweep up all those who are unfortunate enough to encounter the modern criminal justice system in the name of deterrence, regardless of whether they are calculating or irrational.

FUTURE RESEARCH

To summarize, the theory of deterrence may be grounded in sound logic, yet policies designed to deter offenders by increasing the potential risks of crime do not always yield their intended results.[45] Additional research across multiple populations and jurisdictions is needed to determine whether policies designed to deter criminality are effective, and if so, what type of individual is most responsive to which policy and at what point does the severity of the punishment have the greatest deterrent impact on crime. Well-formulated research on the efficacy of deterrence policies should also take into account the process by which sentencing policies are conveyed to the public through formal and informal communication channels.

In addition, future studies should examine if and how the impact of abolishing discretionary parole—in conjunction with other sentencing structures, such as presumptive sentencing, mandatory minimums, and three-strikes laws—affects individuals' decision-making. The overall consequences of the sentencing structural changes that have occurred in the past 30 years may not yet be discernable and may also vary throughout the country. Finally, recidivism rates of individuals sentenced under TIS/no parole should be compared to those incarcerated prior to the enactment of such laws to identify any specific deterrent effect. So far, Cullen states, "correctional programs based on the principles of specific deterrence are notoriously ineffective."[46] Policies designed to deter individuals from illegal behavior are far from influencing changes in serious crime rates for certain offenses. For many crimes, argues Hughes, we have exceeded the point where increasing sentence lengths produces "an efficient return" in decreasing deterrence.[47] Furthermore, a plethora of demographic, biological, and socioeconomic factors have a significant impact on crime rates, such as poverty, substance abuse, education, personality, and genetic predispositions. Even the most rational individuals are not immune to these forces.

In conclusion, sentencing policies should be based on justifications other than the traditional goals of deterrence. If offenders are not deterred by mandatory sentencing statutes and threats of lengthy periods of incarceration, then why perpetuate our "tough on crime" position through harsh sentencing practices? Ongoing research is needed to assess the deterrent capability of sentencing statutes that are enacted in the name of deterrence. For now, however, those who espouse the deterrent potential of draconian punishments need to reexamine their underlying assumptions.

NOTES

1. Fisher 1993.
2. See Pierce and Bowers 1981; Loftin and McDowall 1984; Loftin et al. 1983 (cited in Parent et al. 1997).
3. Beccaria 1819.
4. Ellis and Ellis 1989: 8.
5. Ibid: 32.
6. Ibid: 33.
7. Sutherland 1947.
8. See Santos (2004) for his own observations on prison violence and gang protection.
9. Ahn-Redding 2005.
10. Levitt 2002: 436.
11. Becker 1968 (cited in Levitt 2002: 436).
12. See Ehrlich 1975 (cited in von Hirsch et al. 1999: 12).

13. Hughes 1993: 56–57 (cited in Forst 1993).

14. Sutherland and Cressey's 1960.

15. Ellis and Ellis 1989: 23.

16. Von Hirsch et al. 1999.

17. See Beyleveld 1979a, 1979b, 1980; Murray 1997; Nagin 1998; Levitt 2002; Hughes 1993.

18. See Blumstein et al. 1978 (cited in von Hirsch et al. 1999: 12).

19. Von Hirsch et al. 1999: 12.

20. Ibid: 13.

21. Ibid: 25.

22. Murray 1997 (cited in von Hirsch et al. 1999: 25).

23. Farrington and Langan 1992; Farrington et al. 1994; Langan and Farrington 1998 (all cited in von Hirsch et al. 1999: 25).

24. von Hirsch et al. 1999: 27.

25. Ibid: 17–19.

26. Wright and Decker 1994; Ross 1992.

27. Death Penalty Information Center (www.deathpenaltyinfo.org).

28. Walker 2006: 110.

29. Roberts and Stalans 1999: 43.

30. See Nagin 1998 (cited in von Hirsch et al. 1999).

31. See von Hirsch et al. 1999: 35.

32. Von Hirsch 1999: 49.

33. Cook 1980 (cited in von Hirsch 1999).

34. Nagin 1998 (cited in von Hirsch et al. 1999).

35. Lyons and Scheingold 2000.

36. Ibid: 107.

37. Hughes 1993: 52 (cited in Forst 1993).

38. Ibid: 55 (cited in Forst 1993).

39. Piliavin et al. 1986.

40. Ibid: 115.

41. Von Hirsch et al. 1999: 47.

42. USSC 2004b.

43. Ibid: 108.

44. Loftin and Wiersema 1992 (cited in Parent et al. 1997).

45. Walker 2006: 129.

46. Cullen 2002: 287.

47. Hughes 1993: 55 (cited in Forst 1993).

11

Prison Rehabilitation and Treatment: Where is The Correction in Our Correctional Facilities?[1]

Chapter 4 reviewed the history of sentencing in the United States and the declining faith in the rehabilitative potential of prisons. Yet, prisons continue to provide psychological and treatment programs to inmates, often without examining empirical literature to determine what practices have shown promise and merely relying on practices used by previous prison administrations.[2] Have recent studies shown any treatment and rehabilitation programs to be effective, or at least effective *enough*, to justify mass incarceration and the use of harsh sentencing? This chapter addresses efforts within prison to treat inmates and examines whether incarcerating non-violent offenders yields any rehabilitative benefits.

GOALS

Our nation is founded upon principles that emphasize individuality, hard work, and self-improvement. Humans are malleable creatures—not robotic products of genetic compositions and chemicals—who develop, grow, and self-actualize. In all facets of life and in all areas of functioning we attempt to correct ourselves and others. Children are punished for misbehavior under the assumption that they will learn from their punishments, whether they are given a "time out" for pushing another child or are grounded for missing curfew. All in all, we are continuously adjusting our behaviors, learning from our mistakes, and helping others to improve as well. The "self-help" sections of bookstores are lined with volumes of innovative techniques, strategic plans, and recipes for self-improvement and personal growth. Whether it is to shed those excess 20 pounds or improve our relationships with our spouses, we are always trying to evolve into something greater, something better, and something more complete than we were yesterday. In other words, our society is constantly recognizing the potential for change, facilitating programs and services that enable individuals to obtain their ever-evolving goals, and rewarding the hard work of those who successfully self-improve and actualize their visions.

We naturally gravitate toward encouraging those who break the law to rehabilitate themselves, to better their individual circumstances, to make wiser decisions, and to engage in self-control. We no longer portray offenders as degenerates who are in all physical manners inferior to the law-abiding element of society. We recognize that human behavior is the product of a complex, multitiered amalgamation of genetic influences, social circumstances, and environmental conditions that all contribute to shaping our physical and psychological selves. The philosophy of rehabilitation is grounded in the faith that people can indeed improve themselves with a helping hand, that transgressors are not predestined to live out their lives in the shadows of the law, that as a civilized society we can and should tend to those in need, and that by assisting those who are struggling we are ultimately assisting all of society.

The ebb and flow of our faith in the rehabilitative capacity of the criminal justice system continues to stimulate widespread debate over duty and our capacity to reform misguided individuals. The expenses directed toward treatment efforts in correctional facilities, as well as the continued use of prison over probation in the name of rehabilitation, can be justified if such facilities are able to effectively provide such services. However, there is a pervasive lack of certainty with regards to treatment models in prisons and many of our current facilities only pay lip service to their rehabilitation-related objectives.

While many in favor of rehabilitation support the proclamation that society *owes* individuals who have gone awry treatment, retributivists would not view rehabilitation as an obligation. This latter group would assert that the goal of punishment should not be to fix and reform people—it should be centered on the concept of "just deserts" and proportionality. Punishments should be imposed to restore the social equilibrium that is offset by legal transgressions, not to heal or repair the moral footing upon which the offender stands. Ultimately, this is a philosophical issue, one that will not be casually resolved. Whether we are morally obligated to treat offenders or not, the rehabilitative ideal is nonetheless still used to justify incarceration. If we are unable to follow through on our treatment efforts, if we are not able to amass the resources, knowledge, and time necessary to implement effective rehabilitation programs, then this is a very costly undertaking.

COSTS

There are two explicit costs associated with rehabilitation programs. The first cost is in providing useless treatments. Latessa et al. have identified several programs that have yielded ineffective results in treating offenders, such as boot camps, "scared straight" programs, programs of intensive supervision, wilderness programs, and psychoanalytic treatments.[3] Without highly organized environments, funding, empirically driven strategies, structured monitoring, and professionalism, many correctional treatment programs have amounted to nothing more than what they call *"quackery."*[4] "Correctional quackery," according to Latessa et al. is "the use of treatment interventions that are based on neither 1) existing knowledge of the causes of crime nor 2) existing knowledge of what programs have been shown to change offender behavior."[5]

The second cost is accrued by incarcerating offenders but then failing to provide treatment at all, thereby denying offenders the opportunity to receive otherwise effective treatment within the community. Of the inmates who exit the prison system, 75 percent have a history of drug or alcohol abuse.[6] However, only 40 percent of prisons and jails provided any form of substance abuse treatment in 1997.[7] Prison is far from a cure and offers little in the way of psychological treatment and social services. Many facilities provide educational and vocational classes, support groups, bible classes, and other life skills training opportunities, but these services are secondary to the facilities' primary functions, which are still control and confinement.

In a way, prisoners and the public have been duped by the rhetoric employed by the correctional community. However, the joke has been on us— the public. We *hear* the phrase "correctional facility" and it comforts us to know that offenders are being sent away to be "fixed" or "corrected," yet Johnson asserts that "in very many cases there is very little correction going on."[8] Adjustment centers are another example of this duplicity, where inmates are often placed in solitary confinement as punishment rather than for treatment or "adjustment." Overall, this visible disconnect between language and function reflects our general inability to provide both confinement and rehabilitative services under the same roof.

RESEARCH

Originally, rehabilitation served to mediate the effects of a "purely retributive justice system" by "counteracting" or "compensating for" the harsh aspects of our sentencing practices.[9] Rehabilitation was therefore implemented to increase sentencing fairness. However, its effectiveness has experienced waning confidence among academics, inmates, and administrators alike.

Much of the public's mistrust of ex-inmates originates from earlier research that has found rehabilitation and treatment programs within the correctional system to be ineffective.[10]

Robert Martinson's well-known declaration that rehabilitation has little effect on recidivism, as presented in his essay *What Works?—Questions and Answers about Prison Reform*, became known as the "nothing works" doctrine.[11] These findings were based on a meta-analysis which analyzed 231 studies of rehabilitation programs from 1945 and 1967 that included psychotherapy and group therapy, vocational training, and treatment programs within correctional facilities.[12] While half of the studies demonstrated reductions in recidivism, Martinson claimed that there was no specific category of treatment that was effective. His conclusion that "our present strategies . . . cannot overcome, or even appreciably reduce, tendencies of offenders to continue in criminal behavior"[13] was also supported by a panel commissioned by the National Academy of Sciences. Sarre reminds us, however, that Martinson published this article "peremptorily and without [Lipton and Wilks's] specific consent."[14] Despite the statement that came out a year later by Lipton et al. that "the field of corrections has not as yet found satisfactory ways to reduce recidivism by significant amounts"[15] Martinson's earlier conclusion propelled our nation into a new era of correctional reform that would ultimately change the functions of prison. While many of the studies reviewed by Martinson employed poor methodology or lacked any theoretical basis, his analysis contributed to the radical shift from the earlier rehabilitative and treatment-oriented approach to incarceration to a more retributive and punitive criminal justice system that currently focuses little on rehabilitation efforts.[16] Despite any evidence that would suggest otherwise, the public continues to maintain a perception that all inmates who are released from prison are unrehabilitated, dangerous, and at risk for reoffending. With this in mind, it is not surprising that individuals in certain communities distrust their neighbors or discontinue their participation in certain civic activities when many of the neighbors are known to be ex-inmates.

Cullen purports that "rehabilitation works" in reducing recidivism among prison inmates,[17] while Blumstein states that "prisons are generally ineffective for rehabilitation of adults and may have serious criminalizing effects on those who come out."[18] As such, the rehabilitation question has undergone cycles of public acceptance and skepticism. During the 1970s, faith in rehabilitation diminished as treatment programs were criticized for their ineffectiveness. Around the time that rehabilitation programs were losing public support, parole practices were also attacked when studies reported the failure of correctional programs to reduce recidivism rates and the inability of parole boards to identify which inmates were rehabilitated.[19]

RECENT STUDIES

Ehrlich's economic approach to examining rehabilitation efforts concluded that "Numerous studies indicate little success, if not outright failure, of most programs in bringing about any enduring rehabilitative outcomes for treated offenders."[20] However, researchers have not abandoned their quest to develop effective rehabilitation programs both in and outside of prison.

Cullen reviews several studies on the effect of prison rehabilitation and treatment programs on recidivism rates.[21] In 1993, Lipsey and Wilson reported findings from 302 meta-analyses of intervention programs that they examined and noticed "a strong, dramatic pattern of overall effects."[22] While only ten of these meta-analyses included criminal offenders, they concluded that "there was no evidence that offenders cannot be rehabilitated."[23] Other studies[24] have found positive effects from cognitive-behavioral programs,[25] multi-modal treatments,[26] educational programs,[27] and vocational education and community employment programs.[28]

Still, we are struggling to identify and strengthen programs that effectively reduce rates of recidivism. Gaes et al.[29] review recent studies examining rehabilitation in prison, including a project by Lipton et al.[30] that focused on 1,500 correctional treatment programs. Lipton et al.'s preliminary findings, based on adult and juvenile studies, indicate that community treatment, rather than "treatment in public facilities, custodial institutions, and the juvenile justice system,"[31] may be efficacious in reducing recidivism. Furthermore, "treatment that was behavioral, skill-oriented, or multimodal . . . was associated with larger effect sizes than treatment that was based on deterrence, family counseling, group counseling, or individual counseling."[32] Lipton et al.'s findings have important implications for how our system handles nonviolent inmates. At best, Gaes et al.'s review of treatment and rehabilitation literature concludes that "correctional treatment for adults has modest but substantively meaningful effects."[33]

Morris and Tonry describe the relationship between crime, substance abuse, and mental illness as "intimately related"[34] and Cullen argues that prisons should remain committed to rehabilitation efforts.[35] Such efforts require more than what prisons can offer, such as drug-free environments, medication, evaluation and assessments, and individualized treatment plans. Morris and Tonry also suggest that community-based sanctions in addition to treatment may be more appropriate for certain offenders with psychological or substance abuse problems. Providing rehabilitation services to individuals in a controlled environment where they have little or no autonomy, where their sense of identity is eroded, and where they cannot feel safe contradicts some of the main premises upon which rehabilitative programs are based. For example, Alcoholics Anonymous, is largely based on personal responsibility and making reparations,[36] which is difficult to do when an individual is behind bars and hundreds of miles away from family and friends.

If nonviolent inmates can be successfully treated or rehabilitated outside the confines of prison, then community-based sentences may be more appropriate and less expensive penalties for low-risk, first-time offenders. By treating them within the community and sentencing them to probation or other nonincarcerative punishments, nonviolent offenders can remain within their families and communities, thus reducing the financial burden they place on state correctional systems. As Rotman observes, "Interrupting a criminal career has little benefit without the creation of a purposeful rehabilitative environment, which includes the offer of meaningful opportunities."[37] Undoubtedly this holds true for many, especially nonviolent offenders who in addition to their illicit activities and engagements may also have legitimate careers.

Overall, we must assess the current state of our prison rehabilitation programs to determine whether they are effectively reducing crime rates and decreasing rates of substance abuse among offenders. Studies offer little indication that our correctional system is actually meeting any rehabilitative goals. *So, is it worth sending petty drug offenders to correctional facilities where the prospect of successful treatment is slim? Should we continue to send nonviolent drug offenders to prison when community-based treatment programs can not only provide better treatment modalities, but offset the costs of criminal activity among drug users?* If we answer "no" to these questions, society as a whole must be willing to preserve prisons for the "worst of the worst" rather than small-time offenders who often fare worse in prison than they would in community treatment programs.

HAVE THE GOALS OF REHABILITATION BEEN MET?

Considering that society has largely forgone rehabilitation as a goal of incarceration, the most obvious answer to this question is *no*. However, perhaps it is time to start reconsidering rehabilitation as a desirable goal of our criminal justice system, at least for certain populations of offenders.

First, though, we need to identify which offenders are susceptible to successful rehabilitation and under what conditions rehabilitation programs should be offered. For example, *should we focus treatment efforts on sex offenders or to nonviolent offenders, such as substance abusers?* Certainly there are some offenders whose rehabilitation may require the structured and regimented environment that prisons can provide, whereas other offenders may be conducive to rehabilitation within community settings. Many of the current treatment models that are based on unempirical theories have adopted several beliefs that drive their treatment programs, including: "offenders lack discipline," "offenders have low self-esteem," and "offenders (males) need to get in touch with their feminine side" theories.[38] As Cullen comments, "virtually every prison continues to have an array of rehabilitation programs—perhaps to keep inmates busy, perhaps because it would have been too much effort to get rid of them."[39] Currently, our society is not conducive to the social reentry of prisoners, especially when so many are susceptible to relapsing into their prior illegal or self-destructive behavior. Nor have we significantly reduced recidivism rates through replicable and effective treatment and rehabilitation programs. Yet, there is hope, as Rotman states, for "Rehabilitation is not incompatible with fair punishment."[40]

NOTES

1. To quote Dr. Robert Johnson at American University.
2. Latessa et al. 2006.
3. Ibid: 362.
4. Ibid: 359.
5. Ibid: 359.
6. Durose and Mumola 2004.
7. Senna and Siegel 2002: 31.
8. Johnson interview 2002.
9. Rotman 1998: 284.
10. Petersilia 2002; Blumstein 2002.
11. Martinson 1974 (cited in Sarre 1999).
12. See Lipton et al. 1975.
13. Martinson 1974: 49 (cited in Sarre 1992: 2).
14. Sarre 1999: 3.
15. Lipton et al. 1975: 627 (cited in Sarre 1999: 3).
16. Cullen 2002.
17. Ibid: 287.
18. Blumstein 2002: 480.
19. Tonry and Hatlestad 1997.
20. Ehrlich 1981: 314.
21. Cullen 2002.
22. Cited in Cullen 2002: 263.
23. Cullen 2002: 264.
24. Studies cited in Cullen 2002: 268–72.
25. See Losel 1995 (cited in Cullen 2002).
26. See MacKenzie 2000 (cited in Cullen 2002).
27. See Gaes et al. 1999 and Wilson et al. 2000 (cited in Cullen 2002).
28. See Bouffard et al. 2000 (cited in Cullen 2002).
29. Gaes et al. 1999.
30. Lipton et al. 1998.
31. Gaes et al. 1999: 369.
32. Ibid: 369.

33. Ibid: 414.
34. Morris and Tonry 1990: 187.
35. Cullen 2002: 288.
36. Alcoholics Anonymous 1972.
37. Rotman 1998: 295.
38. Latessa et al. 2006: 361.
39. Cullen 2002: 255.
40. Rotman 1998: 284.

V

CONCLUSION

12

The Benefits of Incarceration—
Real and Perceived

This book was not written with the intent of discounting the benefits of prisons. The previous four chapters addressed the shortcomings of the justifications that we use to incarcerate—retribution, deterrence, incapacitation, and rehabilitation—and the limitations to each of these proclaimed functions of prison. Yet, prisons are not without purpose or function. We incapacitate many dangerous offenders who have committed unspeakable crimes; we embrace retribution by differentiating misdemeanors from felonies and scaling our sentencing structure so that murderers, for example, are dealt with more severely than minor property offenders; we have delivered disturbed individuals into the auspices of facilities that can provide the treatment and services that they would not normally seek on the streets; and we have created correctional facilities that most individuals normally try to avoid. Indeed, without these prisons to assuage society's fear of dangerous offenders and predation, we would live amidst an atmosphere of constant suspicion and trepidation. Nonetheless, the question of what to do with nonviolent and minor offenders remains widely debated, with a multitude of fragmented views and strategies.

This book charges that incarceration is being used excessively and that states' correctional systems are pushing the boundaries to the extreme, thus compromising prisons' functionalities. Indeed, there are many disturbed and violent individuals who *do* deservingly belong behind bars and should probably remain there for the duration of their natural lives; however, prisons do serve purposes other than public safety. Some would go so far as to argue that prisons enable the powerful and wealthy segments of society to exert control over the lower class and minority groups,[1] while others depict prisons as a dumping ground for social deviants, the mentally ill, addicts, etc. While we need some way of controlling individuals who threaten the stability of society, any instrument we employ must be administrated effectively, fairly, and in moderation.

Are prisons bad? No. This book is not a harangue against the existence of prisons, nor is its intention to undermine the abilities of prison administrators and staff; instead, I have argued that many nonviolent offenders do not belong in such institutions. There are several strong arguments for reducing the nonviolent prison population and developing or expanding community-based sanctions. How we manage to do that remains up to the public. Ultimately, the public drives policy and has the upper hand in deciding how we want to shape our system of punishments. As a society, we *can* emerge from our "tough on crime" mentality by acknowledging certain truths, such as declining crime rates, and relaxing some of our assumptions. Most of us have been victims of violent or nonviolent crime at some point during our lifetimes, but we must complement our own emotions with reason. As much as we desire to punish the segment of society who chooses not to abide by our laws, as much as we want them to pay for their wrongdoings through exposure to symbolic or actual suffering, we must make sure that we are not also sweeping up the *wrong* people. Too often, the public demands action without taking the time to explore various issues, check facts, or consider the ramifications of their decisions. We are always on the lookout for quick fixes to social problems, despite the long-term consequences. So, to change the system, we must align the conscious choices that we make to reduce crime and punish offenders with realistic expectations.

Ultimately, we must ask ourselves if the benefits of increased incarceration are worth the costs that have been discussed in previous chapters. To do so, however, requires a well-informed public that can examine the criminal justice system objectively, with emotions aside, and evaluate the efficacy of the policies that they are supporting. Before examining the public's perceptions of crime and punishment, let us take a look at the parties who benefit from tough on crime policies.

WHO BENEFITS?

When analyzing any sort of social institution, it is important to ask *"who benefits?"* from the implementation, maintenance, and popularity of public policies and changes to the legal system. The "Million Dollar Inmate" is an expensive individual who incurs financial and social losses, paid for largely by the public or their families. So, who benefits from the laws that create them?

Politicians

Edwin Bender of the National Institute on Money in State Politics reports that in 2000, private prison industries paid $1.13 million to 830 candidates—most of whom were incumbents and likely to win the elections—throughout 14 states in the south.[2] Their motivation? Private prison industries such as Wackenhut Corrections, Correctional Services, Corp., and Corrections Corporation of America, by lobbying candidates during the election cycle, were after what any other large industry desires—political clout and money. Thus, politicians have ample reasons to support correctional enterprises.

Furthermore, few politician can hope for re-election by espousing "soft on crime" initiatives; to do so would be tantamount to political suicide. Moral panics play out well in the public arena when the social context is just right. Reinarman has extensively described the fluctuating periods of heightened fear and subsequent "crusades"[3] that have marked our history. Much of this fear has been drug- or alcohol-related, although Reinarman adds that these scares are "relatively autonomous from whatever drug-related problems exist or are said to exist."[4] Instead, these scares are embedded within a broader historical framework; they emerge when certain groups or classes pose a perceived threat to our economic or social stability. For example, according to Reinarman, the Prohibition era was largely a movement launched by "native-born, middle-class, nonurban Protestants" against "Catholic immigrants who were filling up American's cities during industrialization."[5] Opium laws passed in California at the end of the nineteenth century were fueled by a widespread fear of Chinese immigrants, and our most recent war has targeted users of crack cocaine, who tend to be the "inner-city, minority-poor."[6] Out of these panics and drug crazes emerge politicians with great battles to fight, with bolstered public support, and who rally around plans (that are sometimes efficient, sometimes not) to remedy the social ills that are concerning taxpayers. Scares of this type are still pervasive throughout society—today, we have turned our attention to crime, regardless of declining crime rates. Politicians have much to gain when the public is scared and when quick-fix solutions are readily available. As Beiser succinctly states, "For politicians, crime pays."[7]

Potential Victims

Not all correctional expenses are sunk costs. Incarceration not only allays our fears and comforts us by swiftly sweeping violent criminals off the streets, but it reduces the overall toll that violent crime takes on society. Incarceration is not a one-way stream of expenditures—it also prevents crimes that would otherwise be committed by those who are incarcerated.[8] As Forst observes, the social costs of crime can be mitigated by the expenses saved when repeat offenders are unable to recidivate.[9]

Measuring the crimes that have been prevented through incapacitation—especially of repeat offenders—is not an easy undertaking, so let's narrow our focus to property crimes. In 2000, there were 262,000 state felony convictions for property offenses (see table 3.4) of which 37 percent, or 96,940, resulted in prison sentences. Table 3.5 indicated that property offenders sentenced in state courts in 2002 were given an average sentence of 41 months but that they would serve an estimated 20 months (1.67 years), or 49 percent of their sentences, on average. In 2001, prisons spent an average of $22,650 in annual operating costs per prisoner (see table 5.9). Each of these property offenders, therefore, cost over $37,000 to incarcerate. Given these figures, we can estimate that incarcerating these 96,940 property offenders for 20 months each, at a rate of $22,650 per year, cost our nation $3.6 billion!

Is spending $37,000 to incarcerate a property offender for 1.6 years warranted? In 2004, there were 2,143,456 burglaries, 6,947,685 larceny-theft, and 1,237,114 motor vehicle thefts reported to the police.[10] The FBI estimates that in the same year, property offenses cost our nation $16.1 billion;[11] broken down by offense categories, $3.5 billion was attributed to burglary, $5.1 billion due to larceny-theft, and $7.6 billion from motor vehicle theft. The average burglary cost each victim $1,642,[12] and items stolen (larceny-theft) were worth, on average, $727 each.[13] Additionally, the average vehicle that was stolen was worth $6,143.[14]

Spending $3.6 billion annually to incarcerate property offenders may appear justified considering the estimated $16.1 billion in costs accrued by victims of property crime in 2004 alone, but we can only speculate as to whether those who are incarcerated would reoffend if released and how much crime is actually prevented by their incapacitation. In 2000, there were 79,300 burglary convictions in state courts resulting in 41,236 prison sentences. If we multiply the number of individuals sent to prison (41,236) by the average loss from burglaries ($1,642), what we have is a grand total of $67,709,512 possibly saved, *assuming* that each of the inmates were to recidivate at least once (see table 12.1). However, the cost of incarcerating these 41,236 individuals for 1.9 years at an annual rate of $22,650 per inmate was over $4 billion. Similarly, if we were to hypothetically estimate that each of the 4,879 individuals sentenced to prison for motor vehicle theft would have stolen an additional two vehicles (each valued at $6,143) had they not been incarcerated, the total value of their offenses would have reached $59,943,394. To incarcerate these 4,879 individuals for 1.4 years costs taxpayers a total of $154.4 million. This is clearly an overly simplified way of estimating and calculating the potential costs of future crimes, but in both cases—burglaries and motor vehicle thefts—the costs of incarceration exceeded the costs of the hypothetical crimes that were prevented.

There are several additional variables involved in calculating the costs and benefits of incarcerating nonviolent offenders. On the one hand, we have operating costs, forfeited labor and taxes during periods of incarceration, family disruption that may involve child welfare services, possible unemployment immediately after release, and community anomie in high crime areas. On the other hand, incapacitating those offenders could possibly save the American public billions in property value over time. Furthermore, we saw in table 3.4 that only 54 percent of violent offenders convicted in state courts were sentenced to prison, whereas the same was true of 60 percent of violent offenders in 1992.

Whether it is worth spending $22,650 to send a property offender to prison for a year for stealing $1,642 or even $6,143 worth of goods (or vehicles) is ultimately up to the public, but the money saved could be diverted to other areas of the criminal justice system that are in need of increased funding.

Communities

The stimulation of fear of crime, which inevitably leads to greater support of incarceration, is not without its own benefits. The community hypothesis argues that the movement to reduce crime and fear of crime has a functional purpose and provides a forum through which communities can come together.[15] Perhaps crime scares bolster community cohesion and strengthen social networks. It has also been suggested that crime and punishment are inevitable, if not necessary, social elements that have positive properties at the macrolevel. Kai Erikson argued that society must publicize and maintain its boundaries, especially when the norms that constitute its perimeters are constantly in flux.[16] By testing social norms through deviation, Erikson argues, acts of transgression reinforce boundaries that are otherwise used to define and solidify each community. Punishment then is "a formal ceremony to deal with the responsible offender, it sharpens the authority of the violated norm and restates where the boundaries of the group are located."[17] Because crime does provide certain benefits, institutions that are designed to curb crime and deviance may unintentionally reinforce and maintain it, thus perpetuating a cyclical process of criminality, imprisonment, and recidivism.[18] Erikson turns to prisons as an example, suggesting that they do a poor job of rehabilitating inmates, and as a result society expects nothing short of recidivism to take place among ex-prisoners. When former inmates are stigmatized, when they are expected to fail, often that is exactly what they do.

Durkheim, in his functionalist-oriented approach to framing the role of crime and deviance in society, argued that crime is "integral," "useful," and even "necessary."[19] Crime, in other words, paves the way for social change and for the "evolution of morality and law."[20] Others, however, would argue that the legal system promotes, reflects, and protects the interests of the dominant or wealthy class[21] while widening the inequities between social classes.

Let's turn to a specific practice that until recently profited from high incarceration rates. Prisons have generally been infamous when it comes to phone call privileges; inmates must always call collect and can never receive personal telephone calls. Only until recently did departments of corrections arrange special deals with telephone companies who would apply excessively high rates to inmate collect calls, thus profiting both the phone company and the prison. Families receiving these collect calls would often pay hundreds of dollars to speak with their family members in prison. In the late 1990s, lawsuits were filed in Illinois, Kentucky, Missouri, Arizona, and Indiana by families and attorneys who were paying for these collect calls.[22] Plaintiffs alleged that these deals were violating the Sherman Anti-Trust Act, 15 U.S.C. § 1, the Telecommunications Act of 1996, the Robinson-Patman Act, 15 U.S.C. § 13, and constitutional amendments. On October 1, 1999, the Federal Communications Commission enacted a new regulation[23] forcing phone companies to disclose to consumers how much they are being charged for their phone calls and how the rates were being calculated.[24]

There will always exist segments of society and various institutions that benefit from incarceration practices, so we should ask ourselves whether incarceration is advantageous to society on a whole.

Local Economies?

It is often argued that prisons bring jobs to depressed areas and therefore yield positive economic functions. Who wouldn't support an institution that can generate hundreds of jobs and economic stimulation? However, the dangers of working in prison, mental health conditions of workers, increasing crime rates, loss of local shops, and high turnover rates fail to be mentioned. In a study conducted by King, Mauer, and Huling, the researchers set out to examine the effects of prisons on local economics.[25] The belief that opening a prison within a depressed region will stimulate the economy is widely pervasive, yet King et al.'s study indicates otherwise. By examining data in 14 rural areas of New York from 1977 to 2000, the researchers looked at the effects of "prison siting" on per capital income and unemployment rates. There was no significant difference in unemployment trends between the seven rural counties with "prison sitings" and the seven without prisons. Rural counties without prisons experienced an increase in per capital income by 141 percent, while the same figure was 132 percent in counties with prisons. King et al. speculate that these findings could reflect differences in the regions where prison staff live and work, the inability of local residents to secure employment within the prison due to a lack of skills and/or competition, and the outsourcing of materials needed to build the prisons.

Farrigan and Glasmeier's study on prison construction in rural areas during the 1980s and 1990s yielded similar findings.[26] In their analysis of the effect of prison construction on poverty rates, employment, and other economic indicators, they concluded that "the economic impacts of the prison development boom on persistently poor rural places, and rural places in general, appear to have been rather limited."[27] While they did observe decreased poverty rates in certain areas, they suggested that this change was more likely due to the general presence of a new institution—which happened to be a prison—instead of the prison industry's specific ability to instigate significant economic change in rural areas. Ultimately, current evidence suggests that the building of prisons to revitalize depressed economies may not yield the expected benefits.

PUBLIC AWARENESS OF CRIME AND INCARCERATION

Prison construction receives a tremendous amount of public support, as do harsh sentencing initiatives. Though policies are implemented and revised on a continual basis, the public is often unaware of their specific details and their potential consequences. Chaffee has argued that political communication "should presumably be studied in connection with changes *over time* in the state of a system, or of individuals within a system"[28] while Bloom and Novelli have recognized the difficulty of transferring "the technology of marketing to the arena of social problem solving."[29] While the criminal justice system is not commonly perceived as a public service, it *is* just that—a governmental service designed to protect and provide for the welfare of the public. Yet, little attention has been given to the manner by which information regarding criminal laws, practices, and changes in policies are disseminated to the public.

Research on general knowledge of criminal justice issues has consistently revealed a widespread misunderstanding among the public. This is no surprise, as our legal system is intricate, multifaceted, and confusing to most people. Donziger identifies a common myth among the American public, a belief that street-level offending costs society more than white-collar crime.[30] Perhaps this is because less attention and fewer resources are directed toward what Simon calls "elite crime"—harmful acts carried out by wealthy individuals that may or may not be illegal but that carry "relatively little risk"[31]—than street crimes. Among the ramifications of elite deviance identified by Simon is the statistic that "five times as many persons die each year from illnesses and injuries contracted on the job . . . than are murdered by all street criminals."[32] Furthermore, Simon reports,

"Street crime, for example, is miniscule in terms of economic costs when compared to the illegal activities by corporations."[33] Even so, our attention is mostly tuned to reports of violent and stranger crimes that make sensational, exciting, emotional, and easily understood media stories. These stories are raw and passionate, unlike the trials of white-collar criminals, which tend to be technical, complicated, and dry. The Zacarias Moussaoui trial in 2006 did not induce sleepiness; the Enron-related trials did.

Roberts and Stalans have shown grave errors in the public's estimation of crime statistics and several public misperceptions of criminal justice issues.[34] For example, one common misperception is that crime rates are consistently increasing, though we have seen that crime rates have been on the decline since the early 1990s. Further, Roberts and Stalans find that "significant discrepancies exist between the true state of the sentencing system and public knowledge. This seems to be true in all Western nations."[35] Studies that assess public knowledge of sentencing issues in California and Arizona have found that the public has little understanding and awareness of sentencing policies.[36] In California, approximately 80 percent of the population was unaware of a policy passed by the state legislature that increased the minimum sentences for certain crimes.[37] Also common in Arizona was an underestimation of penalties for certain crimes. Their findings also suggest that while respondents in the United States, the United Kingdom, and in Canada are largely uninformed of sentencing procedures, they "consistently *under*-estimate the severity of the sentencing process."[38] Roberts and Stalans conclude that increases in sentencing severity have little deterrent effects.

It is unclear as to how accurate people's knowledge of the criminal justice is today. Yet, with clarity comes reason, and today we have many reasons to slow or even reverse the tough on crime era in which we currently find ourselves.

NOTES

1. Aptheker 1971.
2. Bender 2002: 1.
3. Reinarman 2003: 137.
4. Ibid: 138.
5. Ibid: 138.
6. Ibid: 138–41.
7. Beiser 2001 from "How We Got to Two Million: How Did the Land of the Free Become the World's Leading Jailer?" July 10, 2001 from MotherJones.com.
8. See Forst 2004.
9. Forst 2004.
10. Schmalleger 2007: 42.

11. Federal Bureau of Investigation 2006.
12. Schmalleger 2007: 49.
13. Ibid: 52.
14. Ibid: 53.
15. Fisher 1993: 182.
16. Erikson 1966, 2003.
17. Erikson 2003 (cited in Adler and Adler 2003: 14).
18. Erikson 2003 (cited in Adler and Adler 2003: 15).
19. Durkheim 1938 (cited in Adler and Adler 2003: 57–58).
20. Durkheim 1938 (cited in Adler and Adler 2003: 58).
21. See Bonger 1916.
22. *Prison Legal News.* "Law Suits Challenge Prison Phone Rates. Suit Filed in Illinois" and "Phone Rates Challenged in KY, MO, IN and AZ," Seattle, WA. Cited on *The November Coalition* website (http://www.november.org/razorwire/rzold/14/1409.html).
23. Operator Services for Prison inmate phones (47 C.F.R. § 67.710 ').
24. *Prison Legal News.* "FCC cracks down on prison phones." Cited on *The November Coalition* website (http://www.november.org/razorwire/rzold/14/1409.html).
25. King et al. 2004.
26. Farrigan and Glasmeier n.d.
27. Ibid: 24.
28. Chaffee 1975: 86.
29. Bloom and Novelli 1981: 69.
30. Donziger 1996: 66.
31. Simon 2006: 12.
32. Ibid: 39.
33. Ibid: 126.
34. Roberts and Stalans 1999: table 4.
35. Ibid: 43.
36. See Roberts and Stalans 1999: 44.
37. Roberts and Stalans 1999.
38. Ibid: 45.

13

Policy Recommendations

Can we continue to justify the use of a prison system for nonviolent offenders given the tremendous costs that have been explored throughout this book? Are we justified in sending these individuals to prison in the name of retribution when we are still questioning whether the objectives of the other utilitarian-related functions of prisons—deterrence, incapacitation, and rehabilitation[1]—have been served? If we as a society are willing to pay the price of building and maintaining prisons, and are willing to accept the impact that incarceration has on families, neighborhoods, communities, and the labor force, then perhaps we might answer *yes*. If we believe that prisons are adequately correcting the behavior of nonviolent offenders, again, we should answer *yes*. If we believe that incarceration entails "just deserts" for nonviolent drug and property offenders and that the prison experience is an adequate punishment, then we can answer *yes* and best prepare ourselves for what is to come. But, if we answer *no* to any of the above statements, then it is time to implement changes in the way the criminal justice system handles nonviolent offenders.

Part of our disdain for criminal offenders stems from our country's attitude toward crime. We marginalize and stigmatize, but not all countries share this perspective. For example, in Sweden, "Prisoners are criminal patients and thus viewed in many ways the same as unemployed persons—a group whose existence detracts from the complete functioning of society and who thus must be trained and guided to fill useful positions once again."[2] While I am not advocating the coddling of nonviolent offenders and disregarding the harms that they have inflicted, perhaps we too need to reconsider how the incarceration of this nonviolent population also derails our society's ability to maintain a well-balanced equilibrium of crime and punishment, undermines the potential that many law-violators have to reform and adjust their lifestyles, and paralyzes society with fear and anger that only drives more intense and less forgiving policy.

VIOLENT VERSUS NONVIOLENT OFFENSES

When an act is committed that violates a law that society has created to protect person and property, it is an established duty of the state to counteract with punitive and (financially or symbolically) reparative measures. Harmful behaviors necessitate some form of identification, admonishment, and counterforce. Our reaction has historically been embodied in corporal punishment, torture, and death—all of which are intended to inflict extreme physical pain. More recently, sanctions have been oriented toward the temporary elimination of freedom, identity, and comfort, or the more permanent act of taking someone's life. Now that we have entered the twenty-first century, the United States has reduced its reaction to serious offenders by relying on the assumption that incapacitation is the most effective way of ensuring public safety, and for those who commit nonviolent offenses, that imprisonment is still the most effective way of exacting punishment. Today, society's perception of punishment is nearly synonymous with prison. Among nonviolent offenders we value the removal of an individual's freedom as an adequate and effective method of exacting punishment. We are comfortable with the concept of prison, with the temporary banishment of criminals that these institutions provide, and the notion that the longer a prison sentence is, the more punitive it becomes.

However, can we in all certainty equate severity of punishment with lengths of time in prison? Intuitively, yes, for ten years in prison by most standards is harsher than one year. But the total costs of incarceration (social and financial) may be greater for a first-time prison inmate serving one year than for a recidivist serving a third prison term. Who is to say that the recidivist with the three-year sentence is immersed in a more punitive experience than the person serving one year? The point is that we view punishment through incarceration as linear and highly correlative with severity. We automatically assume that ten years is harsher than eight years, that two years is more punitive than one year, that six months is more severe than one month. We assume that the longer the sentence, the greater the deterrent potential and the worse the prison experience will be. But if our assumption is not correct, wherein serving seven years instead of six years for a crime does not necessarily punish more, then we need to focus more of our efforts on strengthening the proportionality of our sentences and concentrate less on equating sanction severity with the duration of prison terms.

We tend to react to nonviolent and violent offenders with disregard, disgust, and intolerance. But in many ways, our system was designed to systematically discriminate nonviolent from violent offenders and then process them accordingly. We recognize the differential damage caused by acts of violence versus crimes directed toward property; likewise, we categorize offenses into misdemeanor or felony categories. Generally, we fine, jail, or place on probation misdemeanants. Felons, on the other hand, are often fined, placed on probation, or confined in correctional facilities rather than jails. So why subject nonviolent offenders to the punishments that are designed to incapacitate violent individuals and to increase the overall safety of the public? Nonviolent and violent felons pose very different threats to society and should be treated as such. The manner with which a rapist or murderer is dealt with *should* be much different from the way property felons are handled by the court system, but this discrepancy is narrowing as our proclivity to use prison—the most severe punishment (aside from capital punishment)—escalates among all types of offenders. If we are concerned with public safety, then clearly incapacitation is a logical choice. The property offender poses a threat to society, but these concerns generally involve objects and replaceable items. The fear that burglars instill in the American public is manifested through security systems, car alarms, and bolted doors, whereas the fear produced by habitually violent offenders is of an entirely different magnitude and nature. The objectives of protecting Americans and reducing fear of violence can be achieved through the use of incarceration for violent and repeat offenders, but they cannot be reached in the same light through the use of prison for low-level nonviolent offenders.

RECOMMENDATIONS

Arguing that our prisons are filled with too many nonviolent offenders is an easy academic exercise, yet devising a solution that suits the needs of all relevant parties is a different story given that they include taxpayers, politicians, policymakers, academics, prison administrators, offenders, and families of offenders. Whether we believe in increasing or decreasing the severity of specific sentences, we need to consider the financial ramifications of these decisions. As we have seen, the costs of imprisonment are staggering. Crime rates have been decreasing, a trend that cannot be attributed in whole to increasing incarceration rates. It is time to reexamine our current practices and prioritize the needs of our nation.

Is it possible to change course and head toward a less incarceration dependent era? Yes. Some states are taking steps to spearhead efforts that can reduce budget crises by altering their sentencing policies. Austin and Fabelo[3]

Table 13.1.   Summary of Recent State Experiences

State	New Policies	Results
Connecticut	• Fewer technical violators • Increased parole rate for low risk prisoners	Reduced the prison population by 800, allowing the return of hundreds of prisoners housed in Virginia to return to Connecticut.
Kentucky	• New parole guidelines that take into account risk assessment • Increased parole rate	Prison populations is stabilized and early release program eliminated.
Maryland	• New inmate classification system • More prisoners sent to prerelease centers • Increased rate of parole for low risk prisoners • Expedited parole hearings	Reduced prison population by over 800 within one year.
New Mexico	• More inmate participation in treatment programs • Prisoners who complete programs awarded more good time • Decreased rate of parole technical violation	Prison population stable despite expectation that it would increase by 400 inmates.
Texas	• New parole guidelines that take into account risk assessment • Increased rate of parole grants • Reductions in technical violations through progressive sanctions and expanding parole revocation centers	$544 million in new prison construction and $300 million for new prison operations annually was averted due to reduction in expected need for prison beds.

Source: See Austin and Fabelo. 2004: table 5, page 20 (reprinted with permission).

describe many state policy changes that have notably reduced prison populations and spending, as seen in table 13.1. The Women's Prison Association also reports that Arizona saved $2.6 million in the span of only 12 months by mandating that nonviolent drug offenders receive treatment rather than imprisonment.[4] So strategies to reduce prison populations, enact cost-saving measures, and reduce prison construction *do* exist, and several states are beginning to actualize these objectives.

Our correctional systems are increasingly overcrowded, expensive, and challenging to manage. There are remedies, however, and states are finding ways to reduce costs and prison populations. Reducing the number of non-violent inmates appears to have the potential to relieve our overcrowded system and save states millions of dollars. To do so would require a host of other changes within the system, such as those addressed in the next section.

WHERE SHOULD WE GO FROM HERE?

In an effort to quench our thirst for tough-on-crime policies, states have swept up millions of nonviolent offenders in hopes of reducing crime rates and satisfying the public's clamor for justice. And we did this only within the last few decades, a record-breaking demonstration of the powers behind the political machinery of the war on drugs and our ceaseless intolerance of crime. Yet, in this whirlwind of activity, the parties who are making these decisions and implementing these changes have not paused to observe this incarceration era's impact on individuals, families, communities, and the economy. Perhaps mass incarceration has satisfied our need for retaliation against those who dare breach our laws, but our criminal justice system exists in order to control these exact sentiments. Our legal framework, which is designed to be equitable and objective, exists to preclude our emotional interference with justice. Yet, are tough on crime initiatives that send non-violent offenders to prison for decades truly objective and proportionate? Are they just? As this book has suggested, our system of punishment has become too retaliatory, too politicized, and too emotional, and it relies upon philosophies of justice that are perhaps more applicable to violent than nonviolent offenders. We must place a cap on our willingness to impose draconian sentences on individuals who are not physically dangerous to society, who have families to care for, and who can still contribute to society while paying for their crimes. We must reduce the number of these non-violent offenders in prison by reversing the current direction and goals of our sentencing practices.

We cannot, nor should we attempt to, revamp sentencing and correctional policies overnight. Any changes that are made must be deliberate, fully debated, and supported by the public who at least until recently has been overwhelmingly supportive of harsh sentencing policies. When and if the public decides that changes are necessary, that the resources we use to incarcerate nonviolent offenders would be better directed toward other social functions, and that alternatives to prison are worthy of exploration, there are numerous ways to instigate these reforms. The rest of this chapter examines and describes a nonexhaustive list of recommendations that could contribute toward the reduction of nonviolent prisoners. Not all of these suggestions will be received with equal enthusiasm; some are more difficult to implement; some are not in complete alignment with the values held by a majority of society; some may appear too lenient; and some may not be feasible given our current resources. However, they should be entertained nonetheless as gateways to an improved, more balanced and proportionate, and equally effective approach to corrections. These recommendations are:

1. Utilize alternative sentencing options for low-level drug offenders;
2. Increase our use of parole and early release;
3. Increase funding of research on the efficacy of alternative sanctions and identification of which inmates are likely to benefit from such programs;
4. Increase funding for probation services;
5. Reduce the population of low-risk geriatric inmates;
6. Explore the concept of restorative justice and identify ways to incorporate its principles into sentencing structures; and
7. Reduce the use of prison for first-time nonviolent offenders.

Sentencing of Drug Offenders

One of the most logical populations to target in attempting to reduce prison growth and increase the use of alternative sanctions is nonviolent, nondealing drug offenders. Our nation cannot possibly fight its war on drugs by incarcerating low-level drug offenders whose positions are instantaneously replaced by many more eager, budding dealers. The drug war must be waged on other fronts as well—on the border, in airports, in the work place, in classrooms, in the home, etc. Placing these low-level dealers in prison only exacerbates any existing financial problems that may have initially propelled them into the world of dealing. Once released, and faced with financial hardships and stressors, the allure of dealing becomes all too tempting.

Sevigny and Caulkins have recently classified drug offenders in state and federal prisons by "functional role and drug group participation, type and amount of drugs, firearms involvement, and criminal conviction and arrest history."[5] Their findings indicate that the majority of drug offenders are neither "ambiguously low-level," nor are they "kingpins." Sevigny and Caulkins categorize "ambiguously low-level" offenders as "nonviolent/nongun, small drug amount, minor role, first- or second-time drug-only offenders," thus reporting that only 750 of the 48,343 federal and 10,000 of the 174,744 state drug offenders meet that criteria.[6] Those who are "ambiguously low-level" drug offenders, observe Sevigny and Caulkins, therefore make up 1.6 and 5.7 percent of federal and state prison populations, respectively. These offenders may be good candidates for drug courts, early release programs, or intermediate sanctions. Sevigny and Caulkins's analysis also showed that 17.4 percent of state-incarcerated drug offenders (30,404) and 31.6 percent (15,266) of federal drug offenders were categorized as "Nonviolent, Nongun [and]

First- or Second-Time Drug Offender Only." Approximately 46.7 percent (81,536) of state and 36.7 percent (17,754) of federal drug offenders were similarly categorized as "Nonviolent, Nongun [and] Repeat Drug or Other Nondrug Conviction Record."[7] Based on this broader categorization, there were 144,960 federal and state inmates who fit this description. Although Sevigny and Caulkins acknowledge that their findings "dampen hopes of dramatically reducing prison populations,"[8] these populations are nevertheless possible starting points.

Another approach to reducing prison populations is through "capacity-sensitive policies" in which sentencing decisions are made in accordance with available prison space.[9] Determining the appropriate "safety valve"[10] through which inmates can be identified, assessed, and released in order to make room for more serious offenders is a difficult process, yet one that could result in substantial alleviation of prison crowding. In Kentucky, for example, Austin and Fabelo report that the state "has stabilized prison population growth by simply making smarter release decisions."[11] Using empirical data from a study on recidivism, the Parole Board adopted new parole guidelines in 2003 which have "served to increase the number of low-risk prisoners who are eligible for parole."[12] Low-level, low-risk, and non-violent drug offenders could be a target population in searching for eligible early release candidates.

One approach to diverting drug offenders from prison involves the use of drug treatment courts. In 2000, there were 116,300 state felony convictions for drug possession, of whom only 36 percent received probation.[13] Among those convicted of drug possession and sentenced to prison in 2000, 38 percent had no prior felony conviction.[14] Furthermore, only 12 percent were also sentenced to treatment.[15] In attempts to decrease "crowded felony dockets and case processing time, and [provide] a mechanism for more creative and effective dispositions," many states are experimenting with the use of drug courts.[16] The Bureau of Justice Assistance has listed the major elements of drug courts, which include the following:[17]

- Integrating alcohol and drug treatment services into the judicial process by using a multiphased treatment process
- Promoting of public safety and protecting defendants' due process rights through a process that is not adversarial
- Early identification of eligible candidates
- Provision of ongoing access to treatment services
- Monitoring abstinence through testing
- Responding to participants' compliance through a coordinated strategy
- Facilitating continuous interaction between the court and participants
- Monitoring and evaluation of the program goals
- Utilizing interdisciplinary education

- Creating partnerships that include drug courts, public agencies, and community-based organizations.

In 1998, the Bureau of Justice Statistics reports that there were 327 drug courts in 43 states and the District of Columbia.[18] One analysis of a drug court in Oregon was found to not only be a "cost effective use of criminal justice system and taxpayer resources"[19] but also cost saving. Other data indicate that drug courts have been working to reduce methamphetamine addiction in federally funded courts in "California, Oregon, Hawaii, Nevada, Oklahoma, and Kentucky."[20] McCarthy et al. also review findings from drug courts around the nation. They report, for example, that clients cost only $700 per year in Miami and the participants "had a longer time before re-arrest and were re-arrested for less serious offenses."[21] They also provide findings from a report published by the National Drug Court Institute Review, which stated, "Drug courts provide closer, more comprehensive supervision and much more frequent drug testing and monitoring during the program, than other forms of community supervision. More importantly, drug use and criminal behavior are substantially reduced while offenders are participating in drug courts."[22] Overall, drug courts appear to hold promise in diverting offenders from traditional prosecution, supplying appropriate treatment and services to appropriate offenders, and reducing the number of drug offenders who are sent directly to prison.

Early Release and Reentry

The practice of incarcerating individuals who have outlived their criminal careers has diminishing returns when the goal is to increase public safety and prevent future crimes. Many such offenders who age out of their criminal lifestyles—whether due to maturity levels, increased commitments to family, or any number of reasons—pose little or no threat to society. Because 47 percent of female state prisoners are in their thirties, the Women's Prison Association suggests that "most women in prison are past their prime years for committing crime."[23] Can we justify the continuation of their imprisonment and the perpetual financial drain on the public? Releasing certain nonviolent prisoners after a reasonable length of incarceration not only increases space in prison for more violent offenders, but also returns the individuals to their communities where they can contribute to society by assuming law-abiding lifestyles.

By offering early release options and good time credits, prisons can provide positive incentives for prisoners to attend substance abuse programs, take GED or college courses, maintain positive contact with family members and supportive friends, avoid becoming involved in physical violence against staff and other prisoners, and seek employment opportunities upon their release.

Providing prisoners with the goal of obtaining good time credit can also assist them psychologically by arming them with hope.

For many inmates, early release is not a reality, especially in the wake of determinate and mandatory sentencing. However, to enact sound changes in our prison populations, the types of sentences we impose must have a degree of flexibility. The Sentencing Project has provided estimates of the costs in 2008 and 2013 of maintaining truth-in-sentencing in the federal system, which requires 85 percent of a sentence served.[24] However, the Sentencing Project also notes that individuals entering the federal system in 1997 were more likely to serve 87 percent of their sentences.[25] Based on 2003 data, they estimate that if the expected 87 percent of time served in 2008 was reduced to 50 percent, there would be a prison population reduction of 37.1 percent and a cost reduction of $1.7 billion. Looking ahead to 2013, reducing the expected 87 percent to 50 percent of sentences served would reduce the prison population by 41.5 percent and save $2 billion. Thus, making small, incremental adjustments in sentencing expectations can yield vast population changes and savings over time.

Prisoners who are released—whether early or on their expected release dates—need assistance in creating or reestablishing lives for themselves (and often their children). Social workers should be available to specifically assist and advise ex-inmates or soon-to-be-released prisoners as they seek housing, jobs, mental health and substance abuse treatment, and reunification with their children. Ross and Richards suggest that prisoners should receive "a correctional experience that prepares them for successful reintegration back into the community."[26]

INTERMEDIATE, COMMUNITY-BASED, AND ALTERNATIVE SANCTIONS

The American public appears to be at odds with its stance on crime and punishment. Many Americans believe that crime is a serious problem and we should therefore increase the severity of sanctions, however, society does not appear willing to sacrifice their children's education for the sake of incarcerating more offenders. For example, a national survey found that 72 percent of Californians opposed averting spending from higher education to fund three strikes sentencing laws.[27] Even 92 percent of the surveyed wardens believed that we should increase the use of alternatives to incarceration.

Intermediate sanctions, which were recognized as early as the 1960s as potential beneficial supplements to traditional sentencing practices, are legal consequences that can be categorized as neither prison nor probation. They involve practices such as intensive probation, financial punishments, and community service[28] and therefore offer numerous possible combinations of punishments. However, Morris and Tonry state that these sentencing options have been underused.[29] Lavine et al. have reported other forms of intermediate sanctions in place today, such as electronic monitoring, boot camps, day reporting centers, and drug courts.[30]

At its inception, intermediate sanctions were viewed as potentially capable of impacting major areas of sentencing issues.[31] First was the dwindling loss of faith in the rehabilitative capacity of prisons during the 1970s. Intermediate sanctions offered a range of punishments, including treatment options *outside* of prison. Second, intermediate sanctions were thought of as having additive value by developing an entire range of sentences that would reflect the philosophy of proportionality. Intermediate sanctions could be used to complement or replace traditional sentencing options, thereby providing more sentencing combinations that could retain the tough-on-crime position without the use of prison. Judges would have a greater range of options in sentencing offenders who they felt were undeserving of prison but whose punishments should be more severe than probation.

The use of alternative sanctions can result in potentially significant cost reductions. For example, in North Carolina, per day expenditures from 2000 to 2001 on each inmate were estimated to be $12.69 for intensive supervision, $7.16 for electronic house arrest, and $61.36 for boot camp, whereas the average cost per prison inmate was $65.29 per day.[32] To address its problems in overcrowding, Maryland's use of alternative sanctions has reduced the yearly cost of incarcerating offenders to $4,000, an annual reduction of $16,000.[33] The state has done this through its Correctional Options Program that was created in 1994.[34] The program involves boot camps, a regimented offender treatment center, electronic monitoring, a day reporting center, intensive probation, aftercare programs for offenders who have finished treatment, and a drug court. Lavine et al. report that the program has effectively diverted nonviolent offenders who would have otherwise found themselves in prison.[35]

Likewise, in response to the tripling of its correctional population during the 1980s, Connecticut has seen significant cost reductions by diverting offenders through its Office of Alternative Sanctions.[36] The program involves the use of inpatient substance abuse programs, offender programs for women, centers for youth and day incarceration programs, electronic monitoring, and community service programs.[37]

The use of monetary sanctions has been explored, yet a system of pecuniary punishments poses dilemmas. Classical criminologists would argue that individuals respond to rewards and punishments in a calculating manner and are guided by maximizing personal utility. Morris and Tonry recognize the irony that "a society that relies so heavily on the financial incentive in its social philosophy and economic practices should be so reluctant to use the financial disincentive as a punishment of crime."[38] Yet, the question remains as to how much offenders should pay in fines for committing various crimes. Should all individuals who commit the same crime be required to pay an equal level of compensation, or should the wealthy pay more than the poor?

Morris and Tonry have argued for the increased use of intermediate punishments, yet they acknowledge that the widespread belief that "nonincarcerative sentences"[39] are less expensive than prison is inherently problematic. However, as more methodologically sound empirical data are able to identify which alternative sanctions are most effective, and for whom, the costs of our current experimental phase may dwindle. In addition to several overlooked considerations in calculating cost savings, Morris and Tonry argue that the marginal costs of incarcerating an additional inmate are small, and only when enough inmates are diverted from prison to enable an institution to shut down some or all of its operations will nonincarcerative options be cost saving. However, in correctional systems where inmates are tripled to a cell and sleeping in hallways, the building of additional prisons is often the most visible solution. By reducing overcrowding in prison, correctional systems may be able to bypass the construction of new facilities, which costs taxpayers millions. Furthermore, diverted prisoners are able to work and pay taxes and therefore generate revenue for the state rather than sitting around idle for years. Finally, reducing prison crowding may foster more controllable environments in which inmates and officers are involved in less inmate-on-inmate or inmate-on-staff violence. With smaller prison populations, educational, treatment, and occupational programs may be more available and effective.

There are other troubling, but potentially fixable, dilemmas inherent in the use of intermediate sanctions.[40] One is the problem of ensuring that offenders who do violate the terms of their sanctions are dealt with accordingly. Secondly, many offenders violate technical terms of their sanctions, these violations that would normally go unnoticed if they were under less controlled supervision, such as probation. Should such individuals be sent to prison for violating curfew or drinking conditions? These issues cannot be easily resolved and the solutions will depend on each state, its needs, its priorities, and its resources.

Clear and Braga examined several intermediate sanctions, such as intensive supervision and electronic monitoring.[41] Electronic monitoring, they state, costs the state very little and is increasingly being used as an alternative to prison or probation. Generally low-risk offenders are sentenced to home confinement or monitoring, and studies have shown small re-arrest rates and positive effects on employment.[42] However, other research[43] has found that many offenders are at high risk for nonsuccessful completion of the program due to technical violations. While home electronic monitoring has its inherent problems, it is worth pursuing as an option to probation or prison. Intensive supervision programs have been used as alternatives to probation and prison. Several studies[44] have found intensive supervision programs to have high failure rates. However, Clear and Braga's review of day reporting centers and residential community corrections (RCC) programs indicate some degree of success, yet there is still a need for additional empirical research. For example, McDevitt and Miliano found an 80 percent success rate in one day reporting center.[45] While studies of residential community corrections have yielded "inconsistent results,"[46] "next to nothing is known about the implementation and impact of the latest wave of surveillance-oriented RCC programs."[47] Ultimately, Clear and Braga conclude that intervention programs may be more effective among high-risk offenders and that increasing the use of intermediate sanctions poses no harm to the safety of communities.[48] There is an evident need for more evaluations on the effectiveness of intermediate sanctions in reducing recidivism. Morris and Tonry also recognize the difficulty in measuring the efficacy of intermediate sanctions and suggest asking, "What is the optimum rate of recidivism for this punishment?"[49] Clearly, any program of intermediate sanctions must attempt to operationalize measures of success and clearly define its goals. Evaluations by nonbiased parties should be conducted to determine whether the program is reaching its goals.

Overall, our nation seems to be utilizing community-based prisons and moving toward alternatives to traditional confinement facilities. In 1995, there were 304 community-based prisons, which the Bureau of Justice Statistics defines as facilities in which at least 50 percent of the inmates are allowed to leave the prison grounds without supervision, including "halfway houses, restitution centers, prerelease, work release, and study release centers."[50] By 2000, there were 460 such facilities, an increase of 51.3 percent in a five-year period. Within the same time span, there was only a 4.1 percent increase in the number of traditional confinement institutions in which fewer than 50 percent of the inmates are able to leave the facilities unaccompanied and that include "boot camps; reception, diagnosis, and classification centers; prison hospitals; alcohol and drug centers; and youthful offender facilities."[51] The impact of community-based facilities on recidivism is yet to be determined, but they provide a means of punishing offenders while also permitting them to contribute to society through work or education.

Probation

Another widely used sentencing option is probation. Many states have understandably enacted statutes preventing offenders from receiving probation for certain crimes,[52] including murder, weapon offenses, sex offenses, prior felonies, kidnapping, drug crimes, robbery, and habitual drunk driving.[53]

While these statutes are logical given the nature of the offenses listed, 15 states prohibit probation for drug offenders.

While the public might initially oppose the increased use of probation on the basis that it is too "soft on crime," Crouch argues that many inmates prefer prison over intensive probation.[54] He cites Petersilia's study in which 33 percent of a sample of felons chose prison over "intensive supervision by the probation department."[55] In Crouch's research on inmate preferences, 66 percent of his sample of Texas felon inmates would have chosen to serve one year of incarceration over ten years on probation, and 25 percent would have chosen three years of imprisonment over ten years on probation.[56] His research suggests that many inmates find prison to be more of a severe sanction than extensive sentences to probation.[57] On this note, community-based corrections may not be as "soft" on offenders as many believe. Probationers in some states may also receive fines, be ordered to pay restitution, or be given community service time,[58] thus adding to the overall severity of probation.

Petersilia reports that the probation population has rapidly increased in size, thus overwhelming probation officers with large caseloads of individuals who are "difficult to manage because more . . . are drug users or sexual offenders, are mentally ill, have gang affiliations, and have fewer marketable skills."[59] Despite the rising number of individuals under community sanctions, Petersilia reports that probation agencies remain underfunded. With probation officers only able to provide limited contact with offenders, their cursory supervision "leaves many serious offenders unsupervised and undoubtedly contributes to high recidivism rates."[60] While research indicates that most individuals on probation recidivate, Petersilia asserts, "offenders who fail under community supervision are the fastest growing component of the prison population."[61] Clearly, the probation system and other facets of community corrections can play a large role in crime control given additional empirical research and collaborative cooperation between criminal justice agencies and communities.

With additional funding and support to strengthen the services provided to offenders and conduct research to identify effective programs, community sanctions can reduce prison crowding, restore credibility in the system,[62] provide effective community treatment programs, reduce recidivism rates, and keep offenders within their families and communities. Researchers have identified potentially effective probation practices, such as using advanced technology to monitor probationers; developing intensive behavioral treatment programs that focus on high-risk offenders and that match offenders with counselors based on personality traits; employment programs; intermediate sanctions; and neighborhood-oriented probation programs. However, further empirical analyses are needed to examine the effectiveness of these tactics.

With more individuals diverted from incarceration, neighborhoods can also hope to remain intact by keeping offenders with their families. In addition, alternatives to incarceration that strive to keep mothers and single parents with their children also serve to strengthen communities. Individuals who place more trust in the criminal justice system and in each other strengthen their community's ability to provide effective formal and informal social controls and also foster conditions for social capital.

Ehrlich notes that crime controls "cannot be based merely on their relative efficacy in reducing offenses, but must involve consideration of their relative costs."[63] In many instances, diverting a nonviolent offender to probation rather than prison could be more cost effective for the state. For example, probation costs approximately $1,000 annually.[64] Yet it offers many potential sanctions, such as close supervision, drug and alcohol testing, community service, house arrest, monitoring, and curfews.[65] From 2001 to 2002 in North Carolina, the Department of Corrections estimates the daily cost of probation to be $1.87, whereas the cost per day for each prison inmate ranged from $54.02 to $84.21.[66]

On the other hand, Morris and Tonry suggest that traditional probation is overused and that many offenders on probation need to be under tighter control and supervision.[67] However, Austin and Fabelo have cited efforts in New Mexico to reduce probation technical violations. The risk assessment instrument used to determine early release decisions has been "applied to a probation and parole officer's recommendation to violate a parolee or probationer."[68] These efforts, as well as those oriented around an early release program, have yielded a "dramatic reduction in technical violators being returned to prison."[69] Ultimately, with enough resources to identify strong candidates for probation and enough funding to increase the number of probation officers, some of the problems that we see today can be tackled.

Aging Inmates

With an estimated $69,000 spent on each elderly inmate annually,[70] it is clear that the elderly are *very* expensive to keep in prison. One suggestion, made by the NCIA, is that prisoners should be released on supervision if they are 65 years or older, committed a nonviolent offense, served at least 33 percent of their sentence, and pose no threat to society.[71] We must give heavy consideration to the crime control impact of releasing elderly inmates and its financial savings. Inmates often "age out" of criminal lifestyles as they settle into stable jobs, marry, have families, and no longer have the physical prowess of their youths. The elderly generally commit fewer crimes than any other age group. In 2002, individuals who were age 65 or older made up 12.3 percent of the U.S. population yet only 0.6 percent of arrests.[72] The age group with the highest percentage of arrests consisted of 15- to 19-year-olds (21.3 percent), followed by 20- to 24-year-olds (19.9 percent). Each of those age groups as a percent of the U.S. population were, in respective order, 7.1 and 7.0 percent. Granted, even if elderly inmates are released and cannot find work, they may still be a burden on the state, but at least they will have the opportunity to be with and receive support from their family members.

What sense does it make to incarcerate older inmates who are confined to their beds due to medical reasons? What sense does it make to incarcerate nonviolent inmates for decades, place them in environments where there are no lucrative means of earning money, and then pay for their health care as they age within the system?

Restorative and Community Justice

A relatively nascent alternative to sentencing incorporates the philosophies of restorative and community justice into the diversion of offenders from current punitive approaches toward punishment. The restorative justice philosophy proposes minimizing government intervention and allowing victims, communities, and offenders to determine appropriate sanctions.[73] Rather than focusing on retribution and punishment, advocates of this approach suggest that each crime be addressed individually. According to Kurki, proponents of restorative justice perceive crime as an action much broader than mere defiance of a criminal code and instead focus on the harm done to the victim and/or surrounding community.[74] The primary goal, therefore, is to heal and make reparations to those who were harmed. To determine the appropriate sanction, the community, victim, and offender identify the victim's needs rather than focus on the severity of the crime and the offender. Kurki describes several components of restorative justice, such as mediation between the victim and offender, family group conferencing, sentencing circles, and reparative probation.[75]

McCarthy, McCarthy, and Leone also note that in addition to tending to the victim's needs, restorative justice may also focus on public protection.[76] When community safety becomes a higher priority than integrating the victim's needs into the process, then it is referred to as community justice.[77] Community justice addresses crime prevention and community collaboration, and advocates strategies very similar to those used in community policing.[78] Criminal justice officials engage in broader responsibilities and expand their strategies to include neighborhood stations, community empowerment, building partnerships, community prosecution, and involving the populace in public safety strategies.

While the principles of restorative and community justice may not be widely accepted when dealing with murder, rape, or other sexual offenses, they are worthy of consideration when handling low-level nonviolent offenders because of their potential benefits to the victims of crime and their surrounding communities. Community and restorative justice proponents both view the community as valuable in crime prevention and public safety. By bridging law enforcement agencies with neighborhood residents, individuals assume more responsibilities in crime control, thereby increasing their involvement in the community. While these practices lack empirical evidence demonstrating their effect on crime rates, they offer alternatives to otherwise punitive sentencing measures. Kurki states that restorative justice has mostly been applied in juvenile cases and for minor offenses, while community justice faces many hurdles in building community bridges and creating relationships with the public.[79]

Restoring community-level trust is crucial to building and sustaining social capital, a vital resource especially during this time period in which individualism is encouraged and prevails. When the criminal justice system adopts correctional practices and policies that are perceived as unfair or unjust by offenders and nonoffenders, and when the community responds by pervasive mistrust and increased individualism, the system is regarded as lacking credibility, efficacy, and equity, and is therefore seen as unworthy of respect. When neighborhoods and families are overwhelmingly disrupted by crime and high incarceration rates, trust diminishes, civic participation declines, and social institutions become less effective. When the public fails to enforce appropriate behavior through the use of informal social controls, crime, alienation, and mistrust may be the end result.

The criminal justice system can take considerable measures to restore trust within society. By changing its treatment of inmates, by addressing policies and practices that disproportionately affect minority groups, by focusing on intermediate and community sanctions rather than solely on traditional incarceration, and by helping ex-inmates succeed in society, the system can assist in keeping communities and families active and intact. Only when individuals believe they are being treated fairly by law enforcement agencies, feel safe within their communities, and regard the criminal justice system as a credible entity will they begin to trust each other and take the initiative to participate in collective responses to crime.

Less Prison Use for First-Time Nonviolent Offenders

Another recommendation that merits consideration, although it is guaranteed to provoke criticism, is reducing the use of incarceration for all low-level nonviolent offenders who commit a first offense. Certainly I am not suggesting that we allow these individuals to escape punishment, nor am I recommending leniency; I am merely suggesting that we find and use alternative punishments that do no require uprooting individuals from their families and communities. Our society can definitely design a system of punishments that satisfy the goals of retribution, deterrence, and public safety while reducing the use of incapacitation.

I propose that low-level nonviolent offenders who have no history of felony offenses—violent or nonviolent—and whose damage is assessed at below a specified level,[80] should be given an automatic alternative sentence and should bypass prison altogether. These individuals should instead receive intermediate sanctions that are scaled to the severity of their offenses but that allow them to remain in their communities with their families. Rather than incapacitate low-level first-time nonviolent offenders, deny them the chance to contribute significantly to society through legitimate work, subject them to physical and psychologically dangerous conditions, expose them to other hardened criminals and opportunities to advance their criminal paths, and estrange them from their families, why not enable them to maintain their familial and legitimate social ties while also ensuring that they "pay for" their crimes fiscally and symbolically?

Some might wonder where the deterrent potential is if we eliminate prison for these low-level nonviolent offenders. Fines/restitution, intensive probation, and community service are only a few alternative sanctions that are possible to incorporate into a new system of alternative sanctions. Incarceration is not nor should it be the sole means of exacting retribution upon an individual. As mentioned before, some offenders have chosen prison over probation because the conditions of their probation are deemed harsher than incarceration. It is therefore possible to re-create punitive conditions within society that do not require full-time incarceration and that are less expensive than prison.

CONCLUSION

Certainly not all of the above changes can be evaluated, implemented, and assessed overnight, but I propose that we begin to take small steps that venture toward more cost-effective, safe, and equitable solutions. We must re-examine our priorities in sentencing and punishment, we must acknowledge what works and what does not, we must eliminate or reduce any emotional or retaliatory sentiments that unduly influence policy decisions, and we must explore alternatives to our current practices. We must make a committed and concerted effort—voters, taxpayers, politicians, policymakers, academics, and prison administrators alike—to prioritize fixing our correctional system, to reduce the number of people in our prisons, and to reverse the negative byproducts of our current policies. Only by taking these steps can we create a system that reduces the number of "Million Dollar Inmates" who drain our system of valuable resources without giving anything in return.

NOTES

1. See Pollock 1997.
2. Moyer 1974: 104.
3. Austin and Fabelo 2004: 20.
4. Women's Prison Association (WPA) 2003a.
5. Sevigny and Caulkins 2004: 401.
6. Ibid: 418.
7. Ibid: 420.
8. Ibid: 425.
9. Blumstein 2002: 478.
10. Ibid.
11. Austin and Fabelo 2004: 17.
12. Ibid.
13. Durose and Langan 2003b: 82.
14. Ibid: table 7.
15. Ibid: table 12.
16. McCarthy et al. 2001: 50.
17. BJA 1997.
18. BJS 2001b.
19. Carey and Finigan 2004: 3.
20. Huddleston 2005: 2.
21. McCarthy et al. 2001: 52.
22. U.S. General Accounting Office 1997 (cited in McCarthy et al. 2001: 53).
23. WPA 2003c.
24. The Sentencing Project 2004c.
25. Sabol and McGready 1999 (cited in The Sentencing Project 2004c: 1).
26. Ross and Richards 2002: 177.
27. Ambrosio and Schiraldi 1997.
28. Morris and Tonry 1990.
29. Ibid.
30. Lavine et al. 2001.
31. Tonry 1996: 100.
32. North Carolina Department of Corrections (NCDOC) 2002.
33. Lavine et al. 2001.
34. Ibid.
35. Ibid.
36. Ibid.
37. See Innovative Court Program 1995.
38. Morris and Tonry 1990: 111.
39. Ibid: 232.
40. Tonry 1996.
41. Clear and Braga 1995.
42. Ibid. See Petersilia 1987; Baumer and Mendelsohn 1990; Renzema and Skelton 1990.
43. See Austin and Hardyman 1991.

44. See Petersilia et al. 1992; Petersilia 1987; Tonry 1990.
45. McDevitt and Miliano 1992.
46. Clear and Braga 1995: 437.
47. See Latessa and Travis 1992 (cited in Clear and Braga 1995: 437).
48. Clear and Braga 1995: 444.
49. Morris and Tonry 1990: 240.
50. Stephan and Karberg 2003: table 1.
51. Ibid.
52. McCarthy et al. 2001.
53. Ibid: 103.
54. Crouch 2004.
55. Petersilia 1990 (cited in Crouch 2004: 46).
56. Crouch 2004: 55.
57. Ibid: 50.
58. McCarthy et al. 2001.
59. Petersilia 2002: 487.
60. Ibid: 489.
61. Ibid: 493.
62. Petersilia 2002.
63. Ehrlich 1981: 316.
64. National Center of Institutions and Alternatives (NCIA) 2003.
65. McCarthy et al. 2001: 113.
66. NCDOC 2002.
67. Morris and Tonry 1990.
68. Austin and Fabelo 2004: 19.
69. Ibid.
70. NCIA 2003: 3.
71. Ibid.
72. Sourcebook of Criminal Justice Statistics Online.
73. Kurki. 1999.
74. Kurki 1999.
75. Ibid.
76. McCarthy et al. 2001.
77. Ibid: 5.
78. Kurki 1999.
79. Ibid.
80. Devising a suitable figure naturally segues into a completely different discussion, one that must be considered carefully.

References

Adler, Patricia A. and Peter Adler. 2003. *Constructions of Deviance*, 4th edition. Belmont, CA: Wadsworth/Thomson Learning.

Administration for Children & Families [ACF]. 2002. "Major Provisions of the Personal Responsibility and Work Opportunity Reconciliation Act of 1996" (P.L. 104–93). Washington, DC: U.S. Department of Health & Human Services.

ACF. Fiscal Year 2001. "Characteristics and Financial Circumstances of TANF Recipients." Washington, DC: U.S. Department of Health & Human Services. Retrieved November 21, 2004 (http://www.acf.hhs.gov/programs/ofa/character/FY2001/characteristics.htm).

Ahn-Redding, Heather. 2005. "Learned Violence: Violent and Aggressive Behavior among Nonviolent Offenders in Prison." Ph.D. diss., American University.

Alcoholics Anonymous [AA]. 1972. "A Brief Guide to Alcoholics Anonymous." New York: Alcoholics Anonymous World Services, Inc.

Ambrosio, Tara-Jen and Vincent Schiraldi. 1997. "From Classrooms to Cell Blocks: A National Perspective." Washington, DC: Justice Policy Institute. Retrieved December 6, 2004 (http://www.justicepolicy.org).

American Friends Service Committee Report. 1971. *Struggle for Justice: A Report on Crime and Justice in America.* New York: Farrar, Straus & Giroux.

American Public Health Association. 1976. *Standards for Health Services in Correctional Institutions.* Washington, DC: American Public Health Association.

Andenaes, Johannes. 1974. *Punishment and Deterrence.* Ann Arbor: University of Michigan Press.

Aptheker, Bettina. 1971. "The Social Functions of the Prisons in the United States." Pp. 51–59 from *If They Come in the Morning*, edited by Angela Davis. Retrieved November 11, 2004 (http://www.prisonactivist.org/crisis/aptheker-prisons.html).

Austin, James and Tony Fabelo. 2004. "The Diminishing Returns of Increased Incarceration: A Blueprint to Improve Public Safety and Reduce Costs." Washington, DC: JFA Institute. Retrieved May 30, 2006 (http://www.nicic.org/Library/020130).

Austin, J. and P. Hardyman. 1991. "The Use of Early Parole with Electronic Monitoring to Control Prison Crowding: Evaluation of the Oklahoma Department of Corrections Pre-Parole Supervised Release with Electronic Monitoring." Unpublished report to the National Institute of Justice, U.S. Department of Justice.

Baldus, Pulaski and Woodworth. 1983. Cited by Donziger.

Barbash, Fred. January 12, 2005. "Supreme Court Says Federal Sentencing Guidelines Not Mandatory." Retrieved January 12, 2005 (http://www.washingtonpost.com/ac2/wp-dyn/A3336-2005Jan12?language=printer).

Bauer, Lynn and Steven D. Owens. 2004. "Justice Expenditure and Employment in the United States, 2001." NCJ 202792. Washington, DC: Bureau of Justice Statistics, U.S. Department of Corrections. Retrieved October 2004, 2007 (Http://www.ojp.usdoj.gov/bjs/pub/pdf/jeeusol.pdf

Baumer, T. and R. Mendelsohn. 1990. *The Electronic Monitoring of Non-violent Convicted Felons: An Experiment in Home Detention.* Final Report to the National Institute of Justice, U.S. Department of Justice.

Baunach, P. J. 1985. *Mothers in Prison.* New Brunswick, NJ: Transaction, Inc.

Beccaria, Cesare. 1918. *An Essay on Crimes and Punishment.* Philadelphia, PA: P. H. Nicklin.

Beck, Allen J., Jennifer C. Karberg, and Paige M. Harrison. 2002. "Prison and Jail Inmates at Midyear 2001." Washington, DC: Bureau of Justice Statistics, U.S. Department of Justice.

Beck, Allen and Paige Harrison. 2001. "Prisoners in 2000." Washington, DC: Bureau of Justice Statistics, U.S. Department of Justice.

Beck, Allen and Laura M. Maruschak. 2001. "Mental Health Treatment in State Prisons, 2000." Washington, DC: Bureau of Justice Statistics Special Report, U.S. Department of Justice.

Beck, Allen and Christopher Mumola. 1999. "Prisoners in 1998." Washington, DC: Bureau of Justice Statistics Special Report, U.S. Department of Justice.

Beck, Allen, Darrell Gilliard, Lawrence Greenfeld, Caroline Harlow, Thomas Hester, Louis Jankowski, Tracy Snell, James Stephan, and Danielle Morton. 1993. "Survey of State Prison Inmates, 1991." Washington, DC: Bureau of Justice Statistic, U.S. Department of Justice.

Becker, Gary S. 1968. "Crime and Punishment: An Economic Approach," *Journal of Political Economy* 76: 169–217.

Bedau, Hugo. 1993. "Justice and Punishment: Philosophical Basics," in *The Socio-Economics of Crime and Justice*, edited by Brian Forst. Armonk, NY: M. E. Sharpe.

Beiser, Vince. 2001. "How We Got to Two Million: How Did the Land of the Free Become the World's Leading Jailer?" July 10, 2001 from Mother Jones.com. Retrieved April 18, 2005 (http://www.motherjones.com/news/special_reports/prisons.overview.html).

Bender, Edwin. 2002. "A Contributing Influence: The Private-Prison Industry and Political Giving in the South." Helena, MT: National Institute on Money in State Policies.

Bennett, T. and R. Wright. 1984. *Burglars on Burglary.* Aldershot: Gower.

Bentham, Jeremy. 1962. "An Introduction to the Principles of Morals and Legislation," in *The Works of Jeremy Bentham*, edited by John Bowring. New York: Russell & Russell: Volume 1.

Beyleveld, D. 1980. *A Bibliography on General Deterrence*. Farnborough: Saxon House.

Beyleveld, D. 1979a. "Identifying, Explaining and Predicting Deterrence," *British Journal of Criminology* 19: 205–24.

Beyleveld, D. 1979b. "Deterrence Research as a Basis for Deterrence Policies," *Howard Journal of Criminal Justice* 18: 135–49.

Birmingham News. 2003. "Dying in prison." September 1, 2003. From *The Southern Center for Human Rights* website. Retrieved June 16, 2005 (http://www.schr.org/prisonsjails/newspaper%20articles/Limestone/news_limestone08bham.htm).

Blakely v. Washington, 542 U.S. 296 (2004).

Bloom, Paul N. and William D. Novelli. 1981. "Problems Applying Conventional Wisdom to Social Marketing Programs." Pp. 69–79 in *Government Marketing: Theory and Practice*, edited by Michael P. Mokwa and Steven E. Permut. New York: Praeger Publications, p. 69.

Bloom, Barbara and David Steinhart. 1993. *"Why Punish the Children?"* Oakland, CA: National Council on Crime and Delinquency.

Blumstein, Alfred. 2002. "Prisons: A Policy Challenge." Pp. 451–82 in *Crime*, edited by James Q. Wilson and Joan Petersilia. Oakland, CA: ICS Press.

Blumstein, Alfred. 2001. "Why Is Crime Falling—Or Is It?" Presentation on February 14, 2001, Washington, DC. Published in *Perspectives on Crime and Justice: 2000–2001 Lecture Series*, Volume 5, March 2002. Washington, DC: National Institute of Justice, U.S. Department of Justice.

Blumstein, Alfred, Jacqueline Cohen, and Daniel Nagin. 1978. *Deterrence and Incapacitation: Estimating the Effects of Criminal Sanctions on Crime Rates*. Washington, DC: National Academy Press.

Bobbitt, Mike and Marta Nelson. September 2004. "The Front Line: Building Programs that Recognize Families' Role in Reentry." New York: Vera Institute of Justice.

Bohm, Robert M. 2005. "'McJustice': On the McDonaldization of Criminal Justice." *Justice Quarterly* 23(1): 127–46.

Bonczar, Thomas P. 2003. "Prevalence of Imprisonment in the U.S. Population, 1974–2001, Special Report." Washington, DC: Bureau of Justice Statistics, U.S. Department of Justice. Retrieved June 8, 2006 (http://www.ojp.usdoj.gov/bjs/abstract/piusp01.htm).

Bonger, William. 1916. *Criminality and Economic Conditions*, abridged ed. Bloomington: Indiana University Press.

Bottoms, Anthony E. 1999. "Interpersonal Violence and Social Order in Prisons." Pp. 205–79 in *Prisons*, edited by Michael Tonry and Joan Petersilia. Chicago, IL: University of Chicago Press.

Bouffard, Jeffrey A., Doris Layton MacKenzie, and Laura J. Hickman. 2000. "Effectiveness of Vocational Education and Employment Programs for Adult Offenders: A Methodology-Based Analysis of the Literature." *Journal of Offender Rehabilitation* 31: 1–41.

Bourdieu, P. 1983. *"Forms of Capital."* From Handbook of Theory and Research for the Sociology of Education, edited by J. C. Richards. New York: Greenwood Press.

Bowker, Lee H. 1991. "The Victimization of Prisoners by Staff Members." Pp. 121–44 in *The Dilemmas of Corrections: Contemporary Readings*, edited by Kenneth C. Haas and Geoffrey P. Alpert. Prospect Heights, IL: Waveland Press, Inc.

Bowker, Lee H. 1982. "Victimizers and Victims and American Correctional Institutions." Pp. 63–76 in *The Pains of Imprisonment*, edited by Robert Johnson and Hans Toch. Prospect Heights, IL: Waveland Press, Inc.

Bowker, L.H. 1980. *Prison Victimization*. New York: Elsevier.

Bowker, L.H. 1979. "Victimization in Correctional Institutions: An Interdisciplinary Analysis." In *Theory and Research in Criminal Justice: Current Perspectives*, edited by J. A. Conley. Cincinnati, OH: Anderson.

Brehm, John and Wendy Rahn. 1997. "Individual-Level Evidence for the Causes and Consequences of Social Capital." *American Journal of Political Science* 41: 999–1023.

Brown, Jodi M. and Patrick A. Langan. 1999. "Felony Sentences in the United States, 1996." Bureau of Justice Statistics Bulletin, NCJ 175045. Washington, DC: Bureau of Justice Statistics, U.S. Department of Justice.

Brown, Jodi M., Darrell K. Gilliard, Tracy L. Snell, James J. Stephan, and Doris James Wilson. 1996. "Correctional Populations in the United States, 1994." NCJ 16009. Washington, DC: U.S. Department of Justice, Bureau of Justice Statistics. Retrieved December 7, 2004 (http://www.ojp.usdoj.gov/bjs/pub/pdf/cpius94.pdf).

Bureau of Justice Assistance [BJA]. 1998. "1996 National Survey of State Sentencing Structures." Washington, DC: Bureau of Justice Assistance, U.S. Department of Justice. Retrieved June 8, 2006 (http://www.ncjrs.gov/pdffiles/169270.pdf).

BJA. 1997. "Defining Drug Courts: The Key Components." Washington, DC: Bureau of Justice Assistance, Office of Justice Program, U.S. Department of Justice in collaboration with the National Association of Drug Court Professionals, Drug Court Standards Committee. Retrieved June 10, 2006 (http://www.ojp.usdoj.gov/BJA/grant/DrugCourts/DefiningDC.pdf).

Bureau of Justice Statistics [BJS] (website). 2006a. "Key Crime and Justice Facts at a Glance." Washington, DC: Bureau of Justice Statistics, U.S. Department of Justice. Retrieved May 22, 2006 (http://www.ojp.usdoj.gov/bjs/glance.htm#Crime).

BJS website. 2006b. "Criminal Victimization." Washington, DC: Bureau of Justice Statistics, U.S. Department of Justice. Retrieved May 22, 2006 (http://www.ojp.usdoj.gov/bjs/cvictgen.htm).

BJS 2006. "The Number of Adults in the Correctional Population has been Increasing." Washington, DC: Bureau of Justice Statistics, U.S. Department of Justice. Retrieved October 24, 2007. (http://www.ojp.usdoj.gov/bjs/glance/corr2.htm)

BJS website. 2005a. "Key Facts at a Glance: Incarceration Rate, 1980–2004." Washington, DC: Bureau of Justice Statistics, U.S. Department of Justice. Retrieved May 24, 2006 (http://www.ojp.usdoj.gov/bjs/glance/tables/incrttab.htm).

BJS website. 2005b. "Criminal Sentencing Statistics, Summary Findings." Washington, DC: Bureau of Justice Statistics, U.S. Department of Justice. Retrieved May 24, 2006 (http://www.ojp.usdoj.gov/bjs/sent.htm).

BJS website. 2005c. "Key Facts at a Glance: Suicide and Homicide Rates in State Prisons and Jails." Washington, DC: Bureau of Justice Statistics, U.S. Department of Justice. Retrieved May 30, 2006 (http://www.ojp.usdoj.gov/bjs/glance/tables/shipjtab.htm).

BJS website. 2004a. "Criminal Sentencing Statistics, Summary Findings." Washington, DC: Bureau of Justice Statistics, U.S. Department of Justice. Retrieved December 2, 2004 (http://www.ojp.usdoj.gov/bjs/sent.htm).

BJS website. 2004b. "Key Facts at a Glance: Direct Expenditures by Criminal Justice Function, 1982–2001." Washington, DC: Bureau of Justice Statistics, U.S. Department of Justice. Retrieved November 21, 2004 (http://www.ojp.usdoj.gov/bjs/glance/tables/exptyptab.htm).

BJS website. 2004c. "Key Facts at a Glance: Incarceration Rate, 1980–2003." Washington, DC: Bureau of Justice Statistics, U.S. Department of Justice. Retrieved December 6, 2004 (http://www.ojp.usdoj.gov/bjs/sent.htm).

BJS website. 2004d. "Key Facts at a Glance: National Crime Victimization Survey, Property Crime Trends, 1973–2003." Washington, DC: Bureau of Justice Statistics, U.S. Department of Justice. Retrieved December 7, 2004 (http://www.ojp.usdoj.gov/bjs/glance.tables/proptrdtab.htm).

BJS website. 2004e. "Key Facts at a Glance: National Crime Victimization Survey, Violent Crime Trends, 1973–2003." Washington, DC: Bureau of Justice Statistics, U.S. Department of Justice. Retrieved December 7, 2004 (http://www.ojp.usdoj.gov/bjs/glance.tables/viortrdtab.htm).

BJS website. 2004f. "Courts and Sentencing Statistics." Washington, DC: Bureau of Justice Statistics, U.S. Department of Justice. Retrieved December 10, 2004 (http://www.ojp.usdoj.gov/bjs/stssent.htm).

BJS website. 2004g. "Data for Analysis, State-Level Crime Trends Database: *Crime in 2002* and *Crime in 1980*." Washington, DC: Bureau of Justice Statistics, U.S. Department of Justice. Retrieved December 12, 2004 (http://bjsdata.ojp.usdoj.gov/dataonline/Search/Crime/State/StateCrime.cfm).

BJS website. June 2004h. "Data Collections for the Prison Rape Elimination Act of 2003." Status Report. Washington, DC: U.S. Department of Corrections. Retrieved December 14, 2004 (http://www.ncjrs.org).

BJS website. December 2004i. "Probation and Parole Statistics: Summary Findings." Washington, DC: Bureau of Justice Statistics, U.S. Department of Justice. Retrieved January 27, 2005 (http://www.ojp.usdoj.gov/bjs/pandp.htm).

BJS website. 2004j. "Key Facts at a Glance Demographic Trends in Jail Populations." Washington, DC: Bureau of Justice Statistics, U.S. Department of Justice. Retrieved January 31, 2005 (http://www.ojp.usdoj.gov/bjs/glance/tables/jailagtab.htm).

BJS website. 2004k. "Prison Statistics, Summary Findings." Washington, DC: Bureau of Justice Statistics, U.S. Department of Justice. Retrieved January 31, 2005 (http://www.ojp.usdoj.gov/bjs/prisons.htm).

BJS website. 2004l. "Homicide Trends in the U.S.: Age Trends." Washington, DC: Bureau of Justice Statistics, U.S. Department of Justice. Retrieved April 29, 2005 (http://www.ojp.usdoj.gov/bjs/homicide/teens.htm).

BJS website. 2004m. "Homicide Trends in the U.S.: Infanticide." Washington, DC: Bureau of Justice Statistics, U.S. Department of Justice. Retrieved April 29, 2005 (http://www.ojp.usdoj.gov/bjs/homicide/children.htm).

BJS website. 2004n. "Violent Crime Rates Have Declined since 1994, Reaching the Lowest Level Ever Recorded in 2003." Washington, DC: Bureau of Justice Statistics, U.S. Department of Justice. Retrieved May 2, 2005 (http://www.ojp.usdoj.gov/bjs/glance/viort.htm).

BJS website. 2004o. "Homicide Trends in the U.S.: Long Term Trends." Washington, DC: Bureau of Justice Statistics, U.S. Department of Justice. Retrieved May 22, 2006 (http://www.ojp.usdoj.gov/bjs/homicide/tables/totalstab.htm).

BJS. 2003. *Compendium of Federal Justice Statistics, 2001.* Washington, DC: U.S. Department of Justice: page 104, cited in *Sourcebook of Criminal Justice Statistics Online,* table 6.55. Retrieved November 21, 2004 (http://www.albany.edu/sourcebook/pdf/t655.pdf).

BJS. 2003b. *Key Facts at a Glance: Correctional Populations.* Downloaded from website. Washington, DC: Bureau of Justice Statistics, U.S. Department of Justice. Retrieved May 16, 2005 (http://www.ojp.usdoj.gov/bjs/glance/tables/corr2tab.htm).

BJS website. 2003c. "Reentry Trends in the US: Success Rates for State Parolees." Washington, DC: Bureau of Justice Statistics, U.S. Department of Justice. Retrieved December 6, 2004 (http://www.ojp.usdoj.gov/bjs/reentry/success.htm).

BJS website. 2003d. "Key Facts at a Glance: Number of Persons in Custody of State Correctional Authorities by Most Serious Offense, 1980–2001." Washington, DC: Bureau of Justice Statistics, U.S. Department of Justice. Retrieved December 7, 2004 (http://www.ojp.usdoj.gov/bjs/glance/tables/corrtyptab.htm).

BJS. 2002a. "Correctional Populations in the United States, 1998." Washington, DC: Bureau of Justice Statistics, U.S. Department of Justice.

BJS. 2002b. *Trends in Justice Expenditure and Employment.* NCJ 178278. Washington, DC: Bureau of Justice Statistics, U.S. Department of Justice. (http://www.ojp.usdoj.gov.bjs.data.eetrnd11.wk1).

BJS. 2001a. *Trends in State Parole, 1990–2000,* Special Report. Washington, DC: U.S. Department of Justice: p. 6. Cited in *Sourcebook of Criminal Justice Statistics 2002,* page 505, Table 6.37.

BJS website. 2001b. *Court Organization Statistics.* Washington, DC: Bureau of Justice Statistics, U.S. Department of Justice. Retrieved June 10, 2006 (http://www.ojp.usdoj.gov/bjs/courts.htm).

BJS. 2000a. "Incarcerated Parents and Their Children," Special Report NCJ 182335. Washington, DC: Bureau of Justice Statistics, U.S. Department of Justice. Cited in *Sourcebook of criminal justice statistics 2002,* p. 504, table 6.36.

BJS. 2000b. "Correctional Populations in the United States, 1997." NCJ 177613 Washington, DC: Bureau of Justice Statistics, U.S. Department of Justice. Retrieved December 7, 2004 (http://www.ojp.usdoj.gov/bjs/pub/pdf/cpus97.pdf).

BJS. 1999. *Special Report: Women Offenders.* Washington, DC: Bureau of Justice Statistics, U.S. Department of Justice.

BJS. 1982. *Prisoners in Year-end Annual: 1925–1981.* Bulletin NCJ-85861. Washington, DC: Bureau of Justice Statistics, U.S. Department of Justice. Retrieved from Paper Only Publications website June 6, 2006 (http://www.ojp.usdoj.gov/bjs/paperonly.htm).

Bursik, R. and H. Grasmick. 1993. *Neighborhoods and Crime.* New York: Lexington.

Bushway, Shawn and Peter Reuter. 2002. "Labor Markets and Crime." Pp. 191–224 in *Crime,* edited by James Q. Wilson and Joan Petersilia. Oakland, CA: ICS Press.

Bushway, Shaw. 2000. "The Stigma of a Criminal History Record in the Labor Market." In *Building Violence: How America's Rush to Incarcerate Creates More Violence,* edited by J. P. May. Thousand Oaks, CA: Sage.

California Department of Corrections and Rehabilitation [CDCR]. 2006. "Weekly Report of Population as of May 10, 2006." Sacramento, CA: Offender Information Services Branch, Estimates and Statistical Analysis Section, Data Analysis Unit. Retrieved May 16, 2006 (http://www.corr.ca.gov/ReportsResearch/OffenderInfo Services/WeeklyWed/TPOP1A/TPOP1Ad060510.pdf).

California Department of Corrections and Rehabilitation [CDCR]. 2005. "Second and Third Strikers in the Adult Institution Population." Sacramento, CA: Offender Information Services Branch, Estimates and Statistical Analysis Section, Data Analysis Unit. Retrieved April 3, 2006 (http://www.cya.ca.gov/ReportsResearch/docs/Quarterly/Strike1/STRIKE1d0512.pdf).

California Department of Corrections [CDC]. 2004a. "Characteristics of Felon New Admissions and Parole Violators Returned with a New Term, Calendar Year 2003." Department of Corrections Policy and Evaluation Division, Offender Information Services Branch, Estimate and Statistical Analysis Section, Data Analysis Unit, Sacramento, Reference Number ACHAR-1. Retrieved September 22, 2004 (http://www.corr.ca.gov/OffenderInfoServices/Reports/Annual/ACHAR1/ACHAR 1d2003.pdf).

California Department of Corrections [CDC]. 2004b. "Facts and Figures, Third Quarter 2004." Retrieved September 22, 2004 (http://www.corr.ca.gov/Communications Office/facts_figures.asp).

California Department of Corrections [CDC]. June 30, 2004c. "Second and Third Strikers in the Institution Population." Department of Corrections, Policy and Evaluation Division, Offender Information Services Branch, Estimates and Statistical Analysis Section, Data Analysis Unit, Sacramento, CA. Retrieved September 23, 2004 (http://www.corr.ca.gov/offenderInforServices/Reports/OffenderInformation .asp).

California Department of Corrections [CDC]. December 2003. "Inmate Incidents in Institutions, Calendar Year 2002." Reference Number BEII-1. Sacramento, CA. Policy and Evaluation Division.

California Department of Corrections [CDC]. December 31, 2001. "Second and Third Strikers in the Institution Population." Department of Corrections, Policy and Evaluation Division, Offender Information Services Branch, Estimates and Statistical Analysis Section, Data Analysis Unit, Sacramento, CA. Retrieved September 23, 2004 (http://www.corr.ca.gov/offenderInforServices/Reports/Quarterly/Strike1d0212.pdf).

Camp, George and Camille Camp. 1992–2001. *The 1992–2001 Corrections Yearbook.* Middletown, CT: Criminal Justice Institute.

Camp, Camille Graham and George M. Camp. 1999. *The Corrections Yearbook, 1998.* Middletown, CT: Criminal Justice Institute.

Camp and Camp cited in McCorkle, Richard C., Terrance D. Miethe, and Kriss A. Drass. 1995. "The Roots of Prison Violence: A Test of the Deprivation, Management, and 'Not-So-Total' Institutional Models." *Crime and Delinquency* 41: 317.

Carey, Shannon and Michael Finigan. 2003. "A Detailed Cost Analysis in a Mature Drug Court Setting: A Cost-Benefit Evaluation of the Multnomah County Drug Court." Portland, OR: NPC Research. Prepared for Office of Research and Evaluation, National Institute of Justice.

Castellano, Thomas and Irina Soderstrom. 2004. "Self-Esteem, Depression, and Anxiety Evidenced by a Prison Inmate Sample: Interrelationships and Consequences for Prison Programming." Pp. 63–81 in *The Inmate Prison Experience*, edited by Mary Stohr and Craig Hemmens. Upper Saddle River, NJ: Pearson Education, Inc.

Centers for Disease Control and Prevention [CDC]. 2004. "Sexual Violence Surveillance: Uniform Definitions and Recommended Data Elements." National Center for Injury Prevention and Control. Retrieved June 16, 2005 (http://www.cdc.gov/ncipc/pub-res/sv_surveillance/sv.htm).

Centers for Disease Control and Prevention [CDC]. 2001. "Providing Services to Inmates Living with HIV." Retrieved online June 16, 2005 (http://www.thebody.com/cdc/services.html).

Chaffee, Steven H. 1975. "The Diffusion of Political Information." Pp. 85–128 in *Political Communication: Issues and Strategies for Research*, edited by Steven Chaffee. Beverly Hills, CA: Sage Publications, p. 86.

Chesney-Lind, Meda (ed.). 2002. "Imprisoning Women: The Unintended Victims of Mass Imprisonment." Pp. 79–94 in *Invisible Punishment: The Collateral Consequences of Mass Incarceration*, edited by Marc Mauer and Meda Chesney-Lind. New York: New Press.

Clark, John, James Austin, and D. Alan Henry. 1997. "'Three Strikes and You're out': A Review of State Legislation." *Exhibit 1. Comparison of Washington and California Strikes Laws*, p. 2. Washington, DC: National Institute of Justice, U.S. Department of Justice.

Clarke, R. G. V. and P. Mayhew (eds.). 1980. *Designing Out Crime*. London: HMSO.

Clear, Todd R. 1996. "Backfire: When Incarceration Increases Crime." *Journal of the Oklahoma Criminal Justice Research Consortium* 3(2): 1–10. Retrieved June 6, 2006 (http://www.doc.state.ok.us/DOCS/OCJRC/Ocjrc96/Ocjrc7.htm).

Clear, Todd R. and Anthony A. Braga. 1995. "Community Corrections." Pp. 421–44 in *Crime*, edited by James Q. Wilson and Joan Petersilia. San Francisco, CA: ICS Press.

CNN. 2001. "In-Depth Specials: Are U.S. Schools Safe?" Cable News Network. Retrieved May 22, 2006 (http://www.cnn.com/SPECIALS/1998/schools/).

Cohen, Stanley. 2002. *Folk Devils and Moral Panics: Thirtieth Anniversary Edition*. London: Routledge.

Coleman, James S. 1990. *Foundations of Social Theory*. Cambridge, MA: Harvard University Press.

Coleman, James S. 1988. "Social Capital in the Creation of Human Capital," in "Issue Supplement: Organizations and Institutions: Sociological and Economic Approaches to the Analysis of Social Structure," *American Journal of Sociology* 94: S95–S120. Retrieved November 23, 2001 (http://www.jstor.org).

Cook, Philip, Donna Slawson, and Lori Gries. 1993. "The Costs of Processing Murder Cases in North Carolina." Terry Sanford Institute of Public Policy, Duke University. Retrieved November 21, 2004 (http://www-pps.aas.duke.edu/people/faculty/cook/comnc.pdf).

Cook, P. J. 1980. "Research in Criminal Deterrence: Laying the Groundwork for the Second Decade." *Crime and Justice: An Annual Review of Research* 2: 211–68.

Cooper, Colin and Sinead Berwick. 2001. "Factors affecting psychological well-being of three groups of suicide-prone prisoners." *Current Psychology: Developmental, Learning, Personality, Social* 20: 2. Abstract. Retrieved October 2001, Available: PsycInfo.

Cormier, B., M. Kennedy, and M. Sendbuehler. 1967. "Cell Breakage and Gate Fever." *British Journal of Criminology* 7: 317–24.

Couturier, Lance and Frederick R. Maue. 2000. "Suicide Prevention Initiatives in a Large Department of Corrections: A Full-Court Press to Save Lives," *Jail Suicide/ Mental Health Update*. National Center on Institutions and Alternatives. Retrieved October 2001 (http://www.nicanet.org).

Cox, Verne C., Paul B. Paulus, and Garvin McCain. 1984. "Prison Crowding Research: The Relevance for Prison Housing Standards and a General Approach Regarding Crowding Phenomena." *American Psychologist*, 39: 10. Abstract. Retrieved October 2001. Available: PsycInfo.

Crawford, Krysten. 2004. "Martha: I cheated no one: Lifestyle diva invokes Mandela as she, ex-broker prepare to appeal 5-month sentences." Retrieved from CNN Money, November 8, 2005 (http://money.cnn.com/2004/07/16/news/newsmakers/martha_sentencing/).

Cromwell, P .F., J. N. Olson, and D. W. Avary. 1991. *Breaking and Entering: An Ethnographic Analysis of Burglary*. Newbury Park, CA: Sage.

Crouch, Ben. 2004. "Is Incarceration Really Worse? Analysis of Offenders' Preferences for Prison over Probation." Pp. 45–62 in *The Inmate Prison Experience*, edited by Mary Stohr and Craig Hemmens. Upper Saddle River, NJ: Pearson Education, Inc.

Crouch, Ben. 1993. "Is Incarceration Really Worse? Analysis of Offenders' Preferences for Prisoner Protection," *Justice Quarterly* 10(1): 67–68.

Cullen, Francis. 2002. "Rehabilitation and Treatment Programs." Pp. 253–89 in *Crime*, edited by Wilson and Petersilia. Oakland, CA: ICS Press.

Cunniff, M. and M. Shilton. 1991. *Variations on Felony Probation: Persons under Supervision in 32 Urban and Suburban Counties*. Washington, DC: United States Department of Justice.

Davis, Kenneth Culp. 1969. *Discretionary Justice: A Preliminary Inquiry*. Baton Rouge: LSU Press.

Dawson, J. 1990. *Felony Probation in State Courts*. Washington, DC: National Institute of Justice, U.S. Department of Justice.

Dear, Greg E., Donald Thomson, and Adelma M. Hills. 2000. "Self-Harm in Prison: Manipulators Can Also Be Suicide Attempters." *Criminal Justice and Behavior* 27: 2. Retrieved October 2001 (http://www.ncianet.org).

Death Penalty Information Center [DPIC]. Website: www.deathpenaltyinfo.org.

Department of Health and Human Services [DHH]. 1997. "Major Provisions of the Personal Responsibility and Work Opportunity Reconciliation Act of 1996." Retrieved May 11, 2005 (http://library.findlaw.com/1997/Apr/28/130301.html).

Dexter, Polly and Graham Towl. 1995. "An Investigation into Suicidal Behaviours in Prison." *Issues in Criminological and Legal Psychology* 22. Abstract. Retrieved October 2001. Available: PsycInfo.

Deyoung, Mary. 2003. "Moral Panics." Pp. 160–68 in *Constructions of Deviance*, eds. Patricia A. Adler and Peter Adler. Belmont, CA: Wadsworth/Thomson Learning.

Dieter, Richard. March 27, 2003. "The Costs of the Death Penalty." Testimony of Richard C. Dieter, Executive Director, Death Penalty Information Center to the Joint Committee on Criminal Justice, Legislature of Massachusetts. Retrieved November 15, 2004 (http://www.deathpenaltyinfo.org/MassCostTestimony.pdf).

DiIulio, John J. 1987. *Governing Prisons*. New York: Free Press.

Ditton, Paula M. and Doris J. Wilson. 1999. "Bureau of Justice Statistics Special Report: Truth in Sentencing." Washington, DC: Bureau of Justice Statistics Special

Report, U.S. Department of Justice. Retrieved October 23, 2002 (http://www.ojp.usdoj.gov/bjs/pub/pdf/tssp.pdf).

Donziger, Steven R. 1996. *The Real War on Crime: The Report of the National Criminal Justice Commission*. New York: Harper Perenial.

Dooley, Enda. 1997. "Prison suicide—politics and prevention: A view from Ireland." *Crisis* 18: 4. Abstract. Retrieved October 2001. Available: PsycInfo.

Dubois, W. E. B. 1903. *The Souls of Black Folk*. Dover Publications.

Duff, Anthony and David Garland. 1998. "Introduction." Pp. 1–43 in *A Reader on Punishment*, edited by Duff and Garland. Oxford: Oxford University Press.

Dunlop, Burton D., Max B. Rothman, and Gretchen M. Hirt. 2001. "Elders and Criminal Justice: International Issues for the 21st Century." *International Journal of Law and Psychiatry* 24: 285–303.

Durkheim, Émile. 2003. "The Normal and the Pathological." Pp. 55–59 in *Constructions of Deviance*, 4th edition, edited by Adler and Adler. Belmont, CA: Wadsworth/Thomson Learning.

Durkheim, Émile. 1938. *The Rules of Sociological Method*. Translated by S. A. Solovay and J. H. Mueller. Chicago: University of Chicago Press. Translation of 1895a (1901c). Edited with Introduction by G. E. G. Catlin.

Durkheim, Émile. 1933 [1883]. *The Division of Labor in Society*. Translated by George Simpson. New York: Free Press.

Durose, Matthew R. and Patrick A. Langan. 2005. "State Court Sentencing of Convicted Felons, 2002: Statistical Tables." Washington, DC: Bureau of Justice Statistics, U.S. Department of Justice.

Durose, Matthew R. and Christopher J. Mumola. 2004. "Profile of Nonviolent Offenders Exiting State Prisons." Washington, DC: Bureau of Justice Statistics, U.S. Department of Justice.

Durose, Matthew R. and Patrick A. Langan. 2004. "Felony Sentences in State Courts, 2002." Washington, DC: Bureau of Justice Statistics, U.S. Department of Justice. Retrieved May 24, 2006 (http://www.ojp.usdoj.gov/bjs/abstract/fssc02.htm).

Durose, Matthew R. and Patrick A. Langan. 2003a. "Felony Sentences in State Courts, 2000." NCJ 198821. Washington, DC: Bureau of Justice Statistics, U.S. Department of Justice. Retrieved May 24, 2006 (http://www.ojp.usdoj.gov/bjs/pub/pdf/fssc00.pdf).

Durose, Matthew R. and Patrick A. Langan. 2003b: 8. "State Court Sentencing of Convicted Felons, 2000, Sentencing Tables." NCJ 198822. Washington, DC: U.S. Department of Justice. Retrieved December 10, 2004 (www.ojp.usdoj.gov/bjs/abstract/scsc00st.htm).

Durose, Matthew R., David J. Levin, and Patrick A. Langan. 2001. "Felony Sentences in State Courts, 1998." Washington, DC: U.S. Department of Justice.

Economic Policy Institute. 2005. "Minimum Wage, Frequently Asked Questions." Economic Policy Institute. Retrieved June 8, 2005 (http://www.epinet.org/content.cfm/issueguides_minwage_minwagefaq).

Ehlers, Scott, Vincent Schiraldi, and Eric Lotke. 2004. "An Examination of the Impact of California's Three Strikes Law on African-Americans and Latinos." Washington, DC: Justice Policy Institute (http://www.justicepolicy.org/reports/Racial%20Divide.pdf).

Ehrlich, Isaac. 1981. "On the Usefulness of Controlling Individuals: An Economic Analysis of Rehabilitation, Incapacitation and Deterrence." *American Economic Review* 71: 3.

Ehrlich, Isaac. 1977. "Capital Punishment and Deterrence: Some Further Thoughts and Additional Evidence." *Journal of Political Economy* 85: 4.

Ehrlich, Isaac. 1975. "The Deterrent Effect of Capital Punishment: A Question of Life and Death." *American Economic Review* 65: 397.

Ellis, Ralph D. and Carol S. Ellis. 1989. *Theories of Criminal Justice.* Wolfeboro, NH: Longwood Academic.

Erikson, Kai. 2003. "On the Sociology of Deviance." Pp. 11–18 in *Constructions of Deviance*, 4th edition, edited by Adler and Adler. Belmont, CA: Wadsworth/Thomson Learning.

Erikson, Kai. 1966. *Wayard Puritans.* New York: Macmillan Publishing Company.

Estelle v. Gamble, 97 S. Ct. 285, 291 (1976).

Etzioni, Amitai. 1988. *The Moral Dimensions: Toward a New Economics.* New York: Free Press.

Families to Amend California's Three Strikes [FACTS] website. "California Sentence by Offense by 2- and 3-Strike Laws as of December 31, 2002." Chart from *FACTS: Families to Amend California's Three Strikes* website. (http://www.facts1.com/ThreeStrikes/Stats/).

FACTS. "Sex, Age, Race and other breakdowns as of December 31, 2002." Chart from *FACTS: Families to Amend California's Three Strikes* website. (http://www.facts1.com/ThreeStrikes/Stats/).

Fagan, Jeffrey. 1994. "Do criminal sanctions deter crimes?" In *Drugs and Crime: Evaluating Public Policy Initiatives*, edited by Doris Layton MacKenzie and Craig Uchida. Thousand Oaks, CA: Sage Publications.

Faggins, Barbara. 2001. "Temple University Study Shatters Theory on Neighborhood Decline and Criminal Behavior." Temple University Office of News and Media Relations. Online article.

Families Against Mandatory Minimums (FAMM). 2005 (Winter). "The Case Against Mandatory Sentences." Retrieved October 24, 2007 (http://www.famm.org/Resources/BrochuresandPublications.aspx).

FAMM. "*FAMM primer on mandatory sentencing.*" Retrieved May 24, 2006 (http://www.famm.org/pdfs/Primer.pdf).

FAMM. 2002a. "Justice on Trial: Racial Disparities in the American Criminal Justice System, Leadership Conference on Civil Rights" and "Leadership Conference Education Fund," p. v, both cited in *Race and Mandatory Sentencing.* 2002. From Families against Mandatory Minimums Foundation website. (http://www.famm.org).

FAMM. 2002b. "Punishment and Prejudice: Racial Disparities in the War on Drugs, Human Rights Watch 2000," pg. 10, cited in *Race and Mandatory Sentencing.* From Families against Mandatory Minimums Foundation website. (http://www.famm.org).

FAMM. 2002c. "Women in Prison, Issues and Challenges Confronting, U.S. Correctional Systems," GAO/GGD-00-22, 1999, p. 2. cited in *Race and Mandatory Sentencing.* From Families against Mandatory Minimums Foundation website. (http://www.famm.org.).

Farrigan, Tracey L. and Amy K. Glasmeier. n.d. "The Economic Impacts of the Prison Development Boom on Persistently Poor Rural Places." Poverty in America Project, Pennsylvania State University. Retrieved June 6, 2006 (http://www.povertyinamerica.psu.edu/products/publications/prison_development/prison_development.pdf).

Farrington, D. P. and P. A. Langan. 1992. "Changes in Crime and Punishment in England and America in the 1980s." *Justice Quarterly* 9: 5–46.

Farrington, D. P., P. A. Langan, and P. O. Wikström. 1994. "Changes in Crime and Punishment in America, England and Sweden between the 1980s and 1990s." *Studies in Crime and Crime Prevention* 3: 104–31.

Federal Bureau of Investigation [FBI]. 2006. "Crime in the United States 2004, Property Crime." Washington, DC: Federal Bureau of Investigation, U.S. Department of Justice. Retrieved June 7, 2006 (http://www.fbi.gov/ucr/cius_04/offenses_reported/property_crime/index.html).

Federal Bureau of Prisons [FBOP] [Online]. September 9, 2003. Washington, DC: Federal Bureau of Prisons, U.S. Department of Justice. Cited in *Sourcebook of Criminal Justice Statistics 2002*, p. 516, table 6.54 (http://www.bop.gov/fact0598.html).

Feig, Christy. 2002. "Study explores high cost of HIV care in U.S." *CNN Medical Unit, CNN.com*. Retrieved online June 16, 2005 (http://archives.cnn.com/2002/HEALTH/conditions/07/10/aids.costs/).

Feldman, Lisa, Vincent Schiraldi and Jason Ziedenberg. 2006. "Too Little Too Late: President Clinton's Prison Legacy." Washington, DC: Justice Police Institute. Retrieved October 25, 2007 (http://www.justicepolicy.org/content.php?hmID=1811&smID=1581#a157).

Fellner, Jamie and Marc Mauer. October 1998. "Losing the Vote: The Impact of Felony Disenfranchisement Laws in the United States." Human Rights Watch and The Sentencing Project, updated by The Sentencing Project. Retrieved December 14, 2004 (http://www.hrw.org/reports98/vote/).

Felthaus, Alan R. 1997. "Does 'isolation' cause jail suicides?" *Journal of the American Academy of Psychiatry and the Law* 25: 3. Abstract. Retrieved October 2001. Available: PsycInfo.

Fernandez v. United States (941 F. 2d 1488 [11th Cir. 1991]).

Fields, Gary. 2005a. "Arrested Development: After Prison Boom, A Focus on Hurdles Faced by Ex-Cons." *Wall Street Journal*, Tuesday, May 24, 2005: p. A1. Retrieved June 6, 2006 (http://www.mindfully.org/Reform/2005/After-Prison-Boom-WSJ24may05.htm).

Fields, Gary. 2005b. "Over 400 Cases Returned for Possible Sentencing." *Wall Street Journal*. January 25, 2005: p. A2. Retrieved May 25, 2006 (http://www.nacdl.org/public.nsf/mediasources/20050125a).

Fields, Gary. December 2, 2004. "In Drug Sentences, Guesswork Often Plays Heavy Role." *Wall Street Journal*, Vol. CCXLIV No. 108: A1, column 1.

Fisher, Bonnie. 1993. "Community Responses to Crime and Fear of Crime." Pp. 177–207 in *The Socio-Economics of Crime and Justice*, edited by Brian Forst. Armonk, NY: M. E. Sharpe, Inc.

Fleiser, Mark. S. 1989. *Warehousing Violence*. Newbury Park, CA: Sage Publications.

Florida Department of Corrections website. n.d. Budget Summary (FY 2003–04). Retrieved October 24, 2007 (http://www.dc.state.fl.us/pub/annual/0304/budget.html).

Florida Corrections Commission [Florida]. 1999. "Florida Corrections Commission *1999 Annual Report.*" Tallahassee: Florida Corrections Commission, Retrieved October 8, 2001 (http://www.fcc.state.fl.us/fcc/reports/final99/ap5-6.html).

Food & Nutrition Service. 2004. "Food Stamp Program Participation and Costs." Washington, DC: United States Department of Agriculture. Retrieved November 21, 2004 (http://www.fns.usda.gov/pd/fssummar.htm).

Forst, Brian. 2004. *Errors of Justice: Nature, Sources and Remedies.* Cambridge, UK: Cambridge University Press

Forst, Brian. 1995. "Prosecution and Sentencing." Pp. 363–86 in *Crime,* edited by James Q. Wilson and Joan Petersilia. San Francisco, CA: ICS Press, p. 376.

Forst, Brian (ed.). 1993. *The Socio-Economics of Crime and Justice.* Armonk, NY: M. E. Sharpe.

Foucault, Michael. 1979. *Discipline and Punish.* New York: Random House, Inc.

Frankel, Marvin. 1974. *Criminal Sentences: Law without Order.* New York. Hill & Wang.

Freeman, Kristy, Donald Hines, and Joe Salter. 2005. "Adult Correctional Systems," Report submitted to the Fiscal Affairs and Governmental Operations Committee, Southern Legislative Conference, Council of State Governments. Retrieved April 11, 2005 (http://www.slcatlanta.org/Publications/cdrs/2005/2005_CDR_CORRECTIONS/2005_CDR_Corrections_pt1.pdf).

Freeman, Kristy, John J. Hainkel, Jr., and Charles W. DeWitt, Jr. 2002. "Adult Correctional Systems," Report submitted to the Fiscal Affairs and Governmental Operations Committee, Southern Legislative Conference, Council of State Governments. Retrieved April 11, 2005 (http://www.slcatlanta.org/Publications/cdrs/2002/2002CDRCorrections.pdf).

Frieden, Terry. October 2005. "FBI: Violent Crime Rate Declines Again." Article from CNN.com Law Center. Retrieved April 25, 2006 (http://www.cnn.com/2005/LAW/10/17/crime.rate/index.html).

Friedman, Lawrence M. 1993. *Crime and Punishment in American History.* New York: Basic Books.

Fukuyama, Francis. 1999. *The Great Disruption.* New York: Touchstone.

Fukuyama, Francis. 1995. *Trust.* New York: Free Press.

Fulwiler, Carl, Catherine Forbes, Susan L. Santangelo, and Marshall Folstein. 1997. "Self-Mutilation and Suicide Attempt: Distinguishing Features in Prisoners." *Journal of the American Academy of Psychiatry and the Law* 25: 1. Abstract. Retrieved October 2001. Available: PsycInfo.

Gaes, Gerald G., Timothy Flanagan, Laurence L. Motiuk, and Lynn Stewart. 1999. "Adult Correctional Treatment." Pp. 361–426 from *Prisons,* edited by Michael Tonry and Joan Petersilia. Chicago: University of Chicago Press.

Gainsborough, Jenni and Marc Mauer. 2000. *Diminishing Returns: Crime and Incarceration in the 1990s.* Washington, DC: The Sentencing Project.

Gallagher, Elaine M. 2001. "Elders in prison: Health and well-being of older inmates." *International Journal of Law and Psychiatry* 24: 325–33.

Georgia Department of Corrections [GDOC]. 2004. "Fiscal Year 2003 Annual Report." Retrieved October 26, 2007. (http://www.dcor.state.ga.us/Reports/Annual/AnnualReport.html).

Gibbons, Don C. 2004. "The Limits of Punishment as Social Policy." Pp. 289–303 in *Public Policy, Crime, and Criminal Justice*, 3rd ed., edited by Barry W. Hancock and Paul M. Sharp. Upper Saddle River, NJ: Prentice Hall.

Gibbs, J. P. 1975. *Crime, Punishment and Deterrence.* New York: Elsevier.

Gillard, Darrell K. 1999. "Prison and Jail Inmates at Midyear 1998." NCJ 173414 Washington, DC: Bureau of Justice Statistics, U.S. Department of Justice. Retrieved December 7, 2004 (http://www.ojp.usdoj.gov/bjs/pub/pdf/pjim98.pdf).

Gilligan, James. 1996. *Violence: Our Deadly Epidemic and Its Causes.* New York: G. P. Putnam's Sons.

Glassner, Barry. 1999. *The Culture of Fear.* New York: Basic Books.

Glaze, Lauren E. and Seri Palla. 2005. "Probation and Parole in the United States, 2004." Washington, DC: Bureau of Justice Statistics, U.S. Department of Justice. May 24, 2006 (http://www.ojp.usdoj.gov/bjs/pub/pdf/ppus04.pdf).

Glaze, Lauren E. and Seri Palla. 2004. "Probation and Parole in the United States, 2003." Washington, DC: Bureau of Justice Statistics, U.S. Department of Justice. Retrieved December 7, 2004 (http://www.ojp.usdoj.gov/bjs/pub/pdf/ppus03.pdf).

Goffman, Erving. 1961. *Asylums: Essays on the Social Situation of Mental Patients and Other Inmates.* New York: Anchor.

Gottfredson, Stephen D. and Sean McConville. 1987. "Introduction." Pp. 3–11 in *American's Correctional Crisis: Prison Populations and Public Policy*, edited by Stephen D. Gottfredson and Sean McConville. New York: Greenwood Press.

Greco, Rozann. *The Future of Aging in New York State, Briefs: Older Prisoners.* Project 2015: New York State Office for the Aging. Retrieved February 2, 2003 (http://aging.state.ny.us/explore/project2015/briefOP.pdf).

Greenberg, David F. 1981. "Theft, Rationality and Deterrence Research." Department of Sociology, New York University, July 1974 (unpublished, prepared for presentation at the 1975 Annual Meeting of the American Sociological Association).

Greenfield, Lawrence A. and Tracy L. Snell. 1999. "Women Offenders." Washington, DC: Bureau of Justice Statistics.

Hagan, John. "The Next Generation: Children of Prisoners." Downloaded from Family and Corrections Network website (http://www.fcnetwork.org/). Retrieved December 19, 2004 (http://www.doc.state.ok.us/DOCS/OCJRC/Ocjrc96/Ocjrc19.htm).

Hall, Richard A. Spurgeon. 1999. *The Ethical Foundations of Criminal Justice.* Boca Raton, FL: CRC Press.

Hagan John and Ronit Dinovitzer. 1999. "Collateral Consequences of Imprisonment for Children, Communities, and Prisoners." Pp. 121–62 in *Prisons*, edited by Michael Tonry and Joan Petersilia. Chicago: University of Chicago Press.

Hall, Richard, A. Spurgeon, Carolyn Dennis, and Tere Chipman. 2000. *The Ethical Foundations of Criminal Justice.*

Haney, Craig. 2006. "Mental Health Issues in Long-Term Solitary and 'Supermax' Confinement." Pp. 47–71 in *Behind Bars: A Readings on Prison Culture*, edited by Richard Tewksbury. Upper Saddle River, NJ: Pearson Prentice Hall.

Haney, Craig. 2003. "The Psychological Impact of Incarceration: Implications for Postprison Adjustment." In *Prisoners Once Removed: The Impact of Incarceration and Reentry on Children, Families, and Communities*, edited by Jeremy Travis and Michelle Waul (33–66). Washington, DC: Urban Institute Press.

Hanifan, L. J. 1920. *The Community Center*, Boston: Silver Burdett.

Hanifan, L. J. 1916. "The Rural School Community Center." *Annals of the American Academy of Political and Social Science* 67: 130–38.

Harer, Miles D. and Neal P. Langan. 2001. "Gender Differences in Predictors of Prison Violence: Assessing the Predictive Validity of a Risk Classification System." *Crime and Delinquency* 47(4): 513–36. Retrieved March 2003 (http://www.bop.gov/orepg/oreprharer.pdf).

Harris, David. 1987. "'Driving While Black' and All Other Traffic Offenses: The Supreme Court and Pretextual Traffic Stops." *Journal of Criminal Law and Criminology* 87 Issue 2 (Winter 1997): 562.

Harrison, Paige and Allen J. Beck. 2006. "Prison and Jail Inmates at Midyear 2005." Washington, DC: Bureau of Justice Statistics, U.S. Department of Justice. Retrieved May 30, 2006 (http://www.ojp.usdoj.gov/bjs/prisons.htm).

Harrison, Paige and Allen J. Beck. 2005. "Prisoners in 2004." Washington, DC: Bureau of Justice Statistics Bulletin, U.S. Department of Justice. Retrieved April 20, 2005 (http://www.ojp.usdoj.gov/bjs/prisons.htm).

Harrison, Paige and Allen J. Beck. 2004. "Prisoners in 2003." Washington, DC: Bureau of Justice Statistics Bulletin, U.S. Department of Justice. Retrieved November 15, 2004 (http://www.ojp.usdoj.gov/bjs/prisons.htm).

Harrison, Paige and Allen J. Beck. 2003. "Prisoners in 2002." Washington, DC: Bureau of Justice Statistics Bulletin, U.S. Department of Justice. Retrieved May 30, 2006 (http://www.ojp.usdoj.gov/bjs/prisons.htm).

Harrison, Paige and Jennifer C. Karberg. 2003. "Prison and Jail Inmates at Midyear 2002." Washington, DC: Bureau of Justice Statistics, U.S. Department of Justice. Retrieved May 30, 2006 (http://www.ojp.usdoj.gov/bjs/prisons.htm).

Harrison, Paige M. and Allen J. Beck. 2002. "Bureau of Justice Statistics Bulletin: Prisoners in 2001." Washington, DC: Bureau of Justice Statistics, United States Department of Justice. Retrieved May 30, 2006 (http://www.ojp.usdoj.gov/bjs/prisons.htm).

Hatsukami, Dorothy and Marian W. Fischman. November 26, 1996. "Crack Cocaine and Cocaine Hydrochloride: Are the Differences Myth or Reality?" cited in "*Crack vs. Powder Cocaine Sentencing.*" 2002. From Families against Mandatory Minimums Foundation website (http://www.famm.org).

Hayes. Lindsay M. 1995. "Prison Suicide: An Overview and Guide to Prevention." Washington, DC: US. Department of Justice. Retrieved October 2001 (http://www.ncic.org/pubs/1995/012475.pdf).

Heney, Jan and Connie M. Kristiansen. 1997. "An Analysis of the Impact of Prison on Women Survivors of Childhood Sexual Abuse." *Women and Therapy* 20: 4. Abstract. Retrieved October 2001. Available: PsycInfo.

Henshel, Richard L. and Sandra H. Carey. 1975. "Deterrence, Deviance, and Knowledge of Sanctions." Pp. 54–73 in *Perceptions in Criminology,* edited by Richard L. Henshel and Robert A. Silverman. New York: Columbia University Press, pp. 59–60.

Holden, Ronald R., James D. Mendonca, and Ralph C. Serin. 1989. "Suicide, Hopelessness, and Social Desirability: A Test of an Interactive Model." *Journal of Consulting and Clinical Psychology* 57: 4. Abstract. Retrieved October 2001. Available: PsycInfo.

Honderich, Kiaran. 2003. "The Real Cost of Prisons for Women and Their Children, Background Paper." The Real Cost of Prisons Project, p. 1. Retrieved June 8, 2006 (http://www.realcostofprisons.org/papers.html).

Hughes, Graham. 1993. "Limits of Legal Sanctions." Pp. 51–61 in *The Socio-Economics of Crime and Justice,* edited by Brian Forst. Armonk, NY: M. E. Sharpe, Inc.

Hughes, Timothy and Doris James Wilson. 2003. "Reentry Trends in the United States," from Bureau of Justice Statistics website. Washington, DC: Bureau of Justice Statistics, U.S. Department of Justice. (http://www.ojp.usdoj.gov/bjs/reentry/reentry.htm#highlights).

Human Rights Watch [HRW]. 2004. "No Second Chance: People with Criminal Records Denied Access to Public Housing." Retrieved May 11, 2005 (http://hrw.org/reports/2004/usa1104/usa1104.pdf).

HRW. 2000. "Supermax Prisons: An Overview," from *Out of Sight HRW Briefing Paper on Supermaximum Prisons.* Retrieved November 11, 2004 (http://www.hrw.org/reports/2000/supermax/Sprmx002.htm).

HRW. 1991 (February). *Prison Conditions in the United States: A Human Rights Watch Report.* New York: Author.

Huddleston, C. West. 2005. "Drug Courts: An Effective Strategy for Communities Facing Methamphetamine." Washington, DC: Bureau of Justice Assistance, Office of Justice Program, U.S. Department of Justice.

Innovative Court Program: Results from State and Local Program Workshops. 1995. State of Connecticut's alternative incarceration program. Online at (www.ncjrs.org/txtfiles/portland.txt).

International Centre for Prison Studies [ICPS]. *World Prison Brief.* Data collected from website. Retrieved May 9, 2005 (http://www.kcl.ac.uk/depsta/rel/icps/worldbrief/world_brief.html). (emailed for permission to use statistics: icps@kcl.ac.uk)

ICPS. 2005. *Entire World—Prison Population Totals.* Retrieved May 9, 2005 (http://www.kcl.ac.uk/depsta/rel/icps/worldbrief/highest_to_lowest_rates.html).

ICPS. 2003. *Entire World—Prison Population Totals.* Retrieved December 8, 2004 (http://www.kcl.ac.uk/depsta/rel/icps/worldbrief/highest_to_lowest_rates.php).

Irwin, John, Vincent Shiraldi, and Jason Ziedenberry. 1999. "America's One-Million Nonviolent Prisoners." Washington, DC: Justice Policy Institute. Retrieved December 6, 2004 (http://www.justicepolicy.org/article.php?id=300).

Ivanoff, Andre, Sung Joon Jang, and Nancy J. Smyth. 1996. "Clinical risk factors associated with parasuicide in prison." *International Journal of Offender Therapy and Comparative Criminology* 40: 2. Abstract. Retrieved October 2001. Available: PsycInfo.

Jacobs, Jane. 1961. "The Death and Life of American Cities." New York: Vintage

Janis, I. L. 1969. *Stress and Frustration.* New York: Harcourt Brace Javonovich.

Johnson, Robert. April 1, 2002. Personal Interview at American University, Washington, DC.

Johnson, Robert. 2002. *Hard Time: Understanding and Reforming the Prison,* 3rd Edition. New York: Wadsworth Publishing.

Johnson, Robert and Hans Toch (eds). 1988. *The Pains of Imprisonment.* Prospect Heights, IL: Waveland Press, Inc.

Jones, Richard P. 2001. "Not All at Supermax Are 'Real Bad Actors.'" *Milwaukee Journal Sentinel,* October 21, 2001. Retrieved online June 2, 2005 (http://www.prisoncentral.org/Prisoncentral/Supermax.htm).

JPI. 2000. "The Punishing Decade: Prison and Jail Estimates at the Millennium." Washington, DC: Justice Policy Institute. Retrieved December 6, 2004 (http://www.justicepolicy.org).

Karberg, Jennifer C. and Allen J. Beck. 2004. "Trends in U.S. Correctional Populations: Findings from the Bureau of Justice Statistics," presented at the National Committee on Community Corrections. Washington, DC, April 16, 2004.

Katz, Pamela Covington. September/October 1998. "Supporting Families and Children of Mothers in Jail: An Integrated Child Welfare and Criminal Justice Strategy." *Child Welfare League of America* 2028 (5).

Keilitz, Ingo. 2000. "Standards and Measures of Court Performance," Abstract. In *Measurement and Analysis of Crime and Justice* 4: 559–93.

Kentucky Department of Corrections. 2001. *Recidivism in 1996–1998*. Frankfort: Kentucky Department of Corrections.

Kessler, Daniel and Steven Levitt. 1999. "Using Sentence Enhancements to Distinguish between Deterrence and Incapacitation." *Journal of Law and Economics* 17(1): 343–63.

King, Ryan Scott and Marc Mauer. 2006. "Sentencing with Discretion: Crack Cocaine Sentencing after *Booker*." Washington, DC: The Sentencing Project. Retrieved May 25, 2006 (http://www.sentencingproject.org/pdfs/crackcocaine-afterbooker.pdf).

King, Ryan Scott, Marc Mauer, and Tracy Huling. 2004. "An Analysis of the Economics of Prison Siting in Rural Communities." *Criminology and Public Policy* 3(3): 453–80.

King, Ryan S. and Marc Mauer. 2001. "Aging Behind Bars: 'Three Strikes' Seven Years Later." Washington, DC: The Sentencing Project: 2 (http://www.sentencingproject.org).

Kleiman, Mark A. R. 2004. "Toward (More Nearly) Optimal Sentencing for Drug Offenders." *Criminology and Public Policy* 3(3): 435–40.

Kurki, Leena. 1999. "Incorporating Restorative and Community Justice into American Sentencing and Corrections," No. 3 in *Sentencing and Corrections Issues for the 21st Century*. Washington, DC: National Institute of Justice, U.S. Department of Justice. (Papers from the Executive Sessions on Sentencing and Corrections).

Kupers, Terry A. 1996. "Trauma and Its Sequelae in Male Prisoners: Effects of Confinement, Overcrowding, and Diminished Services." *American Journal of Orthopsychiatry* 66: 2. Abstract. Retrieved October 2001, Available: PsycInfo.

Langan, P. A. and D. P. Farrington. 1998. *Crime and Justice in the United States and England and Wales, 1981–1996*. Washington, DC: Bureau of Justice Statistics, U.S. Department of Justice.

Langan, Patrick and Helen A. Graziadei. 1995. "Felony Sentences in State Courts, 1992." Washington, DC: Bureau of Justice Statistics, U.S. Department of Justice.

Latessa, Edward, Francis T. Cullen, and Paul Gendreau. 2006. "Beyond Correctional Quackery—Professionalism and the Possibility of Effective Treatment." Pp. 358–71 in *Behind Bars: Readings on Prison Culture*, edited by Richard Tewksbury. Upper Saddle River, NJ: Pearson Prentice Hall.

Latessa, E. and L. Travis. 1992. "Residential Community Correctional Programs." In *Smart Sentencing: The Emergence of Intermediate Sanctions*, edited by J. Byrne, A. Lurigio, and J. Petersilia. Newbury Park, CA: Sage.

Lavine, Ashira, Ben Lozowski, Heidi Powell, Maria Sivillo, and Katharine Traeger. 2001. *"Issues in Maryland Sentencing*—The Impact of Alternative Sanctions on Prison Populations.*"* Published by the Maryland State Commission on Criminal Sentencing Policy. Retrieved online May 23, 2005 (http://www.msccsp.org/publications/issues_altsanctions.html).

Lawrence, Sarah and Daniel P. Mears. 2004. "Benefit-Cost Analysis of Supermax Prisons: Critical Steps and Considerations." Policy Brief. Washington, DC: Justice Policy Center, Urban Institute.

Lederman, Daniel, Norman Loayza, and Ana Maria Menendez. 2000. Draft: "Violent Crime: Does Social Capital Matter?": Abstract. *Economic Development and Cultural Change*, vol. 4, Issue 3 (April), 509–39.

Lemgruber, Julita. 2004. "The Brazilian Prison System: A Brief Diagnosis." Online article. Retrieved June 2, 2005 (http://www.uoregon.edu/~caguirre/lembruger_brazil.pdf).

Lester, David. 1990. "Overcrowding in Prisons and Rates of Suicide and Homicide" *Perceptual and Motor Skills* 71: 1. Abstract. Retrieved October 2001. Available: PsycInfo.

Levinson, R. B. 1998. *Unit Management in Prisons and Jails*. Lanham, MD: American Correctional Association.

Levitt, Steven D. 2002. "Deterrence." Pp. 435–50 in *Crime*, edited by James Q. Wilson and Joan Petersilia. Oakland, CA: ICS Press.

Levitt, Steven D. 1998. "Juvenile Crime and Punishment." *Journal of Political Economy* 106: 1156–85.

Lewis, D. 1986. "The General Deterrent Effect of Longer Sentences," *British Journal of Criminology* 26: 47–62.

Lilly, J. Robert, Francis T. Cullen, and Richard A. Ball. 1995. *Criminology Theory, Context and Consequences, 2nd ed*. Thousands Oaks, CA: Sage Publications.

Lipsey, Mark W. and David B. Wilson. 1993. "The Efficacy of Psychological, Educational, and Behavioral Treatment." *American Psychologist* 48: 1181–209.

Lipton, D. S., F. S. Pearson, C. Cleland, and D. Yee. 1998. "Synthesizing Correctional Treatment Outcomes: Preliminary Findings from CDATE." New York: National Development and Research Institutes.

Lipton, D. S., R. Martinson, and J. Wilks. 1975. *The Effectiveness of Correctional Treatment: A Survey of Treatment Valuation Studies*. New York: Praeger.

Lockwood, Daniel. 1991. "Target Violence." Pp. 87–104 in *The Dilemmas of Corrections: Contemporary Readings*, edited by Kenneth C. Haas and Geoffrey P. Alpert. Prospect Heights, IL: Waveland Press, Inc.

Lockwood, Daniel. 1978. *Sexual Aggression among Male Prisoners*. Ann Arbor, MI: University Microfilms.

Loftin, C., M. Heumann, and D. McDowall. 1983. "Mandatory Sentencing and Firearms Violence: Evaluating an Alternative to Gun Control," *Law and Society Review* 17: 287–318.

Loftin, C. and D. McDowall. 1984. "The Deterrent Effects of the Florida Felony Firearm Law." *Journal of Criminal Law and Criminology* 75: 250–59.

Logan, Charles H. 1993. "Criminal Justice Performance Measures for Prisons." Pp. 19–58 in *Performance Measures for the Criminal Justice System*, edited by BJS-Princeton Project. Washington, DC: U.S. Department of Justice.

Losel, Friedrich. 1995. "The Efficacy of Correctional Treatment: A Review and Synthesis of Meta-Evaluations." In *What Works: Reducing Reoffending*, edited by James McGuire, 79–111. West Sussex, UK: John Wiley.

Lubitz, Robin L. and Thomas W. Ross. 2001. "Sentencing Guidelines: Reflections on the Future." Washington, DC: U.S. Department of Justice, Retrieved October 9, 2001 (http://www.ncjrs.org/txtfiles1/nij/186480.txt)

Lynch, James. 1995. "Crime in International Perspective." Pp. 11–38 in *Crime*, edited by James Q. Wilson and Joan Petersilia. San Francisco, CA: ICS Press

Lyons, William and Stuart Scheingold. 2000. "The Politics of Crime and Punishment," from *Criminal Justice 2000, Volume 1*. Washington, DC: National Institute of Justice, U.S. Department of Justice. Retrieved June 5, 2006 (http://www.ncjrs .gov/criminal_justice2000/vol_1/02c.pdf).

Macallair, Daniel and Chuck Terry. 2000. "Drug Policy and California's Prison Population." San Diego Union Tribune. Reported by Center on Juvenile and Criminal Justice. Retrieved May 16, 2006 (http://www.cjcj.org/press/drug_policy.html).

MacKenzie, Doris Layton. 2000. "Evidence-Based Corrections: Identifying What Works." *Crime and Delinquency* 46: 457–71.

Madden, Helen T., Louis F. Rossiter, and Dexter F. Klock. 2003. "Survey of the Older Inmate Population in Virginia and Its Budget Implications." *For the House Appropriations Committee Retreat*, November 19, 2003. Williamsburg, VA: Center for Excellence in Aging and Geriatric Health and the College of William and Mary. Retrieved January 25, 2005 (http://hac.state.va.us/Committee/OtherPresentations/ 2003/November_18-19_Retreat/OlderInmatePopulation—Color.pdf).

Mansbridge, Jane. 1990. *Beyond Self-Interest*. Chicago: University of Chicago Press.

Martinson, Robert. 1979. "New Findings, New Views: A Note of Caution Regarding Sentencing Reform." *Hofstra Law Review* 7: 243–58.

Martinson, Robert. 1974. "What Works?—Questions and Answers about Prison Reform." *The Public Interest* 35.

Maruschak, Laura. 2004. "HIV in Prisons and Jails, 2002." NCJ 205333. Washington, DC: Bureau of Justice Statistics, U.S. Department of Justice. Retrieved December 15, 2004 (http://www.ojp.usdoj.gov/bjs/pub/pdf/hivpj02.pdf).

Maruschak, Laura. 2002. "HIV in Prisons and Jails, 2000." NCJ 205333. Washington, DC: Bureau of Justice Statistics, U.S. Department of Justice.

Maruschak, Laura and Allen J. Beck. 2001. *Medical Problems of Inmates, 1997*. Washington, DC: U.S. Department of Justice. Retrieved January 27, 2005 (http://www .ojp.usdoj.gov/bjs/pub/pdf/mpi97.pdf).

Mauer, Marc and Meda Chesney-Lind (eds.). 2002. "Introduction." Pp. 1–12 from *Invisible Punishment: The Collateral Consequences of Mass Incarceration*, edited by Marc Mauer and Meda Chesney-Lind. New York: New Press.

Mauer, Marc, Ryan S. King, and Malcolm C. Young. 2004a. *The Meaning of "Life": Long Prison Sentences in Context*. The Sentencing Project cited in "Record Number of 'Lifers' Now in U.S. Prisons." July 2004. *Prison Legal News* 15(7).

Mauer, Marc, Ryan S. King, and Malcolm C. Young. May 2004b. *The Meaning of "Life": Long Prison Sentences in Context*. The Sentencing Project. Washington, DC. Retrieved December 6, 2004 (http://www.sentencingproject.org/pdfs/lifers .pdf).

Mauer, Marc. 1999. *Race to Incarcerate, The Sentencing Project*. New York: New Press.

McCarthy, Belinda Rodgers, Bernard J. McCarthy, Jr., and Matthew C. Leone. 2001. *Community-Based Corrections*, 4th edition. Belmont, CA: Wadsworth/Thomas Learning.

McCorkle, Richard C., Terrance D. Miethe, and Kriss A. Drass. 1995. "The Roots of Prison Violence: A Test of the Deprivation, Management, and "Not-So-Total" Institutional Models." *Crime and Delinquency* 41: 317–31.

McCorkle, Richard C. 1992. "Personal Precautions to Violence in Prison." *Criminal Justice and Behavior* 19: 160–73.

McCorkle, Lloyd W. 1976. "Social Structure in a Prison: An Analysis of the Guard's Function and His Relationship to the Inmate." Pp. 204–8 in *The Sociology of Correctional Management*, edited by D. A. Jones and C. M. Jones. New York: MSS Information Corp.

McDevitt, J. and R. Miliano. 1992. "Day Reporting Centers: An Innovative Concept in Intermediate Sanctions." In *Smart Sentencing: The Emergence of Intermediate Sanctions*, edited by J. Byrne, A. Lurigio, and J. Petersilia. Newbury Park, CA: Sage.

McDonald, Douglas C. 1999. "Medical Care in Prisons." Pp. 427–78 in *Prisons*, edited by Michael Tonry and Joan Petersilia. Chicago: University of Chicago Press.

McDowall, D., C. Loftin, and B. Wiersema. 1992. "A Comparative Study of the Preventive Effects of Mandatory Sentencing Laws for Gun Crimes." *Journal of Criminal Law and Criminology* 83(2): 378–94.

McGinnis, Kenneth and James Austin. 2001. *Texas Board of Pardons and Paroles Guidelines Project*. Texas Board of Pardons and Paroles, Austin, Texas.

McNally, Joel. 1999. "Superwaste, or Why We Built a Prison for People Already in Prison." *Shepherd Express*, September 9, 1999. Retrieved June 2, 2005 (http://www.PrisonCentral.org).

McRee, Joseph. 1997. "Crime and Development: Do Crime Rates Influence the Location of Neighborhood Crime Watch Groups?" *Planning Forum*, p. 31.

Mears, Daniel P. and Jamie Watson. 2006. "Towards a Fair and Balanced Assessment of Supermax Prisons." *Justice Quarterly* 25(2): 232–70.

Merlo, Alida. 1997. "The Crisis and Consequences of Prison Overcrowding." Pp. 52–83 in *Prisons, Today and Tomorrow*, edited by J. Pollock. Gaithersburg, MD: Aspen Publishers, Inc.

Milwaukee Journal Sentinel. 2001. "103 at Supermax weren't sentenced for violence." Associated Press, *Milwaukee Journal Sentinel*, November 17, 2001.

Mokwa, Michael P. and Steven E. Permut. 1981. "Preface." Pp. xiii–xvi in *Government Marketing: Theory and Practice*, edited by Michael P. Mokwa and Steven E. Permut. New York: Praeger Publications.

Morenoff, Jeffrey, Robert J. Sampson, and Stephen W. Raudenbush. 2001 (revised). "Neighborhood Inequality, Collective Efficacy, and the Spatial Dynamics of Urban Violence." *Revised Version of Conference Paper*. Report No. 00-451. Population Studies Center at the Institute for Social Research, University of Michigan.

Morton, Joann B. and N. C. Jacobs. 1992. *An Administrative Overview of the Older Inmate*. Washington, DC: National Institute of Corrections, Federal Bureau of Prisons, U.S. Department of Justice.

Morris, Norval. 1993. "The Honest Politician's Guide to Sentencing Reform." Pp. 303–10 in *The Socio-Economics of Crime and Justice*, edited by Brian Forst. Armonk, NY: M. E. Sharpe, p. 306.

Morris, Norval and Michael Tonry. 1990. *Between Prison and Probation: Intermediate Punishments in a Rational Sentencing System*. Oxford: Oxford University Press.

Moyer, Lloyd K. 1974. "The Mentally Abnormal Offender in Sweden: An Overview and Comparison with American Law." *American Journal of Comparative Law* 22(1): 71–106. Retrieved from JSTOR on May 18, 2005 (http://www.jstor.org).

Mumola, Christopher J. 2000. "Incarcerated Parents and Their Children." Washington, DC: Bureau of Justice Statistics, U.S. Department of Justice.

Mumola, Christopher. 1999. "Substance Abuse and Treatment, State and Federal Prisoners, 1997." Washington, DC: Bureau of Justice Statistics, U.S. Department of Justice.

Myers, B., T. Smarsh, K. Hagen, and S. Kennon. 1999. "Children of Incarcerated Mothers." *Journal of Child and Family Studies* 8(1): 11–25.

Nacci, Peter L. and Thomas Kane. 1983. "The Incidence of Sex and Sexual Aggression in Federal Prisons." *Federal Probation* 47(4): 31–36.

Nagin, D. S. 1998. "Criminal Deterrence Research at the Outset of the Twenty-first Century." *Crime and Justice: A Review of Research* 23: 51–91.

National Center on Institutions and Alternatives [NCIA]. 2003. "Elderly Study." Baltimore, MD: National Center on Institutions and Alternatives. Retrieved December 20, 2004 (http://www.ncianet.org/genpubs/cfm).

National Coalition on Health Care. 2004. "Health Insurance Coverage." Retrieved online June 16, 2005 (http://www.nchc.org/facts/coverage.shtml).

National Institute of Corrections [NIC]. 2004a. "Supermax Prisons and the Constitution, Liability Concerns in the Extended Control Unit." Washington, DC: National Institute of Corrections, Federal Bureau of Prisons, U.S. Department of Justice.

NIC. 2004b. "Correctional Health Care, Addressing the Needs of Elderly, Chronically Ill, and Terminally Ill Inmates." February 2004. National Institute of Corrections, Federal Bureau of Prisons, U.S. Department of Justice.

NIC. 1997. "Supermax Housing: A Survey of Current Practice." *Special Issues in Corrections*. Washington, DC: National Institute of Corrections, Federal Bureau of Prisons, U.S. Department of Justice.

NBC Universal website: "Law and Order." (http://www.nbc.com/Law_&_Order/about/index.html).

Neeley, Connie L., Laura Addison, and Delores Craig-Moreland. 1997. "Address the Needs of Elderly Offenders." *Corrections Today* 59(5): 120–23.

Newman v. State, 12 Crim. L. Rptr. 2113 [M.D. Ala. 1972].

North Carolina Department of Corrections [NCDOC]. 2002. "Research Bulletin," Issue No. 44, February 21, 2002. Office of Research and Planning.

Office of Juvenile Justice and Delinquency Prevention [OJJDP]. 1994. *Balanced and Restorative Justice, Program Summary*. Washington, DC: Office of Juvenile Justice and Delinquency Prevention.

Office of Management and Budget [OMB]. 2004. *The Budget of the United States Government, Fiscal Year 2005*. [CD-ROM] (Washington, DC: USGPO): Table 24–12, table adapted by *Sourcebook of Criminal Justice Statistics Online* staff. Retrieved November 21, 2004 (http://www.albany.edu/sourcebook/pdf/t110.pdf).

OMB. "Assistance for Low-Income Families." Washington, DC: Executive Office of the President. Retrieved November 21, 2004 (http://www.whitehouse.gov/omb/pdf/low-income.pdf).

OMB. 2004a. "Education." Washington, DC: Executive Office of the President. Retrieved November 21, 2004 (http://www.whitehouse.gov/omb/pdf/education .pdf).

Office of National Drug Control Policy [ONDCP]. 2001. "Fact Sheet: Drug Treatment in the Criminal Justice System." Washington, DC: Office of National Drug Control Policy, Executive Office of the President. Retrieved May 19, 2006 (http:// www.whitehousedrugpolicy.gov/publications/factsht/treatment/index.html #credits).

Oregon Department of Corrections. May 2000. "Children of Incarcerated Parents Survey."

Ostrom, Elinor. 1998. "A Behavioral Approach to Rational Choice Theory of Collective Action, Presidential Address, American Political Science Association, 1997." *American Political Science Review* 92: 1–22.

Parent, Dale, Terence Dunworth, Douglas McDonald, and William Rhodes. 1997. "Key Legislative Issues in Criminal Justice: Mandatory Sentencing," U.S. Dept. of Justice, NIJ. Washington, DC: National Institute of Justice, U.S. Department of Justice.

Parent, Dale, Terence Dunworth, Douglas McDonald, and William Rhodes. 1996. "Key Legislative Issues in Criminal Justice: The Impact of Sentencing Guidelines." Washington, DC: National Institute of Corrections, Federal Bureau of Prisons, U.S. Department of Justice.

Parisi, Nicolette. 1982. "The Prisoner's Pressures and Responses." Pp. 9–24 in *Coping with Imprisonment*, edited by Nicolette Parisi. Beverly Hills, CA: Sage Publications.

Parke, Ross and K. Alison Clarke-Stewart. 2002. "Effects of Parental Incarceration on Young Children." Paper produced for "From Prison to Home" Conference funded by U.S. Department of Health and Human Services, January 30–31, 2002. Retrieved December 19, 2004 (http://www.fcnetwork.org/reading/parke_Parental Incarceration.pdf).

Paternoster, R. 1987. "The Deterrent Effect of the Perceived Certainty and Severity of Punishment." *Justice Quarterly* 4: 173–217.

Pennsylvania Department of Corrections [DOC]. *Elderly Inmate Profile.* Statistics: Briefing Papers. Retrieved January 25, 2005 (http://www.hawaii.edu/hivandaids/ PA_DOC_Elderly_Inmate_Profile.pdf).

Petersilia, Joan. 2002. "Community Corrections." Pp. 483–508 in *Crime,* edited by James Q. Wilson and Joan Petersilia. Oakland, CA: ICS Press, 483.

Petersilia, Joan, J. Peterson, and S. Turner. 1992. *Intensive Probation and Parole: Research Findings and Policy Implications.* Santa Monica, CA: Rand.

Petersilia, Joan. 1990. "When Probation Becomes More Dreaded Than Prison." *Federal Probation* (March): 23–27.

Petersilia, Joan. 1987. *Expanding Options for Criminal Sentencing.* Santa Monica, CA: Rand.

Phillips, Llad. 1993. "Economic Perspectives on Criminality." Pp. 37–49 in *The Socio-Economics of Crime and Justice,* edited by Brian Forst. Armonk, NY: M.E. Sharpe, Inc.

Pierce, G. L. and W. J. Bowers. 1981. "The Bartley-Fox Gun Law's Short-Term Impact on Crime in Boston." *Annals of the American Academy of Political and Social Science* 455: 120–32.

Piliavin, Irving, Rosemary Gertner, Craig Thornton, and Ross L. Matsueda. 1986. "Crime, Deterrence, and Rational Choice." *American Sociological Review* 51: 1.

Pollock, Jocelyn. 2004. *Prisons and Prison Life, Costs and Consequences.* Los Angeles, CA: Roxbury Publishing.

Pollock, Jocelyn. 1997. *Prisons, Today and Tomorrow,* edited by J. Pollock. Gaithersburg, MD: Aspen Publishers, Inc.

Prison Legal News. "FCC Cracks Down on Prison Phones." Cited on *The November Coalition* website (http://www.november.org/razorwire/rzold/14/1409.html).

Prison Legal News. "Law Suits Challenge Prison Phone Rates. Suit Filed in Illinois" and "Phone Rates Challenged in KY, MO, IN and AZ," Seattle, WA. Cited on *The November Coalition* website (http://www.november.org/razorwire/rzold/14/1409 .html).

Putnam, Robert D. 2000. *Bowling Alone: The Collapse and Revival of American Community.* New York: Simon & Schuster.

Pyle, Kevin and Craig Gilmore. 2005. "How Prisons Are Paid For (and Who Really Pays?)." Chart from Paying the Price. Washington, DC: The Real Cost of Prisons Project: An Activity of The Sentencing Project. Retrieved July 26, 2005 (http://www.realcostofprisons.org/papers.html).

Reiman, Jeffrey. 1998. *The Rich Get Richer and the Poor Get Prison,* 5th edition. Needham Heights, MA: Allyn and Bacon.

Reinarman, Craig. 2003. "The Social Construction of Drug Scares." Pp. 137–148 in *Constructions of Deviance,* 4th edition, edited by Adler and Adler. Belmont, CA: Wadsworth/Thomson Learning.

Reisig, Michael. 1998. "Rates of Disorder in Higher-Custody State Prisons: A comparative Analysis of Managerial Practices." *Crime and Delinquency* 4: 229 43.

Rengert, G. and T. Wasilchick. 1985. *Suburban Burglary.* Springfield, IL: Thomas.

Rennison, Callie. 2002. "Criminal Victimization 2001, Changes 2000–2001 with Trends, 1993–2001." Washington, DC: Bureau of Justice Statistics, U.S. Department of Justice.

Renzema, M. and D. Skelton. 1990. *The Use of Monitoring by Criminal Justice Agencies in 1989.* Final Report to the National Institute of Justice, U.S. Department of Justice.

Ritzer, George. 2004. *The McDonaldization of Society.* Thousand Oaks, CA: Pine Forge Press.

Riveland, Chase. 1999. "Supermax Prisons: Overview and General Considerations." Washington, DC: Bureau of Justice Statistics, U.S. Department of Justice. Retrieved May 13, 2005 (http://www.nicic.org/pubs/1999/014937.pdf).

Roberts, Julian V. and Loretta J. Stalans. 1999. "Public Opinion, Crime, and Criminal Justice." Boulder, CO: Westview Press.

Rodgers, Leslie N. 1995. "Prison suicide: Suggestions from Phenomenology." *Deviant Behavior* 16: 2. Abstract. Available: PsycInfo.

Rosenbaum, Dennis, Dan Lewis, and Jane Grant. 1986. "Neighborhood-Based Crime Prevention: Assessing the Efficacy of Community Organizing in Chicago." In *Community Crime Prevention: Does It Work?* Edited by Dennis P. Rosenbaum. Beverly Hills, CA: Sage Publications.

Ross, Jeffrey Ian and Stephen C. Richards. 2002. *Behind Bars, Surviving Prison.* Indianapolis, IN: Alpha Books.

Ross, H. L. 1992. *Confronting Drunk Driving.* New Haven, CT: Yale University Press.

Ross, H. Laurence. 1973. "Law, Science and Accidents: The British Road Safety Act of 1967." *Journal of Legal Studies* 2: 1.

Rotman, E. 1998. "Beyond Punishment." Pp. 284–305 in *A Reader on Punishment,* edited by Anthony Duff and David Garland. Oxford: Oxford University Press.

Rubenstein, Gwen and Debbie Mukamal. 2002. "Welfare and Housing—Denial of Benefits to Drug Offenders." Pp. 37–49 in *Invisible Punishment: The Collateral Consequences of Mass Incarceration,* edited by Marc Mauer and Meda Chesney-Lind. New York: New Press.

Sabol, W. J. and J. McGready. 1999. *Time Served in Federal Prison by Federal Offenders, 1986–1997.* Washington, DC: Bureau of Justice Statistics, U.S. Department of Justice.

Sack, W. H., J. Seidler, and S. Thomas. 1976. "The Children of Imprisoned Parents: A Psychosocial Exploration." *American Journal of Prothopsychiatry* 46: 618–28.

Saegert, Susan, Gary Winkel, and Charles Swartz. 2002. "Social Capital and Crime in New York City's Low-Income Housing." *Housing Policy Debate* 13(1): 189–226. Fannie Mae Foundation.

Sampson, Robert J. 2002. "The Community." Pp. 225–52 in *Crime,* edited by James Q. Wilson and Joan Petersilia. Oakland, CA: ICS Press.

Sampson, R. J., S. W. Raudenbush, and F. Earls. 1997. "Neighborhoods and Violent Crime: A Multilevel Study of Collective Efficacy." *Science* 277: 918–24.

Santos, Michael. 2004. *About Prisons.* Belmont, CA: Wadsworth/Thomson Learning.

Sarat, Austin. 2001. "When the State Kills." Princeton, NJ: Princeton University Press.

Sarre, Rick. 1999. *Beyond "What Works?": A 25 Year Jubilee Retrospective of Robert Martinson.* Paper presented at the History of Crime, Policing and Punishment Conference convened by the Australian Institute of Criminology in conjunction with Charles Sturt University and held in Canberra, 9–10 December 1999.

Schiarldi, Vincent and Jason Ziedenberg. 2002. "Cellblocks or Classrooms?: The Funding of Higher Education and Corrections and It's Impact on African American Men." Washington, DC: Justice Policy Institute. Retrieved October 25, 2007 (http://www.justicepolicy.org/content.php?hmID=1811&smID=1581#a157).

Schiraldi, Vincent. 2001. "Hype Skews our View of Youth Violence." *Times Union,* March 14, 2001, Albany, NY. Cited by the Center on Juvenile and Criminal Justice Press Room. San Francisco, CA. Retrieved March 31, 2005 (http://www.cjcj.org/press/hype_skews.html).

Schlosser, Eric. 1998. "The Prison-Industrial Complex." *Atlantic Monthly.* Retrieved June 6, 2006 (http://www.csus.edu/soc/kwehr/teach/soc255/pdf/schlosser.pdf)/

Schmalleger, Frank. 2007. *Criminal Justice Today: An Introductory Text for the Twenty-First Century,* 9th edition. Upper Saddle River, NJ: Pearson Prentice Hall.

Schulhofer, Stephen J. 1993. "Rethinking Mandatory Minimums." *Wake Forest Law Review* 28: 207.

Senate Bill 133. December 2002. "Children of Incarcerated Parents Project." Report to the Oregon Legislature on Senate Bill 133. Retrieved December 19, 2004 (http://www.fcnetwork.org/reading/chips-report.pdf).

Senna, Joseph J. and Larry J. Siegel. 2002. *Introduction to Criminal Justice,* 9th ed. Belmont, CA: Wadsworth/Thomson Learning.

Sevigny, Eric L. and Jonathan P. Caulkins. 2004. "Kingpins or Mules: An Analysis of Drug Offenders Incarcerated in Federal and State Prisons." *Criminology and Public Policy* 3(3): 401–34.

Seymour, Cynthia. 1999. "Children with Incarcerated Parents: A Fact Sheet." Child Welfare League of America. (http://www.cwla.org/programs/incarcerated/initiative summary.htm).

Seymour, Cynthia. 1998. "Children with Parents in Prison: Child Welfare Policy, Program, and Practice Issues." *Child Welfare Journal of Policy, Practice, and Program: Children with Parents in Prison.* (http://www.cwla.org/programs/incarcerated/so98journalintro.htm).

Seymour, Cynthia Beatty. 1997. "Parents in Prison: Children in Crisis, An Issue Brief." Child Welfare League of America. (http://www.cwla.org/programs/incarcerated/initiativesummary.htm).

Sherman, Lawrence W. 2002. "Fair and Effective Policing." Pp. 383–412 in *Crime,* edited by James Q. Wilson and Joan Petersilia. Oakland, CA: ICS Press.

Sherman, Lawrence. 1992. "Attacking Crime: Policing and Crime Control." In *Modern Policing,* ed. Michael Tonry and Norval Morris. Chicago: University of Chicago Press.

Siegel, Larry. 2000. *Criminology,* 7th ed. Belmont, CA: Wadsworth/Thomson Learning.

Simon, David. 2006. *Elite Deviance,* 8th ed. Boston, MA: Pearson Education, Inc.

Sloane, Bruce C. 1973. "Suicide attempts in the District of Columbia prison system." *Omega—Journal of Death and Dying,* 4:1. Abstract. Retrieved October 2001. Available: PsycInfo.

Smith, M. K. 2007. "Social capital." *The encyclopedia of information education.* Retrieved May 30, 2006 (www.infed.org/biblio/social_capital.htm).

Smith, Dale E. 1982. "Crowding and Confinement." Pp. 45–62 in *The Pains of Imprisonment,* edited by Robert Johnson and Hans Toch. Prospect Heights, IL: Waveland Press.

Smith, Douglas and Christy Visher. 1981. "Street-Level Justice: Situational Determinants of Police Arrest Decisions." *Social Problems* 26: 167–78.

Sourcebook of Criminal Justice Statistics. 2003. "Federal Criminal Justice Budget Authorities." Table 1.12, p. 15. Edited by Kathleen Maguire and Ann L.Pastore. Retrieved June 6, 2006 (http://www.albany.edu/sourcebook/pdf/t112.pdf).

Sourcebook of Criminal Justice Statistics. 2002. "Prisoners in Federal, State, and Private Adult Correctional Facilities." Table 6.28, p. 500. Edited by Kathleen Maguire and Ann L.Pastore. Retrieved May 13, 2005 (http://www.albany.edu/sourcebook/tost_6.html#6_b).

Sourcebook of Criminal Justice Statistics. 2002b. "Justice system direct and intergovernmental expenditures. Table 1.2, p. 3. Edited by Kathleen Maguire and Ann L.Pastore. Retrieved June 6, 2006 (http://www.albany.edu/sourcebook/pdf/sb2002/sb2002-section1.pdf).

Sourcebook of Criminal Justice Statistics. 2002c. "Justice System per Capita Expenditures." Table 1.6, page 11. Edited by Kathleen Maguire and Ann L.Pastore. Retrieved October 24, 2007.

Sourcebook of Criminal Justice Statistics 2000: Table 6.22, p. 495. Edited by Kathleen Maguire and Ann L.Pastore. Retrieved May 13, 2005 (http://www.albany.edu/sourcebook/tost_6.html#6_b).

Sourcebook of Criminal Justice Statistics Online: "Federal Prison Population, and Number and Percent Sentenced for Drug Offenses." Table 6.54. Edited by Kathleen Maguire and Ann L. Pastore. Retrieved December 10, 2004 (http://www.Albany .edu.sourcebook/pdf/t529.pdf).

Sourcebook of Criminal Justice Statistics Online: "Sentences imposed in U.S. District Courts under the U.S. Sentencing Commission Guidelines." Table 5.29. Edited by Kathleen Maguire and Ann L. Pastore. Retrieved December 10, 2004 (http://www .Albany.edu.sourcebook/pdf/t529.pdf).

Sourcebook of Criminal Justice Statistics Online: "Rate (Per 100,000 Resident Population) of Sentenced Prisoners under Jurisdiction of State and Federal Correctional Authorities on December 31." Table 6.23. Edited by Kathleen Maguire and Ann L.Pastore. Retrieved December 11, 2004 (http://www.Albany.edu.sourcebook/ pdf/t623.pdf).

Sourcebook of Criminal Justice Statistics Online: "Percent Distribution of Total U.S. Population and Persons Arrested for All Offenses." Table 4.4. Edited by Kathleen Maguire and Ann L. Pastore. Retrieved January 25, 2005 (http://www.Albany.edu/ sourcebook/pdf/t44.pdf).

Sourcebook of Criminal Justice Statistics Online: "Characteristics of Federal Prisoners." Table 6.47. Edited by Kathleen Maguire and Ann L. Pastore. Retrieved January May 13, 2005 (http://www.albany.edu/sourcebook/tost_6.html#6_b).

Spohn, Cassia. 2000. "Thirty Years of Sentencing Reform: The Quest for a Racially Neutral Sentencing Process." From *Criminal Justice 2000, Volume 3*. Washington, DC: National Institute of Justice, U.S. Department of Justice.

Stephan, James. 2004. "State Prison Expenditures 2001." Washington, DC: Bureau of Justice Statistics Special Report, U.S. Department of Justice.

Stephan, James and Jennifer C. Karberg. 2003. "Census of State and Federal Correctional Facilities, 2000." Washington, DC: Bureau of Justice Statistics, U.S. Department of Justice.

Stephan, James. 1999. "State Prison Expenditures, 1996." Washington, DC: Bureau of Justice Statistics, U.S. Department of Justice.

Stephan, James. 1997. "Census of State and Federal Correctional Facilities, 1995." Washington, DC: Bureau of Justice Statistics, U.S. Department of Corrections.

Stohr, Mary K. and Craig Hemmens. 2004. *The Inmate Prison Experience*. Upper Saddle River, NJ: Pearson Education, Inc.

Substance Abuse and Mental Health Services Administration, Center for Substance Abuse Treatment, National Evaluation Data Services. August 1999. "The Costs and Benefits of Substance Abuse Treatment: Findings from the National Treatment Improvement Evaluation Study."

Sutherland E. and D. Cressey. 1960. *Principles of Criminology* (6th edition). Philadelphia, PA: Lippincott.

Sutherland, Edwin H. 1947. *Principles of Criminology*. Philadelphia, PA: J. B. Lippincott Co.

Sykes, Gresham. 1958. *The Society of Captives*. Princeton, NJ: Princeton University Press.

Taqi-Eddin, Khaled, Dan Macallair, and Vincent Schiraldi. 1998. *Class Dismissed: Higher Education vs. Corrections during the Wilson Years*. San Francisco, CA: Justice Policy Institute.

Taylor, Ralph. 2000. "Breaking Away from Broken Windows: Baltimore Neighborhoods and the Nationwide Fight against Crime, Grime, Fear, and Decline." Boulder, CO: Westview Press.

Taylor, Ralph, Stephen Gottfredson, and Sidney Brower. 1984. "Block Crime and Fear: Defensible Space, Local Social Ties, and Territorial Functioning." *Journal of Research in Crime and Delinquency* 21: 303–31.

The Real Cost of Prisons Project. n.d. *The Real Cost of Prisons Timeline.* Retrieved June 8, 2006 (http://www.realcostofprisons.org/timeline.pdf).

The Sentencing Project. 2004. "New Incarceration Figures: Growth in Population Continues." Washington, DC: The Sentencing Project. Retrieved May 24, 2006 (http://www.sentencingproject.org/PublicationDetails.aspx?PublicationID=430).

The Sentencing Project (website). 2004. "Felony Disenfranchisement Laws in the United States." Washington, DC: The Sentencing Project. Retrieved December 14, 2004 (http://www.sentencingproject.org/pdfs/1046.pdf).

The Sentencing Project. 2004b. "State Rates of Incarceration by Race." Washington, DC: The Sentencing Project. Retrieved July 25, 2005 (http://www.sentencingproject.org/pubs_08.cfm).

The Sentencing Project. 2004c. "Truth-in-Sentencing in the Federal Prison System." Washington, DC: The Sentencing Project. Retrieved May 24, 2006 (http://www.sentencingproject.org/pubs_02.cfm).

The Sentencing Project. 2002. "Mentally Ill Offenders in the Criminal Justice System: An Analysis and Prescription." Washington, DC: The Sentencing Project. (http://www.sentencingproject.org).

The Sentencing Project. (website) n.d. "'Three Strikes' Laws: Five Years Later." Executive Summary: 1 (http://www.prisonsucks.com).

The Sentencing Project (website). n.d. "Prisoners Re-Entering the Community." Washington, DC: The Sentencing Project. Retrieved May 24, 2006 (http://www.sentencingproject.org).

The Sentencing Project (website). n.d. "The Expanding Federal Prison Population." Washington, DC: The Sentencing Project. Retrieved May 24, 2006 (http://www.sentencingproject.org/pubs_02.cfm).

The Sentencing Project (website). n.d. "The Federal Prison Population: A Statistical Analysis." Washington, DC: The Sentencing Project. Retrieved May 24, 2006 (http://www.sentencingproject.org/pubs_02.cfm).

The Sentencing Project (website). n.d. "Crack Cocaine Sentencing Policy: Unjustified and Unreasonable." Washington, DC: The Sentencing Project. Retrieved May 24, 2006 (http://www.sentencingproject.org/pubs_02.cfm).

The World Bank Project. 1999. "What Is Social Capital?" *PovertyNet.* Washington, DC: World Bank. Retrieved May 12, 2003 (http://www.worldbank.org/).

Toch, Hans. 1992. *Living in Prison: The Ecology of Survival.* Washington, DC: American Psychological Association.

Toch, Hans. 1988. "Studying and Reducing Stress." Pp. 25–44 in *The Pains of Imprisonment,* edited by Robert Johnson and Hans Toch. Prospect Heights, IL: Waveland Press.

Tonry, Michael. 1999a. "Reconsidering Indeterminate and Structured Sentencing." Number 2 in series *Sentencing and Corrections Issues for the 21st Century.* Washington,

DC: National Institute of Justice, U.S. Department of Justice. (Papers from the Executive Sessions on Sentencing and Corrections.)

Tonry, Michael. 1999b. "The Fragmentation of Sentencing and Corrections in America." Number 1 in series *Sentencing and Corrections Issues for the 21st Century.* Washington, DC: National Institute of Justice, U.S. Department of Justice. (Papers from the Executive Sessions on Sentencing and Corrections.) Retrieved October 23, 2002 (http://www.ncjrs.org/txtfiles1/nij/175721.txt).

Tonry, Michael. 1997. "Intermediate Sanctions in Sentencing Guidelines." National Institute of Justice: Issues and Practices. Washington, DC: National Institute of Justice, U.S. Department of Justice.

Tonry, Michael. 1996. *Sentencing Matters.* New York: Oxford University Press.

Tonry, Michael. 1990. "Stated and Latent Features of ISP." *Crime and Delinquency* 36: 174–91.

Tonry, Michael. 1987. *Sentencing Reform Impacts,* Washington DC: National Institute of Justice, U.S. Department of Justice.

Tonry, Michael and Kathleen Hatlestad (eds). 1997. *Sentencing Reform in Overcrowded Times, A Comparative Perspective.* New York: Oxford University Press.

Torny, Michael and Joan Petersilia (eds). 1999. *Prisons.* Chicago, IL: The University of Chicago Press.

Travis, Jeremy, Elizabeth M. Cincotta, and Amy L. Solomon. 2003. "Families Left Behind: The Hidden Costs of Incarceration and Reentry." Washington, DC: Urban Institute, Justice Policy Center. Retrieved December 19, 2004 (http://www.urban.org/UploadedPDF/310882_families_left_behind.pdf).

Travis, Jeremy, Amy L. Solomon, and Michelle Waul. 2001. "From Prison to Home: The Dimensions and Consequences of Prisoner Reentry." Washington, DC: Urban Institute. Retrieved May 22, 2006 (http://www.urban.org/UploadedPDF/from_prison_to_home.pdf).

Travis, Jeremy. 2002. "Invisible Punishment: An Instrument of Social Exclusion." Pp. 1–36 in *Invisible Punishment: The Collateral Consequences of Mass Incarceration,* edited by Marc Mauer and Meda Chesney-Lind. New York: New Press.

Travis, Jeremy. 1996. "Key Legislative Issues in Criminal Justice: The Impact of Sentencing Guidelines." Washington, DC: National Institute of Justice, U.S. Department of Justice.

Useem, Bert and Michael D. Reisig. 1999. "Collective Action in Prisons: Protests, Disturbances, and Riots." *Criminology* 37: 734–57.

Uniform Crime Reports [website]. Washington DC: Federal Bureau of Investigations, U.S. Department of Justice (http://www.fbi.gov/ucr/ucr.htm).

United States v. Booker 543 U.S. 220 (2005) (http://wid.ap.org/documents/scotus/050112booker.pdf).

United States v. Fanfan, 125 S. Ct. 738 (2005).

U.S. Department of Justice, Bureau of Justice Statistics. 2003. Compendium of Federal Justice Statistics, 2001. NCJ 201627. Washington, DC: Department of Justice: 104. Downloaded from *Sourcebook of Criminal Justice Statistics Online.* Retrieved November 21, 2004 (http://www.albany.edu/sourcebook/pdf/t655.pdf).

U.S. Department of Justice, Federal Bureau of Prisons [Online]. September 9, 2003. Available http://www.bop.gov/fact0598.html. Downloaded from *Sourcebook of*

Criminal Justice Statistics Online, 2002: p. 516, table 6.54. Retrieved December 1, 2004 (http://www.albany.edu/sourcebook/pdf/t654.pdf).

U.S. Department of Justice, Bureau of Justice Statistics. 1991. "Report to the Nation on Crime and Justice, Sentencing and Corrections." In *The Dilemmas of Corrections*, edited by Kenneth Haas and Geoffrey Alpert, 2nd edition. Prospect Heights, IL: Waveland Press, Inc.

U.S. General Accounting Office. 1997. *Drug Courts: Overview of Growth, Characteristics, and Results*. Washington, DC: U.S. Government Printing Office.

U.S. Parole Commission. August 15, 2003. *Rules and Procedures Manual*. Retrieved January 25, 2005 (http://www.usdoj.gov/uspc/rules_procedures/rulesmanual.htm).

U.S. Sentencing Commission [USSC]. 2006. "Final Report on the Impact of *United States v. Booker* On Federal Sentencing." Retrieved April 21, 2006 (http://www.ussc.gov/booker_report/Booker_Report.pdf).

USSC. 2004a. "2002 *Sourcebook of Federal Sentencing Statistics*." Washington, DC: U.S. Sentencing Commission. Cited on *Sourcebook of Criminal Justice Statistics Online*, table 5.29. Retrieved December 10, 2004 (http://www.Albany.edu/sourcebook/pdf/t529.pfd).

USSC. 2004b. "Fifteen Years of Guidelines Sentencing: An Assessment of How Well the Federal Criminal Justice System Is Achieving the Goals of Sentencing Reform." Washington, DC: U.S. Sentencing Commission. Retrieved December 10, 2004 (http://www.ussc.gov/15_year/15year.htm).

USSC. 2004c. Datafile, USSCFY04, Pre-Blakely Only Cases (October 1, 2003, through June 24, 2004). United States Sentencing Commission's *Sourcebook of Federal Sentencing Statistics*. Washington, DC. U.S. Sentencing Commission. Retrieved May 30, 2006 (http://www.ussc.gov/ANNRPT/2004/SBTOC04.htm).

USSC. 2000. Datafile, USSCFY2000, figure 3: *Average Length of Imprisonment for Each Drug Type, Fiscal Year 2000, Mandatory Minimums For Each Drug Type, Fiscal Year 2000*; USSCFY96-USSCFY00, figure E: *Average Length of Imprisonment in Each General Crime Category, Fiscal Year 1996–Fiscal Year*; figure D: *Distribution of Offenders Receiving Sentencing Options, Fiscal Year 2000*; USSCFY00, table 34: *Race of Drug Offenders for Each Drug Type, Fiscal Year 2000*; table 43: *Drug Offenders Receiving Mandatory Minimums for Each Drug Type, Fiscal Year 2000*, cited in 2000 *Sourcebook of Criminal Justice Statistics*, USSC.

USSC. 1995. Datafile, MONFY95, figure E: *Type of Guideline Sentenced Imposed (October 1, 1994 through September 30, 1995)*.

Vincent, Barbara S. and Paul J. Hofer. 1994. "The Consequences of Mandatory Minimum Prison Terms: A Summary of Recent Findings." Washington, DC: Federal Judicial Center. Retrieved May 24, 2006 (http://www.fjc.gov/library/fjc_catalog.nsf).

Virginia Department of Corrections [VDOC]. 2005. "Expenditures of the Division of Operations—FY 2004" and "Expenditures of the Division of Administration—FY 2004." Retrieved on June 2, 2005 from DVOC website (http://www.vadoc.state.va.us).

VDOC. 2000. "Statistical Summary, FY99, FY00 and FY01." Richmond, Research and Forecast Drive. Retrieved September 20, 2001 from DVOC website (http://www.vadoc.state.va.us).

Von Hirsch, Andrew, Anthony E. Bottoms, Elizabeth Burney, and P-O. Wikstrom. 1999. "Criminal Deterrence and Sentence Severity. An Analysis of Recent Research." *University of Cambridge Institute of Criminology.* Oxford, England, Hart Publishing.

Von Hirsch, Andrew. 1986. *Doing Justice: The Choice of Punishments.* Boston, MA: Northeastern University Press.

Walker, Samuel. 2006. *Sense and Non-Sense about Crime and Drugs,* 6th ed. Belmont, CA: Wadsworth/Thomson Learning.

Walker, Samuel. 1993. *Taming the System: The Control of Discretion in Criminal Justice, 1950–1990.* New York: Oxford University Press.

Walmsley, Roy. 2003. "World Prison Population List," 5th edition. Research, Development, and Statistics Directorate, Home Office. (http://www.homeoffice.gov.uk/rds/pdfs2/r234.pdf).

Weber, Max. 1978. *Economy and Society.* Edited by Guenther Roth and Claus Wittich. Berkeley: University of California Press.

Western, Bruce, Becky Pettit, and Josh Guetzkow. 2002. "Black Economic Progress in the Era of Mass Imprisonment." Pp. 165–80 in *Invisible Punishment: The Collateral Consequences of Mass Incarceration,* edited by Marc Mauer and Meda Chesney-Lind. New York: New Press.

Wichmann, Cherami, Ralph Serin, and Larry Motiuk. 2000. "Predicting Suicide Attempts among Male Offenders in Federal Penitentiaries." Canada: Research Branch, Correctional Service Canada, Retrieved October 2001 (http://www.csc-scc.gc.ca/text/rsrch/reports/r91/er91/pdf).

Wilson, David B., Catherine A Gallagher, and Doris L. MacKenzie. 2000. "A Meta-Analysis of Corrections-Based Education, Vocation, and Work Programs for Adult Offenders." *Journal of Research in Crime and Delinquency* 37: 347–68.

Wilson, James Q. 1975. *Thinking about Crime.* New York: Vintage Books.

Wilson, James Q. and Joan Petersilia (eds). 1995. *Crime.* San Francisco, CA: Institute for Contemporary Studies.

Winslow, Robert. 2005. "Sweden." from *Crime and Society. A Comparative Criminology Tour of the World.* Retrieved May 24, 2005 (http://www-rohan.sdsu.edu/faculty/rwinslow/index.html).

Wisconsin Department of Corrections website. *Adult Institutions—Wisconsin Secure Prison Facility.* Retrieved June 2, 2005 (http://www.wi-doc.com/index_adult.htm).

Women's Prison Association [WPA]. 2004. "WPA Focus on Women and Justice: Trends in Arrests and Sentencing." New York, NY: The Women's Prison Association.

WPA. 2003a. "WPA Focus on Women and Justice: Trends in Incarceration 1." New York: Women's Prison Association. Retrieved April 20, 2006 (http://66.29.139.159/pdf/Focus_August2003.pdf).

WPA. 2003b. "WPA Focus on Women and Justice: Barriers to Reentry." New York: Women's Prison Association.

WPA. 2003c. "WPA Focus on Women and Justice: A Portrait of Women in Prison." New York: Women's Prison Association. Retrieved April 21, 2006 (http://66.29.139.159/pdf/Focus_December2003.pdf).

Wright, R. T. and S. H. Decker. 1994. *Burglars on the Job: Streetlife and Residential Break-ins.* Boston, MA: Northeastern University Press.

Yen, Hope. 2005. "Report Released on Life Sentences for Kids." *Associated Press,* Wednesday, October 12, 2005. Retrieved October 17, 2005 (http://www.washington post.com).

Zimmerman, S. E. and Harold D. Miller. 1981. "Corrections at the Crossroads: Designing Policy." Pp. 9–24 in *Corrections at the Crossroads: Designing Policy,* edited by S. E. Zimmerman and Harold D. Miller. Beverly Hills, CA: Sage Publications.

Zimring, Frank and Gordon Hawkins. 1994. The Growth of Imprisonment in California. *British Journal of Criminology* 34 (88) (special issue).

Zimring, Frank and Gordon Hawkins. 1973. *Deterrence.* Chicago: University of Chicago Press.

Index

233

About the Author

Heather Ahn-Redding is an assistant professor of criminal justice at High Point University. She received her doctorate in Justice, Law and Society from American University's School of Public Affairs. She received her master's degree in forensic psychology from John Jay College of Criminal Justice and her bachelor's degree in psychology from the University of Michigan. She is coauthor of *Intercountry Adoptees Tell Their Stories* (with Rita J. Simon, Lexington Books 2007), *The Insanity Defense, The World Over* (with Rita J. Simon, Lexington Books 2006), *Illicit Drug Policies, Trafficking, and Use the World Over* (with Caterina Gouvis Roman and Rita J. Simon, Lexington Books 2005), and *The Crimes Women Commit, The Punishments They Receive* (with Rita J. Simon, Lexington Books 2005).

Breinigsville, PA USA
10 October 2010
247027BV00002B/1/P